BEST CANADIAN ESSAYS
2019

BEST CANADIAN ESSAYS

EDITED BY

EMILY DONALDSON

BIBLIOASIS

WINDSOR, ONTARIO

First Edition
ISBN 978-1-77196-332-9 (Trade Paper)
ISBN 978-1-77196-333-6 (eBook)

Edited by Emily Donaldson
Cover and text designed by Gordon Robertson

Published with the generous assistance of the Canada Council for the Arts, which last year invested $153 million to bring the arts to Canadians throughout the country, and the financial support of the Government of Canada. Biblioasis also acknowledges the support of the Ontario Arts Council (OAC), an agency of the Government of Ontario, which last year funded 1,709 individual artists and 1,078 organizations in 204 communities across Ontario, for a total of $52.1 million, and the contribution of the Government of Ontario through the Ontario Book Publishing Tax Credit and Ontario Creates.

PRINTED AND BOUND IN CANADA

CONTENTS

INTRODUCTION

Emily Donaldson

Many cultural events begin these days with an acknowledgment of the traditional territory on which they are about to take place. And so it goes with the introductory-essay-to-the-essay-collection, where it has long been standard practice to honour, or at least name-drop, Michel de Montaigne, the essay's first popularizer and its spiritual Elf on the Shelf. Far be it from me to tamper with a proven formula, but as I knew just a few cursory things about Montaigne when I took on this gig, I figured I'd better bone up. My expectations, of an intellectually salubrious slog, couldn't have been more off the mark. The *Essais*, it will come as no surprise to anyone who did their assigned reading in university, are disarmingly ranty and charmingly scattershot. Montaigne might have been disciplined and well educated, but his essays were apparently about whatever damn thing came into his head.

I also assumed, incorrectly, that they'd be written in the rigidly formal manner still taught in school: a thesis statement followed by a series of idea-developing paragraphs capped off by a final, sum-uppy one. This is so far from the case with Montaigne it's laughable. Montaigne meanders and digresses, chases rabbits and other things down their holes, forgets why

1

he came in the room, armchair psychologizes, shakes a proverbial fist ("Man is certainly stark mad; he cannot make a worm, and yet he will be making gods by dozens"). He can be wilfully obscure ("The titles of my chapters do not always embrace their matter; often they only denote it by some sign"), or petulantly outward-blaming ("'Tis the indiligent reader who loses my subject, and not I"). His declaration that "I myself am the matter of my book" was considered self-indulgent at the time—which, it's easy to forget, overlapped with Shakespeare's—and yet there's an empathetic streak there too: "the very sight of another's pain materially pains me, and I often usurp the sensations of another person. A perpetual cough in another tickles my lungs and throat." He was the kind of guy, in other words, who goes to Texas and picks up the drawl immediately.

Reading Montaigne drove home a few things. One is that what we now refer to as the "personal essay" isn't, in fact, some bastard offshoot of a Talmudic form, but rather the original form itself. Another is that "peradventure" needs to be resurrected in common parlance. A third is that the proper subject for an essay is anything at all. Just put "Of" at the start of your title and you're off to the races. Montaigne's included "Of Smells," in which he humble-brags about his olfactory prowess: "[I am] a great lover of good smells, and as much abominate the ill ones, which also I scent at a greater distance, I think, than other men"; "Of Pedantry," in which he makes the case for quality over quantity, ideas-wise: "We should rather examine who is better learned, than who is more learned"; "Of Drunkenness," in which he calls the latter "an unmanly and stupid vice" but concedes that the ancient Greeks, whom he respects, advocated losing your head from time to time; "Of the Affection of Fathers to Their Children," in which he comes out against unconditional love: "A true and regular affection ought to spring and increase with the knowledge they give us of themselves, and then, if they are worthy of it, the natural propension walking hand in hand with reason, to cherish them with a truly paternal love"; "Of Cripples," a baffling piece, in which "cripple" only ever appears in the title (thankfully), and also seems to mean something other than what you'd assume. And then there's the evergreen "Of Thumbs," which I will return to later. Over in England, Francis Bacon followed Montaigne's example but seems to strive more for the universal ("Of Death," "Of Truth," "Of Love" etc.). It's also easy to imagine some of Bacon's titles adapted to twenty-first-century concerns: "Of Followers and Friends" (social media!); "Of Marriage and Single Life" (relationships!); or "Of Innovations" (tech!)

People like to rail about the infusion of identity politics into art and public discourse, but one of the things reading Montaigne drove home for me is that identity has been intrinsic to the essay since the get-go. And, in a kind of foreshadowing of Whitman, Montaigne seems to see his own identity as containing multitudes:

> If I speak variously of myself, it is because I consider myself variously; all the contrarieties are there to be found in one corner or another; after one fashion or another: bashful, insolent; chaste, lustful; prating, silent; laborious, delicate; ingenious, heavy; melancholic, pleasant; lying, true; knowing, ignorant; liberal, covetous, and prodigal: I find all this in myself, more or less, according as I turn myself about; and whoever will sift himself to the bottom, will find in himself, and even in his own judgment, this volubility and discordance. I have nothing to say of myself entirely, simply, and solidly without mixture and confusion.

Indeed, as I read essays for this collection, the first since Tightrope Books passed the "Best of" torch to Biblioasis, it struck me that, in the very best of them, the imparting of ideas was hog-tied to the imparting of the writer's identity or character (character and identity admittedly not always being the same thing). Whether that identity oozes out as a slow leak, or announces itself as a brash, jazzy-hands "Here I Am!" simply comes down to style. And "style" doesn't have to mean fancy. Compared to, say, the flamboyant locutions of Gore Vidal, a Joan Didion essay might seem denuded of character. But sparse, we see when we read Didion, does not mean arid. The Didion style is often recognizable in just a few short phrases.

If the essay offers an ideal springboard for exploring identity, how much more so for an identity in flux. So it's perhaps not surprising that ten of the hundred or so essays submitted by magazine editors from around the country (the list of publications these were drawn from, plus a list of other notable essays from the past year, can be found at the back of the book) dealt with sexual transitioning (one, "Fierce Inventory" by Ali Blythe, appears on page 121; two by Gwen Benaway received honourable mentions). The issue of identity in art is the focus of both Noor Naga's "Mistresses Should Be Muslim Too" and Tarralik Duffy's "Uvanga/Self: Picturing Our Identity." Duffy's essay concerns contemporary Inuit self-portraiture, and how the demands of a lucrative marketplace traditionally based on romanticized ideals of Inuit life have sometimes butted up against the artist's need to express raw realities, while Naga's is a nuanced probe of the quandaries of representation raised by her family's conflation of her with an adulterous Muslim character in her novel. Bruce Whiteman's "Unc," in which he speculates about whether his late paternal uncle might have been his real father (and even gets a DNA test to satisfy his curiosity) comes at identity from yet another angle by feeding off the sometimes-dichotomy between how we want to see ourselves, and how we really are.

A further thing that characterizes the chosen essays, I think, is that they feel collaborative: the writer's satisfaction seems dependent on our own satisfaction in reading them. That might sound self-evident, but there was a good deal of submitted work that felt distinctly onanistic, an airing of gripes whose aim wasn't to query, explore, or provoke, but to seek an outlet for misery. You know the kind of writing I mean. It shows up under titles like "I love my husband, but I don't love his OCD," or "I got cancer, and everybody said the wrong things to me." There's a place for these pieces, I suppose, but it isn't in these pages.

On the other side of the bell curve were pieces that brimmed with fascinating facts about everything from rare diseases to Doug Ford to endangered fauna (and no, I'm not referring to a single essay here). Those pieces aren't here not because they weren't well-written—many were extremely polished—but because they didn't fit the mould of what I came to think of as an essay, or, at minimum, have essayistic qualities (like, say, Robbie Jeffrey's descriptive but layered "The High and Lonesome Sound"). Some seem to think the non-fiction article and the essay are the same; they aren't, and this became clearer the more I read. In the final accounting, a piece needed to reflect a point of view, to take a chance of some kind, and to do the latter two things with flair and originality. Straight journalism or reportage, which many of the pieces I just mentioned would qualify as, is intended to reflect the world with minimal authorial intrusion. An essay colours the world, probes its contours, and isn't afraid to fall outside them as it does.

Of course, "essayist" is as likely to be someone's declared profession these days as "boulevardier." Most people who write essays also write in other forms, be it novels, stories, poetry—all of which offer unique ways of interrogating the world. So how does the triple-threat writer choose one over the other? Sometimes the choice is clear. Arguing, like Pasha Malla does in "CanLit's Comedy Problem," that the Leacock Prize has failed to keep up with changing times is probably always going to be best done via the essay (though I'd love to see it written as a poem), but it's not hard to imagine Danny Jacobs' "The Weekend God" as either a story or poem, given the painterliness of Jacobs' prose. Sometimes writers make the wrong choice. We've all read non-fiction books that feel suspiciously like a magazine feature in a fat suit (honestly, how often do you read something and think, "I wish this were longer"?), or the novel that should have stayed a short story. As a reviewer well into her woman-who-yells-at-clouds years, I seem to spend a lot of my time railing against issue- or fact-driven novels that, under fiction's finest veneer, are really aimed at enlightening and instructing us about something the writer deems important. These days, a lot of those books can be found on the historical-fiction shelf, the genre having become an attractive dumping ground for those who've spent years researching, say, raisin-making in nineteenth-century Nova Scotia, or an unappreciated watercolourist who once dated a lesser member of the Group of Seven. (It's always confusing when people boast about how much they "learned" reading a novel; isn't fiction by definition a lie, artfully told?) Fiction needs facts, but it needs them as scaffold; not as the temple at which it worships. The same goes for intentionality in fiction: just the tiniest whiff of it and you instantly taste the flax seed in that shake.

There are practical reasons why non-fiction sometimes masquerades as fiction, some of them economic. Non-fiction can take as long as fiction to write, or longer, and though it tends to sell better, requires the added burden of deep research and fact-checking. Charles Foran, the novelist and author of the multiple-award-winning biography *Mordecai: The Life & Times*, wrote a widely shared essay for *Canadian Notes & Queries* a few years ago in which he explained why writing long-form non-fiction just wasn't worth it for him anymore: the time and effort it demanded could all too quickly shrink a decent six-figure advance to a subsistence wage. Given that reality, as well as the erstwhile non-fiction author's fear of getting things wrong, or of even being sued, you can see the why a novel might suddenly seem like a good, safe option (Foran, I should note here, is a very good novelist), even if the net result is a profusion of artless, painfully earnest fiction. To those "novelists" I say: Consider the essay!

Interestingly, the reverse isn't true: the essay has reaped clear benefits from its ongoing game of footsie with fiction, especially in the rise of so-called creative non-fiction, a genre for which no one has yet come up with an adequate definition, but which you can think of, in simple terms, as a license not to be boring. Witness work like Souvankham Thammavongsa's "On Meaning" and Jessie Loyer's lovely "mâyipayiwin." "mâyipayiwin" originally appeared in *ndncountry*, an excellent collection of writing by Indigenous Canadians jointly published last year by *Prairie Fire* and *CV2*. *ndncountry*'s editors, Katherena Vermette and Warrien Cariou, decided not to label individual pieces by category—essays, fiction, poetry, etc.—and while I'm not sure of the reason for this, it made me realize how much the experience of reading is calibrated to our anticipation of *what* we're reading. While the poetry in *ndncountry* is, for obvious reasons, mostly identifiable as such, it isn't always clear if the prose pieces are actually prose, and, if so, if they're fiction or creative non-fiction. Loyer's piece is slippery in that it feels like all three: poem, essay, story, so I was very happy when I (leadingly) asked her if she'd consider it creative non-fiction and she said yes. I'd hoped to get another piece from *ndncountry*, Richard Van Camp's hilarious, parodic "Young Warriors in Love"—but though Van Camp told me he thought it could pass as creative non-fiction, it turned out Caroline Adderson, the editor of *Best Canadian Stories 2019*, had already pounced, so do yourself a favour and read it there.

You may notice, especially now that I'm mentioning it, that a lot of the essays here have a literary bent, either explicitly, in subject (as with Sue Goyette's "Poetent," Danny Jacobs' "The Weekend God," River Halen Guri's "Six Boxes," or Noor Naga's "Mistresses Should Be Muslim Too"), or indirectly, in style (as with Tanya Bellehumeur-Allatt's "Terrorist Narratives," Jessica Johns' "The Bull of Cromdale," or Melanie Mah's

"In Transit"). And that might strike you as partisan—I've spent the bulk of my working life editing books, writing about books, reviewing books, and I'm the editor of a literary magazine. Perhaps it is. But I'd argue that it's because, going back to that "flair and originality" criteria, literary types are, well, literary; most, by dint of their calling, have a feel for language, an investment in it. On the other hand, it completely escaped my notice until I looked at the final list for this book that the majority of the chosen writers are also poets. This surprised me, but only for a second; I've always found that poets write some of the sharpest essays and criticism around (Montaigne again: "I love a poetic progress, by leaps and skips"). But there's also a more mundane reason for the literariness: literary and cultural magazines are among the few outlets still regularly publishing essays, as opposed to the kind of feature writing you find in glossies like *Maclean's*, *Chatelaine*, or *Toronto Life*.

That the majority of the work represented was originally published in small or online publications was a pleasant surprise, attributable, perhaps, to the latter being less shackled by house style, or the necessity of pleasing broad readerships. But publishing in small publications also has its downside. I received a number of essays with great bones but that were done a disservice by poor editing, or, I suspect, no editing. Rejecting those essays was painful, especially when it was obvious all they needed was a few loose screws drilled in. As the editor of one myself, I'm well aware that many small-circulation magazines simply don't have the resources to go through a series of deep edits with their writers. But the task here being to collect essays, not edit or hone them, there was nothing for it but to reluctantly move those sputtering stars to the No pile. On the positive, and more predatory side, I now have a list of writers I plan to ask to write for *CNQ*.

Their bookish cast aside, I think you'll find the essays here run the gamut nicely. Few would be willing to put themselves out on a limb like Meaghan Rondeau does in "Half-Thing," an essay about the experience of being an (unwilling) thirty-eight-year-old virgin so honest and funny it made my toes curl. (Have I over-quoted Montaigne yet? No? Okay, here's another one: "I speak truth, not so much as I would, but as much as I dare"). Academic jargon generally acts like a bucket of cold water to an essay's burning embers, but when Rondeau, a poet, recovered academic, and translator (of Latin!), talked about virginity's semiotic value, I was all ears.

Some don't try to reinvent the wheel, they're just smart and solid in the argument-making sense, like "Our Country—Le Canada" by Jeffrey Donaldson (also a poet, and no relation) and "David Frum's Trump Card" by Andy Lamey. Some, like Lamey's and Mireille Silcoff's (the funny, trenchant "Swedish Death Cleaning and the Anorexic Home") use book reviews as the launch pad for broader observations, while others, like Larissa Diakiw's "Secrets are a Captive Country" derive power from their open-endedness.

Anthony Oliveira's National Magazine Award-winning "Death in the Village," a look at the impact of the serial murders in Toronto's gay village, is an essay that does everything exceptionally well. Liberally borrowing from fictional technique, it begins with Oliveira contemplating a decrepit billboard whose function in the essay is as a physical remnant but also a metaphor: "I have been staring all week at that mutilated poster: another piece of our vandalized history, another scrap pasted onto the palimpsest of this neighbourhood, another fragment forcibly overlaid atop another fragment, out of which we are expected to assemble some measure of coherence." More impressively, that billboard also guides the essay structurally as Oliveira searches for coherence amidst layers of joy and tragedy in his tiny downtown community. "Death in the Village" moves in several directions at once: expanding the present moment while simultaneously boring down and collapsing the past: "To walk in the village, for me," writes Oliveira, "is to walk in these overlapping histories: through my own, through memorials, through the sites of arrests and beatings and a thousand indignities and intimacies." He builds character deftly and efficiently through a judicious use of anecdote. Here's Alex, a young trans man in the village: "Alex's kindness has a ferocity of its own; they are a volunteer for every LGBT cause imaginable, and I quickly learn they have a distressing habit of crying out to interject 'poor thing!' at the exact moment in your anecdote when you are describing the person you are trying most to vilify therein."

There's a literariness, too, to Oliveira's reliance on contrast and juxtaposition to do his story's heavy lifting, as in this description of a press conference for the family of one of the victims, Andrew Kinsman:

> Andrew's sister Karen tells a story about how her brother wanted to be a paleontologist, and how the family once hid a cow femur and convinced him there must be dinosaurs buried in the yard. He dug and dug until, ecstatic, he found the bones.
>
> The room shifts uncomfortably and moves quickly past the infelicitous image.

And while "Death in the Village" is deeply personal, Oliveira talks about his experience coming out, about partying in the same places as the alleged perpetrator ("In his pictures I see an eye gazing where I gazed, and wonder if it gazed on me: darkly complected, stocky, bearded. Gay."), it's never *just* about him; in fact, the historical need for those in the gay community to forge a collective identity is precisely Oliveira's point: "Queer people are so often born in isolation—we have to find each other, have to excavate our history, have to build new families to replace the ones who abandoned us." "Death in the Village" is a masterful bit of writing and a terrific example of the essay's elasticity and omnivorousness, the way it can absorb other forms and strengthen as it does so.

Which brings me back to Montaigne's "Of Thumbs," an essay I was immediately drawn to for personal reasons, my older son having been born with a condition called hypoplastic thumbs (look it up), for which he has had multiple surgeries, and which has made me appreciate the digital dexterity I'd always taken for granted (he now plays piano, so it turned out well, thanks for asking). Still, "Of Thumbs" is a slight thing, primarily informative. Had Montaigne been living in Regina in 2019 and submitted it to *Best Canadian Essays,* it would not have made the cut for reasons I hope I've already explained. I did learn a few things from it though. One was that in ancient Rome it was "a signification of favour to depress and turn in the thumbs . . . and of disfavour to elevate and thrust them outward." What follows, therefore, are the Canadian essays that had me depressing and turning in my thumbs the most. Happy reading.

— *Emily Donaldson*

DEATH IN THE VILLAGE

Anthony Oliveira

"NO_ONE EVER REALLY DIES"

The massive letters are glued to the plywood around the construction site at 582 Church Street, near the centre of Toronto's Church-Wellesley Village. The site used to be a bar called House-Maison. Once at a party a boy kissed me in the bathroom upstairs. He laughed, and then disappeared into the sea of people outside. It is derelict now, under perpetual construction.

The poster was hung there to promote the latest album from hip-hop/rock group N.E.R.D. (the underscore in "NO_ONE" is to make the acronym work), which was released December 15, 2017. You will have trouble reading the sign. Sometime between being affixed in late November and December 4, 2017, the company in charge of patrolling the site—O.B.N. Security and Investigative Consultants—moved its own placard, from where it hung nearby, to a few feet down and to the right, carefully obscuring the word "DIES." There is an owl scowling on it—an image, presumably, of sleepless watchfulness. The outline of where it used to hang persists, its ghostly outline particularly obvious when it rains. Perhaps the word troubled them.

You will have trouble, too, finding out what this acronym "O.B.N." stands for. It is not on the security company's website, though there you will learn that its executive board and founders are all former police officers or law enforcement personnel, and it is then that you might guess. If you haven't, a bit more digging will lead you to a *Toronto Star* article from 2006, in which, amid a pitch from the firm's vice-president for their services in divorce surveillance, it is explained as a joking reference to O.B.N.'s close allegiance with the Toronto Police. I call to their offices to inquire about security work (I have been feeling unsafe lately) and they confirm: "O.B.N. stands for the Old Boys Network."

Walk past this constellation of signage and follow the plywood to where it ends. Squeeze past the cars parked there. On the building's north-most side you will find a small alley, and stone steps down to a basement door. Next to overflowing recycling bins and garbage containers, in a spot that neither O.B.N. patrols nor police bothered to look, you will find a tall heap of dirt festooned with flowers, candles, and birthday cards.

You will find the spot where, on November 29, four days after she went missing, and one day before her birthday, Tess Richey's mother was left to find her daughter's murdered body.

I am walking along College Street near Bay. It is raining. From an alcove entrance, over the railing of the building wheelchair ramp, a woman in a red vest shouts over to me.

"Come inside out of the rain and donate to Canadian Blood Services? It's in you to give!"

"I'm gay," I say.

She grimaces. "Sorry."

He was a Mall Santa. This was the detail, culled from his Facebook page, that obsessed the press. We are still waiting for numbers—we are still waiting for so much—but it seems (it is, my editor wishes me to stress, *alleged*) that once a year, after killing five men and probably many others, he put on a red suit and dandled the children of Toronto on his lap and listened to their fondest wishes. He smiled, and smiled, and still was a villain.

It seems now secondary that there are still gay bodies to be exhumed. That there was blood—gay blood—in the trunk of his car. Gay blood when it is donated is thrown out, and when it is spilt it is easy to forget, running unnoticed in the gutters.

Think instead of the children.

When I look at his Facebook page (it is now locked, but police left it up for several days) I see different angles of parties I attended—photographs taken on Church Street of the same Halloween costumes I had photographed just before him, giant candied skulls moving in a conga line through the crowd that made me tug on my friend's coat: *look, there.* In his pictures I see an eye gazing where I gazed, and wonder if it gazed on me: darkly complected, stocky, bearded. Gay.

Maybe when the headlines shout "MALL SANTA!" this is the heterosexual community's version of the same impulse: *look where you were vulnerable.*

It is mid December, 2017. We have been looking for Andrew Kinsman for seven months. His posters are still outside in the square and in the coffee shops. In all that time the police have insisted there is no connection between Andrew Kinsman and the rash of disappearances we have been seeing for years. Instead, they tell us to "be careful on the apps." They do not explain why.

Project Marie, the 2016 police sting operation to lure gay men into sex in the park and then arrest them, is a year old.

Briefly, Tess Richey's poster hung next to Andrew's. "But I knew she was dead when the police came in to take down her poster," a barista tells me. Outside the window is Crews

& Tango's, the drag club and dance space where Tess was last seen. Just a few steps north is where her body was found.

Do not congregate online; do not congregate in the park; do not congregate in the bar.

Tess's poster has been replaced with one of the person of interest in her case: a slight, white man photographed by blurry CCTV cameras. Another predator, moving through the village.

"Did you talk to them? When they took it down?" I ask.

"Fuck no."

It is mid January, 2018. I am sitting in the press conference for Andrew Kinsman's family. We are in the 519 Community Centre; above the lobby bulletin board hangs a sign: "FAMILIES DEFINE THEMSELVES." The conference is in the ballroom on the second floor. The last time I was here it was full of steamy bodies—the humid rain had moved the TreeHouse Party inside, and we danced in the microclimate of our sweat. I remember a friend's hand in the small of my clammy back that made me wriggle and slap them away.

Now it is cold. Journalists and equipment personnel sparsely laugh and chat, milling near a hastily erected coffee station. One behind me loudly barks: "There's probably a book in this!" The family is huddled, watching them. Watching us, I guess. They have just learned an arrest has been made. They have just learned, for certain, that their brother was killed. They are waiting for the body to be found.

They speak imperfectly, as all of us would. They think aloud of the child that Andrew was. Shelley Kinsman takes no questions after her statement. I watch her anxiously clutching and persistently rubbing a small black stone with both hands throughout. I never find out what it was. She looks like my mother, fretting at her rosary beads.

Andrew's sister Karen tells a story about how her brother wanted to be a paleontologist, and how the family once hid a cow femur and convinced him there must be dinosaurs buried in the yard. He dug and dug until, ecstatic, he found the bones.

The room shifts uncomfortably and moves quickly past the infelicitous image.

"We looked for him in the heat, in the rain, and in the snow," Shelley Kinsman says.

Attend enough press conferences and you learn the strange synesthetic habit of a sudden burst of photos when the subject says something useful—as though the image captured could be made at all congruent to what striking thing was said. A sound like a group of bats taking flight as cameras go off: *heat, rain, snow*—that was everyone's favourite pull-quote. A family in suffering, scouring for their prodigal brother lost in the big city.

I have yet to find an article that quoted what Kinsman said next: "We found homeless men living in tents. We met a transgender person afraid of living in a shelter as she had been assaulted and robbed. She lived under a bridge. We bought her lunch. We saw a young man sleeping under a bridge surrounded by bottles. In the forest we found needles and more. We never found Andrew."

I wonder if the homeless woman they met was Alloura Wells, whose body was found in August in a ravine by a hiker, discovered during a coroner's exam to be trans, and then neglected, no further identified, in a police morgue for months, until the noise from the family about organizing their own searches (as Alloura's father put it, struggling with her pronouns: "It's like [she's] a nobody") led them at last to identify her remains.

Probably not. There is after all no shortage of homeless trans people in Toronto. The moment, in any case, passes unremarked upon.

The Kinsmans talk around the problem of the other victims' families, of the troubling optics of a killer caught after possible decades of activity because he finally killed a white guy. The sisters have reached out to Selim Esen's family in Turkey, they say, but they have apparently long "considered the matter closed." They implore the family to call the police, whom they thank profusely.

"Remember him in your own way," the sisters say. For their own part, "we know that wherever he is, Andrew is looking down on us."

"Andrew did not want to look down from anywhere."

I am sitting with David at the Blake House, a pub just off the village's main drag. The last time I was here was right after the Pride parade with my then-boyfriend. My shorts were ludicrously short and sparkly, and his eyes were very, very blue.

David slept with Andrew Kinsman a handful of times, and they were friends. It is a kind of relationship every gay man recognizes, but which the media has struggled to quantify. The Andrew that David remembers is not the child his sisters recall at the press conference, but a man who knew his mind—ruthlessly unsentimental, and very kind: "If ever there was a person that didn't deserve it, it was him." David looks down. "He was a big man."

It is a peculiarly terrible feeling watching someone you care about picture someone they care about being disassembled.

The police have been busily peddling a vague warning to stay away from hook-up apps for months, to the exclusion of all other information and amid strenuous denial there was any evidence of a serial killer. Their denials, to David, amount to complicity: "Andrew disappeared in June. There's a young man on that list who disappeared in August. If he is one of the victims, that is on the police." He remembers the case of Jane Doe, who successfully sued the Toronto Police for their part in her attack by a serial rapist.

Instead, for David, the horror is that Andrew knew his killer: "The thing that pains me most is that he might have cared for this person, and been betrayed by this person in such a cruel way."

I ask him about Tess Richey, about the queer voices in Black Lives Matter, who I once watched police perfunctorily scuttle the press conference for the unveiling of the mural behind Hair of the Dog when BLM questioned their cosmetic image renovation, about Project Marie, and about the subsequent police uproar about being excluded from Pride. Was this laxity of their mission to serve and protect meant to be punitive?

"All of this has laid bare the fact that we are alone," David says. "We have no superheroes. We are alone. It is the queer community that has done the most work. It is the queer community that has developed strategies.

"And now it is the queer community who mourns."

I am in the Glad Day Bookshop with a Paper Plane (bourbon, amaro, Aperol, lemon juice) and a book (*Midsummer Night's Dream*) when my ex-boyfriend spots me in the window and comes in to say hi. Then: "I hear they might be up to four bodies."

We talk about how they will probably give him a name. The Mall Santa thing, probably, or something about the gardening. My ex tries the cocktail, and I feel the momentary course of a thrill at the gesture's casual intimacy.

His eyes are still so blue.

He is late for something, squeezes me goodbye, and he is gone, and I am alone again with my book.

City TV posts a report about the murders. My cousin, to whose face I once denied I was gay when she cornered me at a wedding years ago ("But I saw you!" she pressed. "I live just near the village, so I'm there a lot," I stammered, my face hot), spots me in the pre-roll, and tags me. I read the Facebook comments.

Del Core Domenico says: "You don't like cops, now you pay the ultimate prize." Laughing emojis.

Sandra Wieland says: "Why does the media say gay men were murdered. Do they say straight man shot last night. Stop the labels. We are the human race."

Wayne Kennedy says: "Leave the police alone they are doing a good gob there [are] other cases to solve."

Andrew Brown says: "So 2 makes u a serial killer?"

Tom Pearson says: "A bit much to say police won't do a thing. Division is not helping."

Chris Kolmel says: "They could have just not bothered looking for the killer. Just coming off as looking stupid."

Dre Khaloo says: "Let's not forget LGBT ppl u were the 1's who told the cops not to show up at pride wearing their uniforms catering to the demands of blm so shut ur holes An deal with it."

Richie Zina says: "Confused gays. What about aids? Why are they still so quiet in that? I'm sure aids kills thousands more than this guy did...."

I close Facebook.

I am sitting on the second floor of the village Starbucks, grading a student's late paper. I become vaguely aware that behind me an older man is explaining to his companion how Grindr works.

"See, these people are all nearby! It changes every time you sign on. I had sex with this guy once. Some of these people are even in this café! Look, there's that guy!"

To my left across the gulf of the stairs a gentleman sitting alone at a table conspicuously pretends not to hear.

Two police officers, a man and a woman in the Toronto Police yellow winter jackets, walk up the stairs holding coffees, obviously on break. The same old man behind me jeers loudly: "Uh oh, the POLICE are here! I hope nobody in here did anything WRONG!"

The police officers, also, pretend not to hear.

When one of them goes to the bathroom, the old man again heckles him: "Better check if there's a MURDERER in that bathroom! Better get him this time!"

The officer tries the door, but does not know the code (it is 962962, but I do not volunteer it). Instead he returns to his partner, and they hastily leave.

I try to follow to ask them if the jeers are typical lately, but when I get outside they are already in their squad car, pulling away.

I wonder if this is their normal patrol, and if so, I wonder if they are the same cops who, when arresting a man at the southernmost margin of the village a year ago were caught on cellphone video tasering a man while down and insisting to an objecting observer to watch out for the suspect, "because he'll spit in your face and you'll get AIDS."

I wonder if they're still mad they didn't get to march in their uniforms in the parade, expecting cheers from the people they've left for eight years to die while a murderer picked us off, while across town they arrested us in parks for having sex, and electrocuted us in the streets.

Maybe that is uncharitable.

Since June 12, 2016, I have not once walked into a gay bar or café or community centre without thinking, "I wonder if today is the day someone decides to kill us."

Not once.

Alex is 23—the age, by five days, that Tess Richey never lived to see.

Alex is non-binary and bisexual, and came to Canada because they believed it was more welcoming and open. They want to ask for my advice about grad school (my advice is what

21

it always is: don't). We are talking in Glad Day, and around us the daytime coffee shop shimmers, dims, and transforms into a quiet night-time pub. This used to be a club called Byzantium, and the floor still has the tracks that split the dancefloor from the more intimate section where the music meant you had to lean in close while lights drew zigzags on the other person's face.

When straight people imagine coming out they imagine a tearful, dramatic revelation all at once, but Alex's story is like mine: by degrees, when it's safe, when it's too late for them to ruin your life. Coming out is brave not because it is vaguely "scary," like a school play; it is brave because it is dangerous. Some people get violent; some punish you financially; some just love you a little less, forever. You let them see the little fraction of yourself that you can trust them with, because you've learned love is almost always conditional. Surviving is brave, too.

Bitterness is always possible. Instead, Alex's kindness has a ferocity of its own; they are a volunteer for every LGBT cause imaginable, and I quickly learn have a distressing habit of crying out to interject "poor thing!" at the exact moment in your anecdote when you are describing the person you are trying most to vilify therein.

More than anything else, Alex loves anime. Their free time (of which their volunteering does not afford much) is devoted to "magical girls"—the genre of which *Sailor Moon* is the most identifiable example to Westerners. They are highly choreographed stories in which the powerless and disenfranchised are transformed into gossamer agents of justice: beauty and love triumphant, never sacrificing an ounce of vulnerability or compassion to do battle against exploitative evils.

I ask about the disappearances, about Tess Richey, and about Alloura Wells.

"The police aren't doing anything but when have they ever?" Alex asks, sadly. "We protect each other."

We talk some more about magical girls.

I leave class at 11 a.m.—a lecture on Shakespeare's *Richard II*—to 14 texts from my friends. The death toll is now at five.

On the TV above the café bar I watch forensic personnel dressed all in white dragging enormous flowerpots from a property in rural Ontario. There are bodies in the soil.

Unbidden my mind flashes back to the end of the play. Full of baroque images of the horrors of power, it ends with a last one—a new king, crying crocodile tears, for the victim whose death he didn't quite order, but tacitly condoned, even as he punishes the murder:

Lords, I protest, my soul is full of woe,
That blood should sprinkle me to make me grow.
   (5.6.45-6)

What is power? A beautiful flower, whose earth is soaked in blood.

In Shakespeare, eulogies are the privilege of murderers. On the TV, the police spokeswoman speaks, but the TV is set mercifully to mute.

In the heart of the village, behind the 519, in the park across from Tess Richey's alleyway memorial, you will find a bank of roses, and among them on plates a list of names. These are Toronto's dead, lost to AIDS, when no one in power cared to act, when the old boys network raided the bathhouses and the parks and the bars.

In the summer we hold a vigil, and by candlelight we recite their names, and we recite the names of those killed at the Pulse massacre, and we recite the names of anyone else who was loved and lost. This year we will recite new names.

Their names were Selim Esen. Skandaraj Navaratnam. Majeed "Hamid" Kayhan. Abdulbasir Faizi. Sorush Marmudi.

Dean Lisowick. Andrew Kinsman. Alloura Wells. Tess Richey.

There are more names. There will be more names still.

And we will forget some. And we will not know how many died in silence and in secret and alone. No one will tell those stories. No one will know how.

"NO_ONE EVER REALLY [THIS PREMISE IS UNDER PHYSICAL AND ELECTRONIC SURVEILLANCE BY OBN 1-866-626-5900]"

I have been staring all week at that mutilated poster: another piece of our vandalized history, another scrap pasted onto the palimpsest of this neighbourhood, another fragment forcibly overlaid atop another fragment, out of which we are expected to assemble some measure of coherence.

It is the product of crass marketers peddling positivity, and then careless old men seeking to conceal anything that might invite the discovery of their own guilt in creating the conditions for a predator to prey.

I have no sense to offer. Maybe offering sense is just another violence—another sign moved to cover something up.

But still: when you make "NO_ONE" into one word you fuse a noun to its adjective, making a new noun—a "no_one" that is nevertheless a *thing*.

Queer people are so often born in isolation—we have to find each other, have to excavate our history, have to build new families to replace the ones who abandoned us. To walk in the village, for me, is to walk in these overlapping histories: through my own, through memorials, through the sites of arrests and beatings and a thousand indignities and intimacies.

We are never one. Not really.

SWEDISH DEATH CLEANING AND THE ANOREXIC HOME

Mireille Silcoff

A few years ago, while researching a magazine article, I began having conversations with Michael Daley, a self-styled art conservation watchdog. Daley has used the term "blockbuster restoration" to describe our era's increasingly common practice of over-cleaning and touching up masterworks by artists such as Leonardo da Vinci or Titian in a way designed to create exciting "before and after" shots, and thus excitement around major exhibits—Vermeer as you've never seen Vermeer, and indeed also Vermeer as *Vermeer* had never seen Vermeer. Every few weeks Daley would send me another example: a Renaissance madonna who looked as if she'd had a nose job, a 17th-century nymph whose face had been made whiter and more lineless, her surrounding putti more perfectly pastel. The Old Masters had entered the obsessively seamless era of Botox and computer-generated imagery, and, said Daley, were coming out looking more new than old. "There is some disordered practice going on," said Daley. "A little dirt is normal. Imperfection does not need correction. People are being conditioned to think otherwise."

And so to the home, where I believe there is increasingly some disorder too—something like anorexia worn on the outside, or an obsessive compulsion directed toward the home, where a person's living quarters become the site for absurd perfectionism, unattainable standards, and distorted perception. Last year, three people told me, completely independently of each other, that either they or their partners could not endure anything on their kitchen or bathroom counters—counters had to be sparkling empty plains, punctuated by no more than, say, a single soap pump. A cleaning woman I'd hired after renting my home out for a couple of weeks looked sadly at the electrical wires hanging behind my desk and television and side tables. The nice houses she cleaned, she said, had no visible wires. Nobody could stand visible wires anymore. A cousin explained to me how he had grown unable to tolerate items in his apartment that he didn't "absolutely, 100 percent need or like." He kept a big brown box on his back balcony and placed a few things in it every week. He said he kept a running query in the middle of his mind nearly all the time. *And this sweater? And this plate?* In all these cases, the behaviour described was not tagged as particularly problematic, more as something falling within the realm of interesting personal tic, possibly hard to live with, but not entirely devoid of virtue.

Back in the 20th century, when many more people had homes with separate living rooms, it was not unusual for the living room to be purposely little used, a kind of pristine set piece that the homemaker hoped would speak over the rest of the more lived-in parts of the house. Bedrooms—with their unmade beds and stacks of magazines and chipped saucers full of single cufflinks and pennies—might have their doors closed when guests came over, but in the living room, every cushion was plumped and every flowerpot or ashtray was carefully angled on the coffee table.

It would not be a stretch to say that in many contemporary homes, this old ideal of the shrine-like living room has infected the rest of the house. Ikea ran an ad campaign a couple of years ago encouraging its customers to leave the bedroom door open, a cheerful (and cheap) siren call to make one's private space ever more public, ever more available to the gaze of the neighbourhood Joneses. "Where is it said," asked the commercial, "that, when everyone comes over, the bedroom door has to be closed? We're for leaving it wide open." Thanks to digital domains such as Apartment Therapy and Pinterest and television home shows (*Trading Spaces, Property Brothers*), the ideal of the relentlessly staged and curated home has become entrenched. Never have so many bookshelves been so artfully displayed. Never have the average citizen's bathroom products been so meticulously arranged on trays, like volatiles in a lab that can never be touched. Paper towel holders and TV controls and toothbrushes have become egregious "eyesores" better hidden from sight. And when did it become normal for people with young children to have white rugs and white sofas? Buying a white sofa is buying a seat of constant maintenance and neuroticism—*Um, ah, let me just put this dishcloth under your feet. No, no, it's no problem at all. It's just, you know, ha ha, the couch*—and yet it seems more people do it now than ever before.

Into this milieu comes *The Gentle Art of Swedish Death Cleaning*, a faux-naïf ruse of a book that is already a bestseller, a supposed guide on how to pare down and beautify your home in preparation for your death so that you do not overburden your loved ones with too much stuff and ugliness after you go. The brief is to live as though you are perpetually on the verge of popping off. Authored by one Margareta Magnusson, a Swedish grandmother who has crafted her bite-sized chapters in a softy-soft voice, so as not to traumatize the children, and who describes herself—I suppose for the street cred of *oldest age*—as "somewhere between 80 and 100" (Magnusson is reportedly in her 80s), the book instructs us to start death cleaning now, whatever one's age, because you never know, you could get run over by a bus tomorrow, and think of how much work your family will have getting rid of your belongings.

In the past few years, I have gone through all the objects of several deceased loved ones, some of them valiant collectors of utter junk, and I can tell you that this exercise is nothing to build the rest of your adult life around. It takes a couple of weeks; it is cathartic; and, in a society chock full of things but increasingly devoid of useful rituals around death, it is a good way to sift through memories and say goodbye. I don't entirely understand why its spectre is so haunting for this book's author. Magnusson's simple musings ("What are vices? I guess habits that are not so good for us") and no-duh instructions ("Regard your cleaning as an ordinary, everyday job. And in between, enjoy yourself as much as possible with all the things you like to do") hardly need the grim reaper as through line. What is clear is that the final shuffling off has become oddly trendy these days. In the past month or two, the same magazines and newspapers, including the *New York Times,* that have written up Magnusson's Nordic sweater of a book as being the last word in charming have also reported the rising popularity of an app called "weCroak," which reminds users, with push-notifications sent five times a day at random, that they are going to die. So this is not a book to read for the writing, or the suggestions. It is a book to know of because of the one big idea hiding behind its muffin-scented Swedish apron: that the only way out of our current mess of anxiety and materialism, of maximalism and minimalism, of schizophrenic messaging about buying humongous messes of things while maintaining homes so exhaustively curated as to be museum-like, is death. Just in the same way that death is the solution to many chronic illnesses.

Four years ago, when Marie Kondo's four-million-copy-selling *The Life-Changing Magic of Tidying Up: The Japanese Art of Decluttering and Organizing* was first published in English, the initial reaction to its extreme form of home minimalism was predictable enough. To her readers, Kondo's endearingly animistic ethos (famously, she writes that rolling up one's socks is cruel to the sock, that socks should be lovingly folded, so they can rest after a long day "trapped between your foot and your shoe") and punishing principle of nothing extra, was a welcome reprieve against the excesses of home-related consumerism. Even though it was an instant bestseller, the book came across as a cult object, countercultural in the way that becoming a monk is countercultural. With Kondo, the key to a happier, more fortunate life is to throw nearly everything away, even useful things, keeping only the very few items that "spark joy" when held. In Kondo's world, one might only need four teacups and two dish towels. After so much bullying Nespresso-and-thread-count lunacy, the sort of thinking that could make a temp office worker making $15,000 a year believe a dual climate-controlled wine locker (available at Wal-Mart for less than $400) is a "home essential," entering Kondo's ladylike realm of precious spareness, where you always know where your keys are because there is nothing else on your hallway table, ever, could feel like tiptoeing into a quiet patch of sanity. You had been choking under an avalanche of stuff, and look! All you'd ever needed was a single river rock in the palm of your hand.

It can sound healthy enough, even sensible, with living space shrinking, and open-plan architecture (which does away with those useful clutter containers called *walls*) still inexorably on the rise. But the problem of a Marie Kondo in a shopaholic consumer society is that even the best-intentioned minimalism turns into more consumerism, just of a more demanding, neurotic sort. The relentless paring down is a convenient and ongoing clearing of the stage for some fresh, as-yet unmet, un-acquired object which—unlike those other familiar ones grown boring or distasteful with time—has the box-fresh ability to give jollies.

And neurotic it is; Kondo herself admits that her need to organize and strip down does not come from a place of great mental health. She writes how, by the age of five, she could not help but compulsively clean not just her personal spaces, but those of her siblings and parents as well; how she was once traumatized—to the point of crying at the very memory—by a shampoo bottle that had developed a slimy bottom in a humid bathroom. "From the fact that I spent my recesses alone, tidying, you can guess that I wasn't a very outgoing child," she writes. "Because I was poor at developing bonds of trust with people, I had an unusually strong attachment to things." No amount of quasi-religious your-socks-have-feelings pillow-talk can turn "It was material things and my house that taught me to appreciate unconditional love first, not my parents or friends" into anything but a good reason to seek therapy. Photos of Kondo's own apartment show not just a white sofa and rug, but white *everything,* an anorexic space meant to be viewed as the apex of serene livability that no average person could—and, I would add, *should*—possibly feel comfortable living in.

Other recent books sit on this same intersection between mental disorder and a house in order. Justin Klosky, a former actor on the soap opera *Guiding Light,* has made a successful L.A. home-organizing business out of the obsessive-compulsive disorder he was diagnosed with when he was an anxious and unhappy child vacuuming lines in his carpet that "were evenly spaced and perfectly parallel." Incredibly, he calls his business O.C.D. Experience. His book, *Organize & Create Discipline* (OCD, get it?), is full of scrappy bro chatter about taking the garbage out every day ("I'll do a lap around the house, emptying every can, spraying my Lysol, because I don't want anything stinking up my space while I'm sleeping"), fixing up your car's glove compartment with special separators and sections, and, poor everyone, creating a habit of vacuuming in straight lines. ("Nothing screams fresh and clean like parallel vacuum lines!") Baldly, Klosky writes, "because of my neurosis and obsessions, [O.C.D. Experience is] the most efficient, effective, and evergreen system out there for transforming your life."

But is your life transformed for the better? The latest book from the collective behind the Remodelista design site, *Remodelista: The Organized Home,* contains so much anxious complexity masked as easygoing simplicity, so much useless, circular puttering posing as good sense, one gets a tension headache just flipping through it. In the highly millennial matte-white-and-untreated-beechwood Remodelista fantasyland, a Scando-Amish stringency is sold as illuminated pleasure. "Stop the encroachment of unappealing, bulky packaging the way chefs and scientists do. New to decanting? Start in the kitchen by storing your olive oil, hand soap, and other liquids in pretty bottles." In a section called Stowing the Unmentionables, we are told that "a toilet-cleaning kit needn't be cringe-worthy. Choose a non-plastic brush, like this Iris Hantverk birch-handled option . . . and stow it in a pleasing container." Perhaps a terracotta planter or an enamelware pitcher resting on a Fog Linen tray, the picture suggests.

First of all, I have children and a job. Second, the rest of this evil book could fall under this very same category—stowing the unmentionables—because almost every human mod con is here an unmentionable. Real life, in all its messiness, is impossibly gauche. So here is a two-page spread on hiding "eyesore" office wires, and another on Where to Put the Blow-Dryer (note: you will have to add an outlet to the back of your drawer, *to hide the wire*), and another on Camouflaging Your Television ("the cable box is hidden in a cardboard box"). In a section called "Use Display-Worthy Vessels and Containers in the Bath," we are told that "a bottle of Ibuprofen fits neatly inside a covered ceramic canister." In another on leftover food, we are instructed—honestly—to use linen bowl covers.

Of course, making your whole house—these days very likely smaller than the one you grew up in; these days very likely more open plan—into a seamless showpiece, a zone of total presentability, with not an unwanted or unsightly thing within eye's view, manufactures an unprecedented crisis of clutter, a problem exacerbated a thousand times over by the fact that, as a species, we are encouraged to buy, and we do buy, more things per person than anyone ever has before. And so here we find ourselves in a terrible schizophrenic wedge. The last third of the supposedly minimalist Remodelista book is dedicated to where you can purchase "essentials." "Here's what you need to achieve a well-organized (and nearly plastic free) existence," write its editors, after which flow 54 pages of natural rubber ties and Shaker peg rails and "lab-style cylindrical glass-covered containers."

Michael Daley, the art restoration expert, told me that most people tend to think of the era they are living in as aesthetically neutral. It's only once the era has passed that a definitive, overarching look becomes more clear (the purple velvet sofa you bought in 1997 did not look like the 1990s until about 2010, when it did, irredeemably). The pristine domestic look of our time surely expresses some desire for escape from the trash compactor's worth of stimuli that crowds us out every day (after four hours staring into your iPhone, how does your brain feel? Not good! Not spacious!). But I would posit it has flown from being the product of an anxious headspace to the creator of more anxiety, a kind of vicious circle. If you look at popular decor books from the 1970s, '80s, and '90s—say, Terence Conran's classic *The House Book*, or any of the influential interior design books by the *New York Times* writer and editor Norma Skurka—most of the photographs of homes featured would not pass muster today with the editors at Rizzoli books or *Veranda* magazine, or, indeed, even the *New York Times*: the sofas look sat in, the hems of bed skirts are not ruler-straight, seat caning may be darkened, and bunches of flowers, weirdly often, are somewhat wilted. Today, in order to look "right" things increasingly need to look untouched, untouchable. Iron-straightened hair in 2018 is straighter than it was in 1968. Manicures are more manicured. To understand what I am getting at, reach, with your mind, into history and take almost any everyday object—toothbrush, placemat— from the house you grew up in, and compare it to the state of the same item today. When I was a kid in the 1970s and '80s, the Tupperware my mother happily used every day was scratched, cloudy, and stained, as was everyone else's. Today, when our disposable-yet-non-disposable Ziploc containers start looking anything but clear, they are due for replacement, because in the lunchroom at work, most people's containers look shiny-new all the time.

In this era of botoxed Leonardos, and bodies worked out to look like seamless stone, and walk-in closets with a hundred shelves that are best left nearly empty, in this time of so much spacious order camouflaging so much interior mess, these books can be seen as rampant overcorrection. Any human feeling inhuman and wishing to return to centre would do best to read none of them. The way to better health and home might be a messy bedroom. The path to fewer headaches: Leave the Advil on the counter.

UNC

Bruce Whiteman

> "Man has undertaken the top job of all,
> *son fin*. Good luck."
> — John Berryman, "Dream Song 46"

> "Don't most of us sometimes wish in the darkest recesses of
> our hearts that we had a different father?"
> — Amos Oz, *Judas*

Everyone who met my Uncle Sydney liked him instantly, and, given enough time, came to love him. He was handsome, tall, urbane, good-natured, and sympathetic to other people. Among the few papers I have from his earlier life, there is a clipping from a magazine of a hair tonic advertisement—it was for the hair tonic Vitalis—and he is the featured model. I know nothing further about this event, but it is obvious that he was chosen for his great good looks. He married late, despite those good looks and his good nature. I believe he was engaged once when he was in his twenties, but religion broke up the relationship. She was Catholic. When he did finally marry, in 1968, I wrote a mock-solemn letter to him about my disappointment—losing him to Terry, a woman, after all those years of having him to myself (I was sixteen.) Terry was a Catholic too, but I guess that, by then, religion was no longer so important a factor.

But at the heart of my thoughts about my Uncle Sydney these days is a strange and deeply unnerving question. I have come to wonder whether he was my father.

Sydney Charles Whiteman, my father's elder brother, was born in Montreal on April 21, 1911, to Emma and Charles Whiteman, the first of their three children. She was a resolute Anglo-Quebecker from a very French part of the province, New Carlisle, in the Gaspé. He, at least according to the old family story, was an immigrant Englishman from London's East End. We now think that his father, my great-grandfather, was a German Jew who perhaps emigrated to England during the philosemitic period, when Disraeli was prime minister. My grandfather, Charles Whiteman, was married in an Anglican church in the Gaspé in 1910, but was not baptized until 1932, and this suggests at least the possibility that he was born into a Jewish family. It is hard to tell from old photographs what my grandfather's national origins may have been, and no one ever remarked on his having any but an English accent. I don't know where my uncle lived in Montreal as a child, apart from an address he wrote into a book at some point: 6701 Stuart Avenue, near the corner of Beaumont Avenue, a house now demolished. I do know he was confirmed in the Church of England at the Church of the Ascension on Park Avenue (now a municipal library) on April 5, 1925, just before his fourteenth birthday, and I have a school "honour card" given to him at the end of grade seven, in 1924, from Fairmont School in Mile End. Fairmont was one of a small group of public schools built after World War I to accommodate a huge influx of recent and mostly Jewish immigrants. His musical talent must have been recognized early, because he was eventually taken to a very good teacher, Stanley Gardner (1890–1945). Gardner studied with Egon Petri and Ferruccio Busoni in Germany, and every · pianist knows that this is a wonderful genealogy to be a part of. I don't remember much about his repertoire in those early days, except that he played Liszt's *Gnomenreigen*, a character piece extremely difficult to pull off, so he must have had excellent technical skills. He won a silver medal in a Royal College of Music competition in London, in 1924, when he was just thirteen years old. I wear that medal around my neck every day as a way to remember him and his passion for the piano. At two examinations, of which I have the record, he played a Mozart Sonata, K. 283, Beethoven's early Sonata, Op. 7, an étude by Moscheles, the famous Prelude, Op. 3, No. 2, of Rachmaninoff, and one or two things I don't recognize.

Unfortunately, my grandfather's early death in 1938, at fifty-two, meant that Uncle Sydney had to begin giving piano lessons to children, a job for which he seems to have been oddly unsuited. The work eventually turned him against the piano and he stopped playing altogether. He also contracted tuberculosis sometime in the 1930s, and, although he recovered, I presume that this was the reason he did not participate in World War II. But it may also be because he was supporting his mother at that time. He lived with her until her death in 1968. Not too long after she died, Uncle Sydney finally got married, to Terry, a widow ten years younger than he who was originally from Prince Edward Island, but who had moved to Montreal for work during the war. He also moved to Toronto from Montreal around the time of his marriage. He and Terry lived in a house in Don Mills, an upscale suburb, on a street called Waxwing Place. Their house overlooked a ravine, and they enjoyed the raccoons that were frequent visitors. (These days Torontonians treat raccoons the way Americans often think of illegal immigrants, but they considered them charming and delightful.)

As children, my sisters and I saw Uncle Sydney quite often, and I cannot remember a single incident of crankiness or bad temper on his part. He always had a good word for us, asked questions about school and friends and what we were interested in. Eventually, when my own musical aspirations became clear, he began to take a determined role in my education—sending me records, taking me to concerts, and even, when my parents acquired a summer cottage, buying an upright piano so that I could continue to practise in the months after the school year finished. He still had not gone back to playing the piano, but his heroes were Arthur Rubinstein and Vladimir Horowitz. Most people preferred one to the other—the Romantic versus the technical wizard—but he would not choose. Because of him I heard both play in concert at Massey Hall in Toronto, Rubinstein once and Horowitz twice, after the latter returned to concertizing in 1965. On one of those occasions, we sat on the stage among some two hundred listeners who had been able to buy special tickets. Horowitz played the Schumann Sonata, Op. 22 that time, among other pieces I can't recall. Unc had earlier sent me a copy of Horowitz's "historic return" concert at Carnegie Hall, a two-record set I all but wore out by playing it so often. The playing was all wonderful—there are big pieces by Bach-Busoni and Schumann that I love to this day—and I was especially entranced by one of his encores, a little technical miracle by Moritz Moszkowski that Horowitz played with such perfection that it never failed to leave me open-mouthed in admiration no matter how often I listened to it. On the record you can hear the audience's collective intake of breath as he finishes the piece.

Eventually he went back to playing. He bought a reconditioned Steinway for the house in Don Mills. While he was never happy with the instrument, he did start to practise again, and worked up the Chopin Scherzo No. 2 to a high level. I remember that we played some Mozart duets together, and I am pretty confident that my own *gradus ad Parnassum* was the reason he decided to take up the piano again after so many years. We went to other concerts together too. At the St. Lawrence Centre in Toronto he bought us tickets to a series called Piano Nine, for the nine fine pianists it presented over the course of a season. Martha Argerich was the one who struck him most forcefully; in part, I think, because she made him abandon a long-held prejudice against women pianists—an attitude not atypical for a man of his generation. She performed Schumann's *Fantasiestucke* and the Prokofiev Sonata No. 7, with something else, too, and he was amazed at her playing. Next in the series came the accomplished Canadian pianist André Laplante, who alas had the misfortune to repeat the Prokofiev Sonata on his programme. He played it well, I'm sure, but no one could come up to Argerich's level of conception and execution.

Although I studied for many years, I never amounted to much as a pianist. I remember that, as a kind of final test of whether I really had it in me to be an accomplished player, I decided to learn the famous Étude by Scriabin, Op. 8, No. 12. It was not the first time I became fixated on a difficult, emotional piece of music that was in truth harder to play than I had the skills for. This happened all the time. But on this occasion I was determined, and felt certain that I could get it into my fingers. The hard thing was not to play it through without practice. This was the ruse that had become a fault with me. I had Horowitz's recording and it was tempting to try to imitate it without real exercise and repetition. I needed to work on one hand at a time, slowly, very slowly, and bring it gradually up to something like the indicated tempo (100 to 112 to the quarter note) before even attempting to put two hands together. It was a challenge that I already had the music in my head, and that it wrenched my feelings side to side and up and down whenever I heard it. I could imagine Scriabin playing the piece himself, his hands moving dreamily over the keyboard, his hair flying around his head like a nimbus out of control, his eyes disappearing upwards under his eyelids in a sort of trance, his feet pressing on the sustaining pedal with a thunderous stomp. How, I wondered, could ecstasy be parsed out one bar at a time? That was always the issue. The piano could easily become the enemy, forcing itself between what I knew was recorded in the notes and the emotions I felt just thinking about the music. Ecstasy and materiality were constantly and irremediably at war. It was patently obvious that I did not have it in me to be a pianist. Unlike you, Unc.

Uncle Sydney died on November 27, 1985, a few months shy of his seventy-fifth birthday. He collapsed on the ground from a heart attack at a car dealership. When they found him he was already dead. His grave is in Toronto's Mount Pleasant Cemetery. When Terry died on Hallowe'en, in 2008, she chose to be buried in Montreal beside her first husband, Jack (Jean Romain) Duquette, who had died in 1961. And so Unc lies alone, which seems somehow unfair. Just a small bronze plaque in the ground, inscribed only on the upper half, marks his place.

When I was growing up, he was always splendidly avuncular to all of us, but perhaps he gave me a little more attention than my four siblings. Our shared musical passion connected us more deeply than with the others. When I chose the French horn as my instrument in grade nine music class, he immediately sent me a recording by Barry Tuckwell of the four Mozart horn concertos. That was in 1965. Other records I remember receiving as gifts were the Tchaikovsky Piano Concerto No. 1 with Rubinstein, Nathan Milstein performing the Mendelssohn and Bruch violin concertos, and, perhaps oddly, Julian Bream playing the *Concierto di Aranjuez*, and a piece by Benjamin Britten. I'm sure there were others. I can remember only one composer whose work he clearly did not like, and that was Mahler. I noticed a complete Mahler symphonies recorded by Leonard Bernstein in a record store in Montreal when I was there (one of two visits on my own during the 1960s), and he dismissed the music as "heavy." I came to Mahler only much later. Those two visits to Montreal were both wonderful, the first in 1965 or 1966, and the second in 1967, when we went to Expo

67 together and his pride in being Canadian was very much in evidence. He took me to International Music on the first visit, where I bought the scores for Mozart's "Turkish Rondo" and the Liszt Hungarian Rhapsody No. 2. We also heard Zubin Mehta conduct the OSM and, on a lighter note, saw both *My Fair Lady* and *The Sound of Music* in the theatre. I am these days more than a little impatient with musical comedies, but back then they seemed magical—a long, long way from Mahler, needless to say. I was later the rehearsal pianist in high school for a local production of *My Fair Lady*, and if I never hear that piece again it will be too soon. As for *The Sound of Music*, a private and intense aversion is now equally not to be dislodged.

One of the only things I inherited from my uncle is a set of the Century Library of Music, eight volumes of piano music arranged in order of progressive difficulty. It is full of once popular but now largely forgotten pieces such as Anton Rubenstein's "Kammenniy-Ostrov" and Adolf von Henselt's "Si oiseau j'étais." I spent many hours uselessly trying to play music from those volumes that was far beyond my abilities, works like Liszt's Hungarian Rhapsodies, the later Beethoven sonatas, the Franck *Prelude, Chorale,* and *Fugue,* and so on. It was good for my musical education, if frustrating for my piano studies. As I say, I never did amount to much as a player. All the same, music has given me an enormous amount of pleasure and consolation throughout my life. Apart from that set I have only one thing to remind me of my uncle: a miniature score of Haydn's Symphony No. 100. He must have used it in an adult-learning class, as it has technical notes added in his handwriting throughout. I am deeply glad to have it, even though Haydn was not, as far as I remember, a composer whom he particularly loved.

If Unc were alive and I asked him the question with which I began this essay, there's no doubt he would have been completely nonplussed, perhaps even shocked and angry, though shocked and angry aren't words I can imagine applying to him, never having experienced him being either. I recognize that this would be a deeply upsetting question. It's upsetting to me to pose it as it is to imply that my uncle and my mother were lovers. It is to imply that both of them kept this from me for decades, perhaps kept it also from my father, and perhaps that my uncle kept it from his wife, Terry. If it were true, then clearly, given the circumstances and the time (the 1950s and afterwards), it would not be a truth he could ever acknowledge openly. Nor could my mother, perhaps not even on her deathbed. My uncle died suddenly, and did not have a chance to confess, if confession was warranted. My mother disappeared into dementia before dying suddenly, too, perhaps also too quickly gone beyond the ability to summon the moral courage to tell me the truth about my paternity. Now there is no one alive who can attest either to the truth of this shocking question, or to its being an implausibility. I am left to confront a question that I cannot settle definitively.

There are no facts, no documentary remains to consult. There are unsettling asseverations and clues. I look less like my father (and my brothers) than I look like him. I am taller than my father, and taller, again, than my brothers, and my hair is similar to his. I am told that my character is close to his, too: caring, a little self-conscious, good-natured, seldom given to anger and never to senseless enmity. And then there is the shared musical passion, especially for the piano. I do assuredly get some of my musical talent, limited as it is, from my mother and father, my mother especially. Yet my passion for the piano is like his, and his desire to nourish it when I was young, with encouragement and gifts, seems clearly to bespeak a parental longing. I am also told that my mother's behaviour in his presence, at family dinners and other events, was suggestive. She always laughed at his jokes, told him how warm and funny he was, almost acted like a lover, without ever going quite so far as to be fawning or obviously amatory. Her comportment never struck me as anything out of the ordinary for a sister-in-law, but it did strike others as unusual. I wonder too about the fact that, after my parents divorced—around the same time that Uncle Sydney finally married—my mother never dated another man, much less remarried. Perhaps she was pining for him. That's a big "perhaps," I realize.

So many contentions, so little to go on. Recently, a friend of my sister's, meeting one of my brothers and me for the first time, remarked to her that there was an obvious resemblance between them; as for me, she joked, was I adopted?

My initial reaction to the idea that Unc,—that's what I used to call him when I got a little older—might be my father was devastation. It seemed to change everything. Every remembered family moment suddenly seemed altered, seemed as though it were false, or compromised; it felt like the air I breathed got thinner and less sustaining. This is not because I have any hesitations about him as a person. Far from it. In many ways he was a more interesting and complex person than my father was; or, to put it differently, since everyone is complicated, his interests were closer to my own than Dad's ever were. In an objective sort of way, and following the not unusual fantasy that children have of wanting to be parented by someone they think of as nicer or more loving or more glamorous or just cooler than their own parents, I might well have said that he was preferable to me as a father had I had the choice. (Of course I didn't. Fathers are fate, not choice. Or so I thought.) No, it's something else. Half of my genetic code suddenly seemed unfamiliar, and every gesture, thought, and word that both he and my father had ever spoken or made or entertained seemed unreliable, if not poisoned.

Perhaps poisoned is too harsh. I suppose we are always in the process of reimagining our childhood. I have tried anyway, tried not to think of mine as engraved on a stele like Hammurabi's laws, a lithic part of the past, my past, as I have also tried not to be reductive, not to assign blame for my shortcomings to the evident pattern set by my father, or at least the man until recently I never had reason to doubt was my father. My fantasy as a young man was about someone else—not my uncle—possibly being my real father. That man was Alfred Laliberté, a composer and pianist who was my mother's singing teacher in the 1930s and early forties. Despite the difference in their ages (he was born in 1882, she in 1917), I liked to think, in the superficial way of artistic young men who resent the obviously bourgeois character of their fathers, that somehow my mother and *le maître* had had a love affair and that I was the result. But when I was conceived, Laliberté was seventy and retired in Montreal, where he lived with his wife Madeleine, admittedly a much younger woman and formerly a pupil, just like my mother, indeed a contemporary of my mother's. Laliberté died on May 17, 1952, one month and one day before I was born. My parents had already been living in Ontario then for two years, first in a newish house in Port Credit, a western suburb of Toronto, and then, from 1953, in Islington, a tonier suburb nearer Toronto and presumably a closer commute for my father to his job. We had a small house on a pretty street near a creek and a golf course. I spent some time in my twenties carrying out research on Laliberté's life and career, and found much to stimulate my musical passions. He was a close friend of the composer Medtner and knew Scriabin and Rachmaninoff well. He wrote an opera based on a Maeterlinck play, although it was never orchestrated, much less performed. That my mother could somehow have skipped out on her domestic situation and had a love affair in Montreal, with two young children already in her life, with a man of seventy who himself was married, and happily as far as I know, is an idea ridiculous if not contemptible. At that age, I was a bit old to be still under the influence of what Freud called the "family romance," but his contention in that essay—that "a boy is far more inclined to feel hostile impulses towards his father than towards his mother and has a far more intense desire to get free from him than from her"—seems on the mark in my case.

So that was a fantasy. Perhaps the possibility that my uncle is my father is just another fantasy too. I used to visit his grave in Mount Pleasant Cemetery from time to time, like a solemn and confused pilgrim. I would sit on a low wall nearby and talk to him. It's good to talk to the dead. They do not answer, of course, but they give one a spiritual address for all kinds of trial balloons and complex, real feelings: cries for help, questionings of the past, emotions with no place to go. Sometimes I felt like John Marcher in Henry James's story "The Beast in the Jungle," restlessly visiting the grave of his friend May Bartram, the woman who knew the secret of his life, who *was* the secret of his life, though he failed to realize that fact until after she died, and thus lost his centre forever. Like him, "fixing with his eyes her inscribed name and date, beating his forehead against the fact of the secret they kept, drawing his breath, while he waited as if, in pity of him, some sense would rise from the stones," I became upset but could get nowhere with my emotions. But at other times I experienced a temporary feeling of serenity in hearing nothing, in getting to no new knowledge about who you were and who I am, accepting the truth of no truth, or rather of truth's inaccessibility. Yet such acceptance is fleeting, and by the time I walked away from your grave and started the trip back out of the cemetery and into the street, it had vanished, and the unkind welter of uncertainty came back to stay.

Returning to my studio apartment near the university to brood, I would inevitably get mired again in the ineluctable limitations of the situation and the truth that there was no incontrovertible evidence and no one to ask. My father is buried in a cemetery in the far northwestern corner of Toronto; my mother in a graveyard on the outskirts of Peterborough, another cemetery named Mount Pleasant; my Aunt Eileen and my Aunt Terry are in Mount Royal Cemetery in Montreal. Birds fly and squirrels and rabbits gambol and people wander quietly among the bushes and the trees in all of these final resting-places of the generation before mine, so oddly and sadly scattered for such a small family. If my mother's brother Edward, her only sibling who lived into adulthood, knew anything about her intimate life, he took such knowledge to an early grave from Hodgkin's disease. He and his wife, my Aunt Delma, lie together in a cemetery in Charlotte, North Carolina. They were my sponsors when I was baptized in June of 1956. Eventually we all become the elder generation, and at that moment, there will be no further answers, no matter how desperate the questions remain or become. No witnesses, no one left to attest to events. As you age, the past becomes more and more predominantly a piece of your life, but a more inscrutable one, too. Is it any wonder that, the older I get, the more unmoored I feel?

With my uncle dead, so many objects from the past are gone too—totemic objects, objects with a speaking voice that whispered to me because they were part of my intimate life, my life in the family. Where are his pianos now, I wonder? He owned an imposing upright in the 1960s that I played on, one that had probably been in the family for decades, that he and my father had played on as children. He had later a rebuilt Steinway grand that disappointed him but was a good instrument in my view, a piano that filled a small nook off the living room in his comfortable Don Mills house, with books and knick-knacks and fancy liquor bottles on glass shelving behind it. And the sofa in the living room in the Town of Mount Royal apartment where I sat and listened to the Mendelssohn and Bruch violin concertos for the first time at fourteen or fifteen? The rotary phone, the Old Spice toiletries in the bathroom, the gloves and hats he wore, the beige trench coat, the brown leather shoes, the old television set (was it an RCA? a Motorola? a Zenith?), the framed photographs on a table in the living room? The big batch of letters and bills brought by the mailman that lay on a polished table? There was a stereo set too, nestled inside a fine piece of Scandinavian furniture with short legs and silver metal wrappings around their base, and many vinyl records and 78s of classical music. Apart from the pianos, whose present owners are as unaware of their history as I am of those men or women who play them today, everything is long gone. History and the heart's intimacies inch away into nothingness and one doesn't really notice until it is far too late. It's normal for this to happen, but it makes me—it makes all of us, surely—deeply sad.

I recently visited the Toronto church where I was baptized and which I attended until I was eleven. I wonder why Unc was not chosen as my sponsor. Perhaps that's a tiny bit of evidence against the idea that he's my father. Yet perhaps he sponsored one of my brothers when they were baptized, or perhaps my mother felt that it would be imprudent to ask him. I thought the sight of the inside of the church would knock loose some memories, but nothing seemed familiar: not the nave and its wooden pews, not the benign stained-glass windows (no *via crucis* here), not the rather modest altar. It was depressing to stand there and not recognize a single thing. Surely growing up is not about forgetting? When the psychoanalyst Adam Phillips once referred to "the insanity of childhood," he meant the openness to feelings, the easy availability of feelings that disturb us, the freshness of sensuous experience, the being able to exist in uncertainty, because uncertainty, in a sense, is what childhood is defined by. "Sanity," Phillips also says, "is the cure for the intensities of childhood," which means that sanity might consist of a great deal of forgetting. Small traumas are the common coin of all childhoods, after all, and children by nature block out things just as adults do in stressful situations. I wonder sometimes whether as a response to my parents' divorce I did not unconsciously begin to forget much of my earlier life as a way to cope with my new and unwelcome one: not just fatherless, but become a father by default to my sisters when I was unready for such a responsibility.

Now the father question is back to unmoor me in a different way. When my father disappeared after the divorce, we moved away from Toronto, so I did not get to see my uncle often. But I think I do remember that he took some pains on our behalf, not to make up for the loss of a father in any extensive way—that would not have been possible—but in small ways, by sending gifts and occasionally visiting us in Peterborough, where my mother had moved us. When eventually I returned to Toronto to start university, we saw each other from time to time. I still have the copy of the *Harvard Dictionary of Music* that he gave me on my eighteenth birthday. I got married too soon, needing perhaps to exchange the role of father for that of husband; and while he agreed to be my best man at the wedding—whose comedy of errors included a thunderstorm that cut the electricity temporarily—once married I saw less of him, living away from Toronto as I did, having a child eventually, and finally hearing about his sudden and unexpected death at the car lot. Many people claim that they prefer the idea of a quick death, but it does mean that there are never any last conversations or final goodbyes. No revelations, no confessions. I am left with the almost unbearable emotional challenge of accepting the hard truth that there will be no truth, no compelling certainty, no comfort. Keats said that a poet is someone who can exist among uncertainties, mysteries, and doubts, without any irritable reaching after fact and reason. I need to learn that lesson, but sometimes it feels disturbingly impossible. The dead remain silent and always will.

Postlude

But the dead do not in fact have to remain completely silent in a postmodern world.

Two friends with whom I shared my memoir early on were quick to suggest that a DNA test might clear up the uncertainty about paternity. It would be possible to disinter my father's and my uncle's ashes, to test them against my own DNA, and to learn beyond conjecture which man was my real parent. But the complications, both emotional and practical, involved in digging up not one but two graves, felt unbearable. Then I learned that a test could easily determine whether one of my sisters and I shared one hundred percent of our DNA. If we did, then we had the same parents; if not, then one parent, obviously the father, was different. The test cost five hundred dollars and the results would be available in less than a week. It involved nothing more than each of us taking a swab from the inside of our cheeks and having them compared in a laboratory.

Faced with settling the matter with scientific exactitude I experienced an unexpected hesitancy. I did wish to know with certainty, and yet I felt that if all of my emotional turmoil and self-examination had been for nothing, and that my father was my father, I would be angry, certainly, but maybe also a little disappointed. Part of me, like an adolescent, like the narrator in Amoz Oz's novel *Judas*, wanted a different father, one who was gentler, kinder, more musical, more suave, more faithful. "Faithful" might sound like the wrong word in the circumstances—if my Uncle Sydney really was my father there wasn't much fidelity in the true history—but I suppose I mean faithful to the emotional substrate, to my emotional need. I recognized that a part of me wanted to rewrite my own history. This left me feeling deeply ashamed, and needing somehow to apologize to my father if the test proved that I was indeed his son. It also left me feeling empty, ignorant of the reasons for my desire to recompose my past, flustered, lacking somehow the gift of self-examination.

The test was positive, with no room for uncertainty. My sister and I shared DNA to within a few thousandths of one per cent, incontrovertible evidence that our mother and our father were the same. I felt empty when the email from the testing company arrived. I still feel empty. The uncertainty

BRUCE WHITEMAN

has vanished, but my emotional investment in it has not; now I have to process the feelings that it originally evoked. I feel they will haunt me forever.

MISTRESSES SHOULD BE MUSLIM TOO

Noor Naga

In 2017, I wrote a verse-novel titled *The Mistress Washes Prays* about a young Muslim woman in Toronto who becomes romantically involved with a married man. In May of the same year, an excerpt of this manuscript won the Bronwen Wallace Award for Poetry. Because my family is so geographically scattered—a brother in Cyprus, a sister in Toronto, parents in Dubai, and extended family in Alexandria—only my sister could attend the ceremony. In a way, I think this was a relief. Perhaps because I write in English instead of Arabic, or because there are no other writers and few readers in my family, I've always thought of my work as a private world, irrelevant, even antithetical, to family. At the ceremony I read an excerpt from the verse-novel, which ended up being recorded and published online as an audio file. A month later, the file was discovered by a well-meaning friend, who sent it to my mother; my mother listened to it with my father and then forwarded it to my grandmother, who I was living with in Alexandria at the time. And then *The Mistress Washes Prays* became a family affair.

Over the course of the summer, I was subjected to a host of interrogations. My mother, a successful pathologist who spends most of her days peering down the eye of a microscope and diagnosing skin cancer, was primarily concerned that the work would be read autobiographically. In her experience of reading material—medical literature and newspapers—the author is the narrator, and all presentations are true. While she might have made an exception to this imaginative restriction for fiction, she was not willing to do so with poetry. One afternoon on a beach in Dubai, my mother pretended to ask what the verse-novel was about and then hissed throughout my explanation, clearly impatient to lunge. "They will think you are the mistress!" she eventually interrupted, "Or that you sympathize with mistresses, or that you are an adulterer-apologist." I could tell from the way she said *they* that she meant young, male, Egyptian bachelors. The subtext was, of course, "You will never get married if this book gets out," and "If it isn't incriminating, it's still unforgivably scandalous." In my mother's mind, published work—being part of the public sphere—demands a level of decorum and propriety that is violated by subjects like extramarital affairs or, really, sex of any kind. Having grown up in the United Arab Emirates, and now living in Egypt, I recognize this prudishness as symptomatic of the Middle East. It is pervasive and infectious. Today, when my aunts and uncles ask me what the verse-novel is about, I feel a shrinking reluctance even just to *say* the Arabic word for "mistress."

My father—slyer, more sensitive, and more religious than my mother—took an alternate, more circuitous route. Although we have very different ideas about the roadmap to hell, he, like myself, is less concerned with matrimony than with the state of the soul. Without broaching the subject of the verse-novel at all, he waited until we were alone in a car together (no escape) to "warn" me that with writing comes a moral responsibility, and that in a few years, my own ethics might evolve in contradiction to something I have already published. "By then," he cautioned, "it will be too late to retract it." He was right, of course. This is, in fact, an aspiration of mine. I hope that my ethics will be always evolving to meet my level of experience, always slipping out from under my feet. But my father's comment begged the question: was the verse-novel I'd written somehow an articulation of my ethics? Does a poetic rendering of an affair inherently involve moral adjudication? If so, how do I avoid the danger of outgrowing whatever position I have unwittingly committed to? Should I delay publication year after year, revising and rephrasing everything I write only to publish a complete oeuvre posthumously?

In that car ride with my father, I recognized the subtext to his warning immediately. There is a belief in Islam that "when a person dies, all their deeds are terminated except three: a continuing charity, beneficial knowledge, and a child who prays for them." The first of these, a continuing charity, is perhaps the most popular, the idea being that if you build a mosque or school, if you pave a road or plant a tree or dig a well, then you have left behind a good that keeps on multiplying in the world long after you depart it. This kind of charity is described in the Qur'an as "a grain of corn which grows seven ears, and each ear has a hundred grains" to indicate its boundless proliferation (2:261). The same is true for beneficial knowledge; leaving behind a work of scholarship that in some way improves the lives (or afterlives) of humankind is considered a source of everlasting yield. Unfortunately, the flip side of this formula, though not given as much emphasis, is undeniably inferred. A wrong committed or a misguidance transmitted can continue to injure both you and others ad infinitum. Islamically, even just airing out your own sins or shortcomings is considered injurious because of the possibility that it will contribute to the normalization of wrongdoing and/or potentially inspire others. While this is a well-known directive within the sphere of verbal communication, how it translates to the written page is unclear.

For a Muslim writer concerned with the devotional reverberations of her work in the world, it is debatable whether any meaningful attempt at autobiography would be possible.

But it seems even fiction and poetry become suspect, insofar as they reflect realities of injustice or moral corruption, and insofar as they exhibit plausible interiorities that are not perfectly saintly. That life imitates art seems obvious. We learn how to interact with others in the world, how to break up with a lover or share a quiet family dinner, in part by watching actors play out these familiar scenes year in year out, or by reading about them in books, or hearing about them in songs. Artistic renderings are our primary windows into other people's lives, and we often need these points of reference to make sure we are being human correctly.

Of course, we also learn how to hurt each other. I am reminded here of how, in the absence of adequate training, U.S. soldiers in Mosul drew on films like *Zero Dark Thirty* for inspiration in their interrogation rooms. Novels like *The Sorrows of Young Werther*, *The Virgin Suicides*, and more recently *Thirteen Reasons Why* are recognized as having inspired strings of copycat suicides. Murderers Ronald Pituch, Richard Ramirez, Curtis Lee Walker, and Michael Miller claimed to be motivated by the music of Metallica, AC/DC, Tupac, and Eminem, respectively. While most writers don't generate the same audience-sizes that these popular works of art do, it seems naïve to believe that any writing that becomes accessible to an anonymous public is not affecting someone, *somewhere,* in a way that is potentially negative.

So how does a Muslim write about a mistress—or better yet, how does a Muslim write about a *Muslim* mistress? The answer that has been insinuated over the years by relatives and religious-types in my acquaintance has been simple: punish her. If you must create characters that sin, then at least do so didactically. I have been frequently encouraged to write parable-like narratives in which good is rewarded and evil punished in order to educate and inspire virtue in my readers. Unfortunately, the pieces of literature that are most transformative and darling (to me), the ones that always merit revisiting, are not those that provide the correct answer to a moral conundrum, but rather those that ask questions; not those that condemn or reward, but those that invite the deepest empathy—and perhaps love—for the most unattractive, unlovable characters.

My biggest challenge when writing *The Mistress Washes Prays* was to architect circumstances painful enough and compelling enough to make the mistress' decision to begin an affair *inevitable* within the arc of her agency. I wanted to surround the idea of her "autonomy" with a crowd of external variables, to squeeze and pressurize it so thin that it almost disappears before the readers' eyes. I wanted readers to step down from their horses and podiums and minarets, into a new body, into a new room of agony, where they would have sex with a married man. I am not, as my mother fears, an adulterer apologist, but I believe that being a good human means being a good empath, and empathy—which is merely a combination of kindness and imagination—is best exercised through literature. I am trying in my small way to invite a complicated forgiveness where there was brute condemnation before.

The composite age of my grandmother and I is exactly one hundred years. We are terribly close and terribly similar, with our long bones and addiction to milk tea. She is perhaps my biggest fan. I had just come home to her flat in Alexandria when I found her sitting on the leather couch with something to say in her mouth. She had heard a recording of me reading from *The Mistress Washes Prays*, forwarded to her by my mother, and I was frightened by the unhappy seriousness of her face.

"If your character is going to be a Muslim, why make her a mistress?" she began. I tried to explain that the whole verse-novel was about an affair, but my grandmother countered, "If she must be a mistress, why make her a Muslim?"

"Muslims can be mistresses too."

"Yes. Okay," she said. "That might be true, but the West is already saying about us what you are now saying about us: that we are wicked and animal and godless. They already hate us and they *love* to see you agree with them. They just love it."

My grandmother didn't say, "You are hurting us," but I heard it in her breathing.

And I understood. It is impossible to be an Arab and Muslim Anglophone, exposed to Western (mostly American) literature and pop culture, without feeling that we are living in a time of representational warfare. From the fanatical caveman terrorist to the tyrannical oil sheikh rolling in pussy and riches, to the oppressed daughter/wife, the stereotypes come in many flavors, none of which are positive, and many of which end up being deadly to people in the region. The US invasion of Iraq and Afghanistan, for example, which collectively resulted in over 200,000 war-related civilian deaths, was predicated on years of diligently pathologizing those same civilians as threatening and subhuman.[1] Given the prevalence of this misrepresentation and the extent of the violence it empowers, there is an understandable anxiety within the Middle East about how to rescue our image on the international stage.

Since 2001, there has been a movement of Arab and Muslim writers, especially those that are Anglophone, scrabbling to produce positive representations of us that demonstrate our peacefulness, victimhood, intelligence, modernity, relatability, agency, even and especially our moral superiority. Horse sense dictates that, in order to prove to someone who thinks you are an animal that you are a human, you have to show them that you are a saint. The resistance is so strong that you have to overshoot the mark in order to land on it; hence the plethora of rose-tinted literature allegedly combatting the demonization of Middle Easterners by idolizing them. If a book written by one of us is not loudly objecting or defending or educating in this way, it is often considered not just irrelevant, but actually incorrect, as though literature were a kind of political mathematics. This is true for works produced in any Western language or for apparent Western consumption, but it is more apparent in English. Among ourselves and in our own languages, we can afford to explore other questions, but among outsiders that are powerful and hostile towards us, there is an expectation that literary works will double as activism.

The problem with this species of protest, however, is that it invalidates itself. I am reminded of a tweet by the Australian poet of mixed Turkish and Lebanese descent, Omar Sakr, in which he says, "If we stay stuck in a news cycle of Muslim Monster v Muslim Human, we lose. To debate your humanity is to implicitly agree it is uncertain."[2] When literature considers itself a corrective prescription for xenophobes, it privileges those readers by respecting their accusations enough to challenge them. The more energy exhausted in communicating with an aggressor, the more their power and centrality is affirmed. Hence, to write in response to hatred is to fail before you've begun. "The function, the very serious function of racism, is distraction," observes Toni Morrison in a similar vein. "It keeps you from doing your work. It keeps you explaining, over and over again, your reason for being." Arabs might have warped stereotypes about Americans but this has not resulted in a nationwide scramble to produce a counter-mythology. We do not distract them in the same way. The British are not sitting around their living rooms and front lawns anxiously fretting over what Egyptians think about them. Any single piece of Australian poetry does not bear the burden of representing Australians at large, and yet this inductive fallacy continues to haunt Arab Anglophone literature.

My grandmother is much more progressive and literary than either of my parents, but her remarks about my writing were in many ways a composite of theirs. Like my mother, she was concerned that the verse-novel would be read autobiographically, but as a collective—rather than individual—

confession on behalf of the entire Middle East. Like my father, her concern was ethical rather than cosmetic. She was less interested in what the work *was* than in what it would *do* in the world. After a year of ruminating, I'm still not sure that I have an answer for her.

For those of us in the Middle East who consider English our mother tongue, we cannot escape the possibility that our work will be read in the service of bigotry, but we can, I think, choose to ignore the bigots. Let them talk to themselves. We elect the imaginary readers that we write for and so we are responsible for the host of expectations or restrictions that they bring to our pages. Personally, I believe there is space in Anglophone literature, between the Muslim terrorist and the Muslim saint, for a Muslim mistress. In fact, I believe that she is necessary if we are going to escape the defense position we have been occupying for years. I realize that in the region I come from and have returned to, writing such a character means crossing into treacherous ground where I may be understood as a native informant, whitewashed, brown-nosing, shamelessly admitting to anyone already hating us that we, too, sin. It is a bit like a period stain on a white dress at the Oscars, or picking one's nose in front of the Queen; like blowing oneself up in a desert via Facebook's live stream; a protest against table manners when one is clearly sitting in a zoo, and all the real people outside looking in. I don't want to hurt anyone, but I am also trying to feel free and unafraid in my craft.

So far it's been as hard as it looks.

Notes

1 "Civilians Killed & Wounded." *Civilians Killed & Wounded | Costs of War*, Watson Institute of International and Public Affairs - Brown University, Mar. 2015, watson.brown.edu/costsofwar/costs/human/ civilians.

2 Sakr, Omar (@omarjsakr). "How many more years of this They're Human, Too stories? This dehumanising surprise. If we stay stuck in a news cycle of Muslim Monster v Muslim Human, we lose. To debate your humanity is to implicitly agree it is uncertain." 25 December, 2017, 11:45pm. Tweet.

HALF-THING

Meaghan Rondeau

How does one begin an essay on almost-middle-aged virginity?

Let's see:

Webster's dictionary defines *virgin* as "a person who has not had sexual intercourse."

*   *   *

Sigh.

*   *   *

The crux of the problem is that what I really really want is *connection*, and yet I have, thus far, 38 years in, not engaged in humanity's most universally engaged-in method of achieving it. Not even close.

What does that say about me? What the hell am I?

*   *   *

I'm a writer, and I'll pretty much write anything, and often it's poems, and lately they're coming out as these very flat-toned, plainspoken, sparse things. No lyricality. Little to no word play. Barely any punctuation even. Just broken statements hanging out naked in the white space. I'm fond as fuck of rhythm, rhyme, assonance, *et al.*, always have been, but certain stories of mine seem to be asking for a different approach. They're unpoems. For the most part they aren't going over well with the literary journals, but a couple of them were published in a local magazine recently. This led to a reading at the Vancouver Art Gallery, and the editor did the inevitable awkward little Q&A beforehand. She was like, "How did you come to write 'unpoems'?" and I launched into an inarticulate thing about how sometimes decoration feels like deception, like hiding behind language; how CanLit irritates me with its unrelenting pretty lyricality and what I perceive as an overall aversion to real risk-taking or badassery; how I feel like I'm not part of the poetry "scene," or any scene, etc.

Really it's not that complicated. I say too much when I'm flustered, and the editor's question flustered me, even though she'd told me in advance that she was going to ask it. Later that day when I redid the conversation in my mind my response was: *I write unpoems because I'm an unperson.*

*   *   *

I'm a translator, as well. *Translate* means nothing more (and nothing less) than *bring across*, carry from one place to another. The word has no etymological link to language. My concept of it is unbounded. Words on a page are translated thoughts. Actions are translated feelings. Actual is translated potential. Age is translated time. Mythology is translated psychology. Metaphors are translated images.

I love languages, I love language. I've done translations of Horace, Sappho, Ovid, Aeschylus, Catullus. I've translated "Mack the Knife" into Latin, the chorus of "Billie Jean" into Greek. With the help of some classmates and professors at a reception, I've Latinized the opening lines of "Baby Got Back" (we got stuck on how to accurately render "You get sprung"). I've done straight translations, liberal translations, adaptations, dramatic modernizations of classical literature, translations of dark tragedy into darker comedy. I translate my own unpleasant experiences into, Muses willing, entertaining reads.

And yet when it comes to emotional closeness and physical contact, I can't do the translation. The distance between them feels untraversable. *How did* that *happen?* I ask myself whenever I see a couple holding hands. *What's the mechanism?*

*   *   *

I know I'm not the only one, but I'm the only one I know, which is pretty much the same thing from where I'm sitting.

*   *   *

(Obviously I'm not counting nuns and whatnot. God knows this has nothing to do with religion.)

*   *   *

There is a lady virgin trope that shows up here and there in literature and on film, but she's usually post-menopausal, usually a side character with a sepia-toned backstory of having decades ago fucked up (via some combination of timidity, vanity, indecision, and unladylike comportment) her one and only golden opportunity for companionship. She is a relic of a bygone era when it was marriage or nothing. Any distress her situation may have caused her is far in the past; she is content now, content and wise, content and wise and old.

Occasionally a non-elderly adult virgin from the modern day shows up on TV or in a movie, but then it's always a man, and his situation comes across as hilarious to the other characters in the show, and to the people watching the show (me included), and, I assume, to the people writing the show.

It doesn't offend or upset me not to be "represented" in popular culture. Honestly, I'd rather represent myself. I'm all the proof I need of how "valid" my (in)experience is. But there's an ontological incongruity to actually existing while at the same time being laughably unimaginable. It's not something that bothers me constantly, or even all that often, but it's always there, floating around, and now and then in the course of its drifting it bumps up against my consciousness, and I can't deny that those moments are pretty unfuckingpleasant.

* * *

An earlier draft of this segment began: *I feel an unspoken pressure to depict myself as a joke to make others comfortable*. But every time I reread the line, it felt disingenuous and inaccurate, like writer BS, calculated vulnerability, one of those aphorisms that sound profound but make less sense the more you think about them.

The truth is, I've always gotten the impression that I experience considerably *less* pressure than other people, women in particular, to make anyone comfortable. I have very few fucks to give in the social obligations department, even fewer to spare for the gender roles department. I have no practical interest in what other people are doing or expect me to be doing. I do what feels appropriate or necessary for me to be doing. I trust myself the most. I'm grateful for this self-reliance now, though not for the years of shit from which it was sculpted.

The truth is, when I depict myself as a joke, it's to make *myself* comfortable.

* * *

I love comedy, the darker the better, ideally dark enough that the reader or audience becomes emotionally unmoored. If there's a consistent philosophy behind my writing it's the concept of comedy and tragedy as identical twins, as each other's reflections. What, if anything, differentiates them? Timing. Time.

* * *

Thirteen years ago, when I told him I hadn't slept with anyone, my University of Washington classmate and purported friend and persistently aspiring deflowerer Alex replied, palpably perplexed: "How is that possible?" A fair question.

*   *   *

I never expected to survive high school, to experience my adult self. I didn't see myself as a person with a future. Things were not good. They'd never been great, but I'd gotten by, and then around grade six I really started to unravel. I'd always been socially weird, introverted AF, and now I was drowning in the effort of attempting to give the impression of comprehending the complex and mysterious social rituals and demands engendered by adolescence. Cliques, dating, crushes, kissing. Brand-name clothes, eyeshadow.

Mainly what I remember from grades seven through twelve is debilitating anxiety, severe depression, migraines that left me immobile with pain or weakness in the middle of class. I assumed I'd kill myself. That seemed like the only rational conclusion, the only believable ending for this character. I was always fantasizing about it, always cutting myself.

It's not that I was *bullied*, exactly. There was one guy, Cory fucking Scott, who harassed me from grade seven onward, sometimes physically, but aside from his bizarrely persistent reliance on insults that played off my, unfortunately for him, unrhymeable name ("Hey Scrondeau!"), it was for the most part a situation of being invisible, negligible, ignored, mocked behind my back (though sometimes within earshot) because I didn't wear the right clothes, was excruciatingly awkward, rarely spoke, had nothing to contribute socially.

I kept my eyes on my textbooks, not (contrary to popular opinion) because I was nerdishly obsessed with my grades or even necessarily all that interested in whatever I was reading. As often as not, "reading" wasn't even the right word. In hindsight, staring at books was a self-preservation tactic that I made heavy use of well into my university life and can still be found employing at readings and other social events. Directing my eyes at any page of text was safer than having to look up and take in all the little daily rejections. I had made a pact with myself to always come across as indifferent. I'd worked out that refusing to give anyone the satisfaction of a reaction would let me keep hold of a small piece of my dignity.

There was never a time when anyone chose me as a gym-class partner or a group member or a friend. Although grudgingly tolerated on occasion, I was not wanted in anyone's presence. I was rarely sought out. Rarely was anyone glad to see me. If there was an assembly I'd cling to the fringes of a certain group of girls who weren't actively terrible to me, sit at their outskirts, feeling guilty that I was imposing on them, contaminating their space by being there.

To never be seen. To be unseeable, to not occupy physical space, to be present only as absence. To nonexist. That was the fantasy.

* * *

My concept of myself, of time, of my self in time, is still pretty fucked up, even though all that stuff was so, so long ago and I went on to eventually make friends and build a highly tolerable life for myself and dare I say achieve things. But even now I sometimes catch a glance at myself in the bathroom mirror and it's like, *You're still here?* Twenty years later, I've still got a foot out the door.

* * *

nam sane cum hanc considero sive meips[a]m quatenus sum tantum res cogitans, nullas in me partes possum distinguere, sed rem plane unam et integram me esse intelligo. (Descartes, *Meditation* VI.19, italics mine, with the masculine pronoun feminized 'cause I'm a lady.)

"But then when I consider [the mind]—I mean, *myself*, insofar as I am plainly a thinking thing—I can distinguish in myself no parts; rather, I understand clearly that I am something *single and whole*."

Unam et integram.

I suppose it's still the fantasy, and to some extent the reality.

* * *

I was introduced to Descartes' *Meditations on First Philosophy* in my first year of university. I don't want to give him a lot of airspace here because in a graduate seminar I took six years later I found out he was a major asshole who went around kicking dogs because he thought animals were automata who couldn't feel pain, but anyway, what he's mainly known for is *cogito ergo sum* ("I think, therefore I am"). In the *Meditations* he serves up his theory of dualism: a person consists of two distinct entities, a body and a mind, and the body is divisible, corruptible, etc., while the mind is divine, immaterial, immortal, the true essence of humanity. Again, I dislike Descartes as a person and I hope he's getting shinbitten by plenty of dogs in the afterlife, but I really latched on to his argument that the mind is what matters, is the *you* of you. His thesis legitimized what I already hoped was true: I was a *res cogitans*, a thinking thing. I'd never believed in God, but the idea of physicality as irrelevant, minds as indivisible and unbound by space, heaven as a place without bodies, made a beautiful, almost religious kind of sense.

* * *

In the beginning was the Word, and so on: one of the great opening lines in fiction. Language as synonymous with God, as the First Thing, as Creation itself, as Immortality. Eternity, Entirety, Entity.

Wow!

Right?

I wish I were a more credulous kind of person so I could have the experience of believing in things like that for more than two seconds before my internal monologue shows up to point out that the concept of language predating and creating everything else in the universe is logically impossible, if not downright meaningless. Anthropocentric. A myth.

*　*　*

In the 8th century BCE-ish, around the same time the *Iliad* and *Odyssey* were working their way up the charts, the poet Hesiod composed the *Theogony*, the graphically disturbing R-rated story of the genealogy of the Greek gods. In his poem, the first entity to come into being is Chaos. In Greek, "chaos" means neither "disorganization" nor "a hectic excess of romantic entanglements and/or emotional problems and/or tasks to complete"; it means kind of the exact opposite of that: "emptiness," "nothingness." Cognate with *chasm*. A void.

Then, spontaneously, simultaneously, come Gaia (Earth), Tartarus (vaguely defined; some sort of prisony dungeony place deep within the Earth), and Eros (self-explanatory).

Some implications: (1) Earth without sex is unthinkable. (2) Both causally and temporally, everything descends from Eros. (3) Without fucking, there's nothing.

The Greek gods are gleefully, shamelessly physical, but even in the more cerebral, less symposiastic Christian tradition, the Word becoming flesh is pretty central to the whole deal, despite the Christian philosophers' and Biblical commentators' proclamations of the superiority of the immaterial and indivisible. Jesus is, among other things, a testament to humankind's dependence on matter for meaning, our species' apparently innate need for something (/someone) to grab on to.

*　*　*

I've never written about this. Well, never straightforwardly, and never at length. Never in a format that could lead to anyone else thinking about it, uninterrupted, for *this long*. I would have liked the story to have reached some sort of conclusion before writing it (or, perhaps better yet, not writing it). Structurally, that would be preferable. Emotionally, likewise.

*   *   *

ludunt formosae; casta est quam nemo rogavit: Ovid, *Amores* I.8.43.

"Good-looking girls play around; the chaste girl is the one no one has—" well, *rogavit* is literally "asked," but here it's meant in an innuendoey winkyface sense: "propositioned," "come on to." "Chased."

*   *   *

Early on in my terrible adolescence I somehow or another came to believe I'd like to learn Latin, a hunch that intensified each time we crossed paths: biological taxonomy, the periodic table, Poe's "The Cask of Amontillado" (*Nemo me impune lacessit!*). So when I ran into the list of Latin classes in the University of Calgary's course catalogue as I made my first-year schedule, it felt like fate, and maybe it was.

On the first day, the prof distributed handouts with the text of the Lord's Prayer, the English on the left and the Latin on the right, and allowed us a silent minute to begin to build the bridge, to connect the philological dots, and that was about as long as it took for me to abandon my nebulous intention to "become a writer" by way of an English degree. Who knows where I'd gotten the idea that that was how a literary life was achieved. I didn't know how anything was achieved. I was seventeen and I'd spent the last six years hanging out with a carpet knife in a bedroom in small-town Saskatchewan.

*   *   *

I went to the U of C because that was where my cousin Jess was. She and I became close in the late '90s, in our late teens. We lived three hours apart and regularly mailed each other long letters with extravagantly decorated envelopes.

Although I talked a decent game in my letters, going right along with, e.g., Jess's positive assessment of the physical attributes of Gavin Rossdale, I had no idea what "a cute guy" was. I didn't have any real feelings about Gavin Rossdale, beyond liking his songs.

I didn't know what I was supposed to be feeling about guys. I was overhearing all kinds of stuff about dates, crushes, sex, love, and so forth, but the sense I always got was that none of it applied to me. I remember being in a sex ed class in grade six or seven, and as the teacher explained, with the help of a crude overhead projection, the basic logistics of intercourse, I said to myself: *I'm not doing that.* Not that I thought it was bad or dirty; it just looked . . . strange. Foreign. Nonsensical. Like, *Why?*

One day during my lunch break in grade eleven or twelve I was sitting alone near a group of people, near enough that when a guy from the group accidentally broke his plastic fork, one of the tines came flying over and either hit me or landed near me. I looked up. He was smiling genuinely, bigly. "Sorry about that!" he said, as though speaking to me was an acceptable thing to do, as though accidentally hitting and/or startling me was apology-worthy, as though I was a human being. I told Jess all about it in my next letter. *I kept his fork tine.* But it wasn't attraction, really. I was just astonished by his kindness.

* * *

Jess was a year ahead of me, and in her first year in Calgary she had nothing but great things to report about residence life. Silly times! Cute guys! Holiday parties! Friendships around every corner! We decided we wanted to room together.

Needless to say, it was a ridiculous disaster. I didn't know how to function socially. I didn't know how to be in a conversation, had nothing but silent confusion to contribute to discussions of dating, drinking, drunken mistakes, clubs, high-school antics, missing one's friends at home. That year I nearly lost Jess as a friend in the process of constantly embarrassing myself and offending others with my feral behaviour.

I belonged nowhere, nowhere except at the back of classics and philosophy classrooms. I did not speak in class. I did not make friends. I drank coffee and took very thorough, colourful notes. I studied Latin verb charts and Greek principal parts lists like my identity depended on it. I did all the readings on Plato and Ockham and Aquinas. I let the gods run around in my head.

* * *

Sounds like something out of a book of unattributed Greek lyric poetry fragments, I think to myself every time I see the tagline on the front of a package of Safeway brand sliced strawberries: "Frozen at the peak of ripeness."

* * *

In mythology, men chase girls in the most literal sense. The girls who decide to hold on to their virginity are always athletic, outdoorsy types. Fast runners.

Times have changed, apparently. I have never entered a gym. I've owned a bike for twelve years and ridden it twice. As we speak, I'm slouched on an armchair spooning a tub of gelato.

* * *

The theory in Ovid's poem—virgins are virgins for a reason—is witty (and sexist), stated with his usual sly elegance (and sexism). But the theory fails to hold. Sure, high school was a bleak writeoff, but there's plentiful photographic evidence to confirm that in the bygone days of my twenties—copulation primetime, I hear!—I was quite sufficiently *formosa*. And plenty of people have asked me out. Friends, strangers, men, women, a couple of students . . . I've said yes to some of them (not the students), gone on some dates. How do you like me now, Ovid?

Say I meet someone tomorrow and—

"Someone" who?

Whatever gender, sex, category, and/or etc. of person you want to imagine me with is fine with me. I don't know, and I have yet to encounter any evidence that I care. In my twenties I became infatuated with a woman, which had a huge emotional impact on me because it was the first time I'd noticed myself being infatuated with anyone, really noticing and being affected psychologically by someone's physicality. Utterly against my will, I acted like a total teenaged doofus whenever she was around, which I found embarrassing but also fascinating because it had never happened in all the years that I'd actually *been* a teenaged doofus. As a result of her being a her I sort of vaguely thought of myself as a lesbian for a few years: told my parents and my closest friends, wounded the heart of a smitten friend with whom I'd accidentally gone on what he considered a date, intentionally went on dates with some women. But the label never felt quite right, although for a while there it did bring some relief in that I felt like it went some of the way toward explaining why my entire romantic CV consisted of one reluctant date and one accidental one.

In conversations with men who want to date and/or sleep with me, I wield my alleged orientation like a shield: combatively, clumsily, unconvincingly. I want it to end the discussion, but it only ever elicits more questions.

*   *   *

I had a poem published in *Plenitude* a few years ago, and even though I'm clearly not straight in any recognizable sense of the term, it felt wrong to be included in an LGBTQ+ publication. Underhanded, like some sort of cheating. Like, *What if they ask me what I am? How could I respond in a way that would make sense? If they find out I'm not any of the things from the acronym will they take down my poem and demand their fifteen dollars back? I've already spent it on ice cream . . .*

It's been a long time since I've felt any affiliation with any of the currently claimable categories or communities. Maybe I'm in the wrong place, or the wrong time, or the wrong language, or the wrong culture. Or maybe I'm something that already does exist and I just don't realize it. Regardless, the best I can do here and now is to espouse a key tenet of propositional logic and "identify as" Meaghan Rondeau.

* * *

I realized recently that I'll never get to have the experience of being a young writer, and articulating that to myself made me a little bit griefy. Thanks to my mental-health-garbage-themed adolescence and the intensity of my academic life, I didn't start writing seriously until I quit my PhD program at 27. I was first published at 30 and started my MFA at 35. I don't regret my background: as both a person and a writer I'm grateful for my education, and for what I've learned about creativity and writing outside of creative writing classrooms. Still, the exaltation of young writers irritates the bejesus out of me. Prizes and contests for writers under 30, "top 25 under 25" lists, that sort of thing.

Am I jealous of how effortlessly they fit in? Of how easily they, and their writing—their voices, their perspectives, their experience—find their place, are granted acceptance?

Of course.

* * *

So. Say I, Meaghan Rondeau, meet someone tomorrow. We hit it off super hard. Immediate connection. Trust! Comfort!

Similar principles! We hang out a lot. We meet each other's cats. We sit in my living room's two adjacent armchairs passing a tub of gelato back and forth. We act like teenaged doofuses (doofi?) around each other. We start to fall in love, however that works. We end up in bed, or something like that. Hurrah!

Now what?

How the fuck do I be and do what a person roughly my age, 38, expects and wants? I don't know what to offer, how much to ask for, what the available positions are. I lack the requisite skills and the prerequisite experience. It's not that I don't know what sex is. I'm well-read. I'm one of the greatest eavesdroppers of my generation. I have friends, we have conversations. I am intellectually cognizant of the salient logistics of what pairs of humans do with/to/for each other. But knowing about something isn't the same thing as having experienced it. How do I not scare and/or amuse the shit out of the person with the fact of what I am? How do I not make it about me? How do I not take it too seriously, ascribe more importance to it than is reasonable or fair to my partner? ("I'm scared this is going to mean too much to you, like, we made out a couple times and you're going to want to get married now."—UW Alex in 2005.) How do I engage in a truly shared, reciprocation-oriented experience, which, though it may not always be everyone's goal, is definitely mine in the context of this hypothetical scenario?

In the same way, for the same reasons, that I'll never be a young writer, I've lost the possibility of mutual discovery, equal footing with a partner, young love. I never get to be a 16-year-old fumbling around on a couch in my parents' basement with another 16-year-old.

* * *

I met my best friend Nicole in the fall of 2002 when she moved to Calgary from California to start the Classics MA program.

Later that semester she told me about an awkward encounter with a guy who had fallen for her really hard at a Grad Studies meet-and-greet during her first week on campus. She was uninterested, but she was also lonely and disoriented, a new student in a new country, recently out of a long-term relationship, on top of which she tends to exude a warm friendliness regardless of how she's actually feeling, so it can be impossible to tell when she wants you to eff off. Anyway, somehow they ended up back in her room in residence, and although she'd been clear that she wasn't going to have sex with him, she agreed to let him stay over because she was too indifferent, tired, nice, whatever to kick him out of her room and make him walk back to wherever he lived at whatever time of the early morning it was. While crammed into her single bed, they made awkward conversation, and he ended up divulging that he'd never been in a relationship.

This being a secondhand anecdote from sixteen years ago, I've forgotten a lot of the details, but what I do remember, still, is the exasperation in Nicole's voice as she told me what went through her mind in response to his confession: "I don't want to have to *teach* you."

She and I were, at the time, 22. And, again, she is *way* above average, friendliness-wise.

It's not that I don't see where she was coming from. I see, and I agree. I don't want to have to *be taught*. I don't want to be a 38-year-old fumbling around like a 16-year-old with another 38-year-old. I'm an independent, almost-middle-aged woman with a schwackload of credentials. And *I'm* a teacher, damn it. Between TA gigs and ESL positions, I've spent thousands of hours at the front of classrooms. Even when I'm taking a course, I can't turn off my teacher brain. *If she had us do a quick group activity occasionally the atmosphere in here would be totally different. We could do so much more with our class time if he'd just spend ten minutes preparing.*

Besides the not speaking in class, I was a model student in my undergraduate days—I bought in to the system, I had an almost blind, uncritical respect for my professors, I was content to look way, way up to them—but that ship sailed a long time ago. And anyway, I'm an equal-footing-or-bust kind of person, and even the most successful teacher-student interactions are rooted in a pretty blatant power mismatch. When I'm teaching, I acknowledge this explicitly, I ridicule it now and again, I do my best to slacken its grip on whatever is going on in my classroom—but it's still there. Whereas, as far as I can tell, the whole thing of a successful relationship is reciprocity, mutual giving and mutual benefit. A sort of balanced . . . I don't know . . . *even-handedness*.

* * *

"You're so exotic," Alex—still the only person I've ever kissed—once said to me, with a certain gleam in his tone, a certain moon-landing flag-plant kind of lust, as we discussed my inexperience.

Thirteen years ago, I was exotic. What would the adjective be today?

(Don't answer that.)

I'm still playing catch-up from things I missed. Not just important interpersonal things but day-to-day stuff. Like, it took me years to figure out how to choose clothes. I still don't know how to do a French braid or a messy bun. I don't have a flaming clue how to use eyeliner; I buy it, try to apply it, say a bunch of swears, and that's the end of that, until the next time. There was no internet when I was growing up, no YouTube tutorials to pick up the slack for a socially non-participating teenager. My little sister is a big help; I'm always asking her to help me pick out sunglasses and lipstick, sending her texts like *Can I wear hot pink tights with a shortish black dress?* (You can. I did.)

There's no YouTube video called "How to fall in love and lose your virginity at 38." Or 39 or 43 or 56. Or "How to maintain your humanness despite never falling in love or sleeping with anyone ever," another possibility.

*   *   *

"This is a universal experience," my nonfiction prof said last year, in response to a classmate's personal essay on his quest for the right partner. "Everyone wants a relationship."

(Is that true??), I wrote in my notebook, frantic enough to bust out a second question mark, after recording the above quotations.

For the next week's workshop, I submitted the first draft of . . . this.

[Awkward silence]

*   *   *

Is that true?

Shouldn't I be able to answer that? I mean, if *everyone* wants something, and I *want* to want it, but I haven't figured out *how* to want it, then . . .

??

*   *   *

The way I once described it to a friend (ex-friend, now) is that back when I was younger I went into my brain's electrical panel and shut off some of the switches, which at the time was a clever move, a strategy to pre-empt total burnout, to outsmart the part of me that yearned for that. Self-sabotage in the service of self-preservation. And now, now that my life is no longer a hellscape, now that I possibly have it in me psychologically to participate in whatever I've been missing universal-experience-wise, I can't reset the breakers. It's too late, the system's been upgraded, that panel is defunct. Mice chewed through the wiring years ago, and I was too busy hiding from my floormates and memorizing Latin verb endings to notice.

*   *   *

Virginity is a symbol: it has semiotic value, conceptual significance that transcends its dictionary definition. Same goes for the loss (" ") of it. It's a fairly arbitrary boundary—hilarious, even—if you take it literally.

But you don't. We don't.

*   *   *

This isn't about the stark fact of not having been fucked. If the problem were that I'm on one end of a dichotomy and would rather be on the other, it would take about twelve minutes to solve, and then I could come home and triumphantly delete this entire document.

The weight of it is this: as a result of never having experienced a sexual relationship, I've never done, felt, suffered, given, or received any of the good or bad or complicated or significant or character-developing or generous or selfish or devastating or life-affirming or death-defying stuff that comes along with getting so intimately tangled up with another human being. And as a result of that, distance exists between me and the people who have, which, at my age, is everyone I know.

The distance is the problem. The growing and growing and growing distance.Because I was friendless for so long, I still and probably always will experience every friendship of mine as miraculous, an ineffable mystery. I value friendship above everything except language. Yet, ironically, I'm in exactly the right position to watch friends drift away from me as they assume the role of partner or parent. To be cut off by friends whose partners don't want them talking to me anymore. To end up at unresolveable impasses with friends who have either come to want, or have secretly wanted all along, a physical relationship with me. (The ex-friend mentioned above, for example.)

* * *

I attract people in the middlespace: the recently divorced or broken-up-with, the emotionally wounded, people looking for a form of exclusive companionship without the dating, for someone incapable of casting judgment on their sexual lifechoices, someone to talk to until two in the morning, someone who's almost always available to exchange texts or go for a drink. I don't go looking for these people. But they find me. Looming over all of these relationships, despite the unusually intense closeness they often generate, is my knowledge that I'm a rest stop, a half-thing, that the person will be moving on once they've recovered enough to go out and find what they really want. They're my friends, I respect them, I fucking love them. I want them to have what they want. And it isn't this. It isn't me.

* * *

I'm not looking for sympathy, my dear good reader. I *am* still here, and I'm strong as fuck, actually. I know all kinds of interesting shit. I have good people in my life. I'm employed, financially stable, debt-free. I rent my home from a landlord who's kind and reasonable, and it's full of meaningful knick-knacks and good books. My sense of humour is as sharp as a carpet knife. I have like two dozen articles of cat-themed clothing, plus two actual cats. I always wanted to be a writer and knew I was one and now I am one. My freezer is full of ice cream and when I run out I can and will go get more.

* * *

My academic life has been a long tour of the arts and humanities, and I have the useless degrees to prove it. I've taken courses in English literature, comparative Indo-European linguistics, medieval Christian philosophy, Old English, Helen of Troy, Plato, Greek and Latin prose composition, Rene dogkicking Descartes, Sanskrit, Thomas Aquinas, Homer, Aeschylus' *Oresteia*, ancient manuscripts, sentential logic, the Greek New Testament, Greek novels, feminist philosophy, women in the ancient world ...

It's as though I've been unconsciously trying to make up for my physical inexperience intellectually. Like if I take enough of these classes, it'll be equivalent to having done the things in real life, I'll understand them as thoroughly as everyone else does. Like if I spend enough time in the humanities I'll eventually be fully human.

* * *

As both a writer and a reader, what I'm most fascinated by, drawn to, is voice. That feeling of knowing within a few seconds, "This is _____'s writing." That's how I want people to feel when they're reading me or hearing me read: *Nobody else could have written this.* The word choice, the structure, the syntax, the rhythms, the placement of humour, the take on the topic, I want them to be unmistakably mine. Otherwise, why bother?

I wonder a lot if the chronic relationshiplessness, the physical aloneness, the untouchedness, is holding me back as a writer. I worry that there may be certain things I can't understand, can't write intelligently about, can't "get right" or describe from a realistic perspective or helpfully comment on in my colleagues' work, because I don't have hands-on experience of anything past the very very tip of human sexuality. The thought that this may be standing in the way of my being able to connect with readers emotionally upsets me whenever I think about it, which I try not to. Are we too far apart, is the bridge unbuildable? Maybe whoever is reading this is feeling the same unsettling sense of oarless floating that grips me as my peers describe their hilariously disturbing one-night Tinder hookups, their agonizing three-month dry spells, their inability to resist sleeping with a certain person despite knowing that it's going to lead to months of ridiculous fallout.

* * *

If all I'm accomplishing is making you feel as far away from me as I feel from you, is that connection, or a parody of connection? Or both?

* * *

On the other hand—no: *at the same time*—maybe my intactness/untouchedness/integrity (a set of etymological triplets) contributes to my voice, or even to some extent defines it. When I'm writing, no-man's-land is where I'm comfortable; it's all hybrid this and fragmentary that and indefinable the other. It would hurt to be seen as unsettling or aberrant by a person whose bed I was in, but I take it as a delicious compliment when people react to my writing with terms like those.

Is genrelessness worth what it costs me as a person, if it makes me a better writer? I've been called a fatalist more than once. Maybe I'm *supposed* to be a half-thing. Maybe there's no other way to get to wherever I'm going.

* * *

Does an "essay" like this have an ending?
    Is it a happy one?

THE WEEKEND GOD:
ALDEN NOWLAN AND THE
POETRY WEEKEND FRAGMENTS

Danny Jacobs

> I've worshipped him myself, climbed the days of
>   the week
> like a ladder, with every rung bringing me closer;
> and if when I got there it was never
> quite as good as I had hoped,
> afterwards it always seemed to have been better.
>   — Alden Nowlan, "The Weekend God"

Nanny says Nowlan *lumbered*. She calls on Christmas, the year after Grampie died, and I tell her I got the *Selected*. It's one of my first poetry books, the one from Anansi, the one with the bland blue-grey fish house. For this Maritime Poet, the cover demands a bland fish house. "He was a big man," Nanny says. "Your Grampie and I would see him lumbering across campus when we visited for functions." Grampie—respected alum, federal minister, his honorary doctorate's black floppy hat hanging on my office wall, flattened and mounted under glass, *Hon. Gerald S. Merrithew, Doctor of Laws, Honoris Causa* sewn on a square of satin. Grampie, MLA for East Saint John during the Hatfield era and reciter of doggerel verse, might've known Nowlan well, might've known his poems, yet he doesn't have his books among his military histories and outdoor guides at the family farm. After he dies, I find a 19th-century Wordsworth with gilt-edged pages and tooled leather cover, the publication page missing. Mountain etchings for *The Prelude*. The last time I see him he's lying on a chaise lounge in the kitchen; he's wrapped in a blanket and it's the first time I've seen him unshaven. He asks about my poetry, asks if I've read T. S Eliot. I wish I'd asked him what he knew about Alden.

Nowlan *lumbered*. Can only the large lumber? I like to think it's the geography of UNB, the hill tuning our gait, nothing to do with size, the hill canting us, feet ahead, steps larger and longer, a lope, a saunter, the slow dip of the Saint John River Valley creating in our bodies a downhill compensation. Nowlan lumbering down Windsor Street—his big beard and big hair catching the snow, his tie blowing out behind him, his post-op neck distended as if he's swallowing the day's weather, his myth trailing behind his gait.

And *we*, too, lumber years later. To his repurposed home— Windsor Castle turned grad house, the downstairs full of formica tables, the upstairs offices where we get our student IDs, file our grievances. Which room was the bedroom? Where he slept, snored off the whiskey? There are framed copies of his best-known poems throughout. "An Exchange of Gifts" is installed by the front entrance: "I will keep on / writing this poem for you / even after I'm dead." And I want this to be true when I walk in after the angst-ridden one-upmanship of seminars, after I leave half in the bag, head down into a snowstorm, the door banging behind me.

See, we can't help but think this way. The myth grows, lumbers. And we grad students lumber, insecure with new poems, cradling moleskines and *Coastlines*, hugging our IPAs and arguing the pronunciation of *DeLillo*; loud talkers and outtalkers, first readers and frequent flyers, *The Fiddlehead*'s xeroxed slush pile under our arms as we lumber across Windsor Castle's back deck at one a.m. for more beer money from the ATM by the bookstore, wilted twenties spat out from the bank loan aether while we stamp our feet and puff our own cold hoppy breath; or we lumber from the library at midnight after typing cramped papers on the poetics of birding; we lumber unsteadily down the winding walkway to the brick and finial gates on Beaverbrook, and then to downtown, to the Tannery, to our messy balled-sock apartments. And we lumber from Poetry Weekend's final hangdog reading, the burnt-dust smell of old rads still in our noses, Mem Hall's stained glass and mic'ed Poet Voice now a memory; we lumber down the hill with the news of who slighted who, who got too drunk, and we still love poems, some knocked us out, really they did, but no more poems for a little while, ok? Shane Neilson lumbers down the hill to a trunk full of chapbooks. Dan Renton lumbers down the hill in his fedora and Italian shoes. Jen Houle lumbers down the hill with her poems of Shediac, poems in Chiac, "Acadian ghosts / boring into the headpond." Tammy Armstrong lumbers down the hill, where at the Taproom we teach Ross our NBer talk: *that's right a good poem.* Brian Bartlett in the early 70's, high-school senior, kid poet of the Icehouse Gang, lumbers down the hill with Fred Cogswell. Lynn Davies lumbers down the hill. Bob Gibbs lumbers down the hill. Travis Lane lumbers down the hill to hunt review copies at the *Fiddlehead* office. Bliss Carman and Charles G. D. lumber down the hill in cape and spats, talking Shelley and planning canoe trips, their leather boots knocking tetrameter crisp on cobbles. We all lumber down the hill, almost falling, our feet leading us, Chucks and brogans, until we're poleaxed with the sleet sheeting off the mighty Saint John, "this fleeced and muffleheaded / snow blindness," and we try and try and try not to write another ode.

It's early fall at UNB, and in Mem Hall the particle board tables are bowed with stacks of thin books; anxious poets shiver and smoke on granite steps outside, their vintage messenger bags sheathing really really nice pens. Upstairs band practice is ongoing despite the readings, the faint sound of an oboe curling down the hand-tooled staircase. The Quad's maples are lit red and match the buildings' Georgian brick. Here's a photograph of three young men at Poets' Corner, UNB's 1947 memorial to its Confederation Poets, the campus' literary omphalos; the cairn, weather-blackened at its bricked seams, backgrounds them: Shane Neilson in the middle, arms draped around Jim Johnstone and Marc Di Saverio. Shane's playing the proud NBer, the prodigal son returned, host to these Ontarians, and he's happy. They pulled in that morning, Fredericton's big blue water tower materializing on the hill.

Marc looks least comfortable in the picture, his full black suit hot, the strap of his bag pulling at his tie and jacket. I imagine the photo snapped after Marc's reading that morning, the first set, a reading where Marc yelled his poems under Mem Hall's neo-gothic proscenium. God —an awesome, awkward, beautiful and attention-demanding performance—"Go, my songs, verse through the ears of the smilers-in-their sleep, bridge them to their wakes…" I listened or tried to, and forgot about what pub we'd go to that afternoon and if they'd have the Picaroons IPA I really thought was fine. I didn't know if I liked his poems, but he cut through the verse-drift, the daydreamt dull stretches. But between poems there were proprietary snickers from the otherwise hushed audience, because Marc said his poems unselfconsciously, like he meant them. Shane calls Memorial Hall the Church of Poetry, with its porticos and cornices, quoined pilasters, its Miltonic stained glass. But Marc's reading was a different witnessing; this wasn't the way they worshipped here?

Critic Geoff Dyer says that the best photographs screw with temporality. Through some perceptual voodoo, they "seem to extend beyond the moment they depict." They can be heard, Dyer suggests, the photo's snapped nanosecond stretched in both directions. The Poets' Corner shot is hardly great. Standard Facebook fare. A record of a clear fall day. Yet let me misread Dyer and take liberties, stretch the moment to breaking. I see Marc losing his smile the instant the cell phone dispatches its ersatz click. He grabs a smoke from his blazer's breast pocket, turns, lights up while reading the oxidizing plaque on the poet's cairn, the bronze text sharp against regal red. He squints through his smoke, fingers scanning the names raised like braille.

I'm paging through my copy of *The Fiddlehead* 137, October 1983—the month I was born. The cover's a graduated off-yellow, what appears to be a deflated scarecrow on the front (title: "Machine II"). The design's simple, the colours hazy and sun-bleached. It's ugly in the way only eighties litmags are ugly. But I like it very much. I like it for this throwback ugliness, its textured paper, the endearing typo in the table of contents (both fiction and poetry are headed "Fiction"—there's "Fiction" and "Fiction"). I like it for its worn spine—not a crack but a deepening crease, hatched and uneven like a hand's heart line. The book's more rigid than newer issues—a crisp *twok!* in its flex—as if it's slowly hardening into its core materials, a ligneous fossil. I like it for its back section, *Atlantic Soundings*, a homey-toned and optimistic bulletin with regional announcements, pronouncements, news from the freshly formed Writers Fed, Alan (sic) Cooper presiding as first president. There's talk of their first successful event in the fall, a literary salon where "Premier Richard Hatfield paid an informal visit." Hatfield emerging from the gull-wing doors of a lime-green Bricklin SV-1. Disco Dick hanging with the poets: dig it.

I like it, too, for its feature on Alden Nowlan. Nowlan had died earlier that year, and here's "About Memorials," a short story where one of Nowlan's many persons named Alden Nowlan visits his hometown for a poetry reading and encounters the backward neediness of his birthplace (a town called

Balmoral, clearly standing in for Windsor, NS). The story's
funny, vindictive and judgemental, a current of nostalgic love
underlying the narrator's bristling. A parade of teachers and
would-be mentors take the mic at his reading, claiming their
part in his success, and the narrator complains bitterly, "What
right did they have to create this caricature of me to give ficti-
tious support to their self-esteem?" It's Nowlan berating all of
us, future readers he resents and loves. It's Nowlan—master
caricaturist— berating himself.

> Here in my living room
> are the twenty most remarkable
> persons in all the world.
> —Alden Nowlan, "The Night of the Party"

Saturday night we gather at Ross's, cram ourselves into the
hallways between rooms, crick necks as we look sideways at
so many spines, bookcases in every room but the kitchen.
The deck's for the smokers, disembodied cherries floating like
fireflies on the arc of forced points. The bathroom line-up is
too long, and we stand tight against the hallway to let people
pass, drinks held to our chests like bouquets. The kitchen is
the nexus, where the booze is, an archipelago of gossip and
shop talk coalescing around the centre island. Wayne Clif-
ford asks me: "Do you want to hear the perfect poem?" To his
snazzy and Blyish vest, I said: "Why not?" A short thing from
Herbert I think— nice enough, but no such thing as a perfect
poem. Tipsy and jostled, I smash one of Ross's fridge magnets,
a small ceramic cactus. "It's ok. It was just from Arizona." This
all to say that Poetry Weekend isn't just Mem Hall but Ross's,
too— the dining-room walls with their full run of *The Fiddlehead*, the living room and its quiet jazz and framed broad-
sides, that blue carpet like Nowlan's blue chair gone planar.
That thin twisty iron stairwell, so Victorian-library. Shane's on
the couch selling M. Travis Lane merch from the end table.

We recite poems. Someone starts in with Larkin ("They fuck you up, your mum and dad.") but they're cut off: "Ah, everyone knows that one." I do "Skunk Hour" by the fireplace, sitting on the hearthstones with a half-empty case of Moosehead between my feet. The year before, I socked my Picaroons in the fridge and they were gone within the hour—thirsty, thirsty poets. It's warm, but this year I keep my beer close. On Sunday a hoarse-voiced Ross takes the podium and tells us he found a pint glass on the edge of his front lawn, stood upright as if carefully placed, filled to the brim with rainwater.

The party would've been at Alden and Claudine's. For sure. The poets filtering in, sitting at Alden's feet while he holds forth on the day's readings. He didn't like conferences ("The real writers write. The phoney writers confer."), but the week-end's slapdash organization and last-minute additions, its inclusivity and sociability, the unintentional theatre of the whole thing, would've appealed to Nowlan. Picture it: Alden still with us, in his eighties, his beard and hair white now, cumulonimbic. He sits with a half-filled whiskey and barely sips. Zealous grad students who hours before poo-pooed Nowlan for his sentimentality are lining up with their two volumes of the *Collected*, twelve-hundred pages. "Jesus," he says. "Too many poems. I'm not signing both volumes." But he enjoys himself this year, doles out honorary Maritime status with abandon. He gets his hackles up but once: "If you waste any more of my whiskey in that turkey-baster, I'll shove it up your ass." The poets keep coming through the front door, let-ting in the autumn draft. "You might as well put these down for a doorstop." He raises each volume of the *Collected* above his head. Arms thin, shaky. He's smirking. "*They'll* certainly hold the doors. Let people know all are welcome."

The book table's packed up. We've spent too much, shelled out just like last year. The dude we had a pint with was cool but now we're not so sure about these erasure poems. We're full of poetry, dyspeptic with it. We've nodded with lowered heads and crossed legs, practiced our relaxed attentiveness, a slouched languor in these unstylish chairs—our best listening pose. Some lines stay with us. Many we miss. We've waited patiently for the signal, the whispered *thank you*. We always applaud. I've watched poets stand in line at the book table with uneven stacks up to their chins, hundreds of dollars' worth, and they have the dogged look of obligation. We've signed our own books, crossed out our names on their title pages, replaced them with garishly illegible signatures. I asked about that once. The crossing out of the name. No one seemed to know.

There's a second party tonight, the Sunday weekend-ender, and we await our second winds. But now we're on stage, thirty or forty of us, and we smile for the group photo, its many takes, someone in the back always blinking, always cut off. One more, okay? The shortest up front, please. Behind us all, a baby grand gathers dust in the shadowed crossover. And we're all smiling politely, brought back to photo day at school, to tense family reunions. From the lit stage we stare at the staggered rows of seats. Aside from partners, supportive friends, the close-talking local who apparently just likes poetry, Mem Hall's darkened pews and folding chairs are empty. We're our own audience.

At a work training in Fredericton, I sneak off during lunch to haunt the public library archives on the second floor, a few rows of glassed bookcases opened with a key from the reference desk. I find *Alden Nowlan: Writer and Poet* (1984), an adult reader published by the Literacy Council of Fredericton, stapled and chapbook-thin. There are pictures throughout, cartoon line-drawings depicting pivotal scenes from Nowlan's life. I sense an attempt at socio-economic resonance, a presumptive connection with the book's inferred demographic. The simple syntax and grammatical structures are kind of beautiful, making this perhaps the most Nowlanesque of all writing on Nowlan:

> But no one told Alden what to do when he was little.
> No one told him what time to go to bed.
> No one told him what time to come home.
> No one told him to study.
> No one told him what to put on.

Each page is headed with its key sight words. Removed from context, these lists, their pedagogical randomness, make their own odd music—woods, logs, years, grandmothers, Nora, Old Em, told, home.

Ross appoints a Presiding Spirit each year at Poetry Weekend. There's no established rubric; it's a designation conferred for dedication, attendance, enthusiasm, distance travelled. I will never earn Presiding Spirit. I'm a wayward and fair-weather participant— missing years, knocking off Sunday mornings and heading back home hung-over, shaky, missing half the readings. For two years during grad school, I lived in Forest Hill Apartments, cutting through a small wood to get to campus. Nowlan was buried just up the street. I never went to pay my respects.

Here's my favourite Poetry Weekend memory: I'm following a red pickup to Oromocto, the Saint John River somewhere to my left—Fredericton's outskirts dissolving into semi-rural-ness, fallow fields, small convenience stores, the lowering sun pulsing through corridors of pine and birch. It's the Saturday of Poetry Weekend, the long break between afternoon sets, and Shane Neilson's taking me to his childhood home for an editing session on my upcoming chapbook with Frog Hollow, a small press he edits. We gather in the back sunroom, Shane in a worn lounger, and we lean over a coffee table with my sheaf of poems. In less than an hour, Shane dismantles habits, cuts lines, drops line-breaks, spends quiet minutes on single words ("how about *arbor vitae* here?"). He carefully and calmly makes my book a much better one. I put the marked-up pages away, and Shane's dad Doug makes us roast pork for supper—pulled and broiled in a roasting pan, the cuboid pieces seared black on their edges. Cream corn and mashed potatoes on the side. It's delicious. Right good.

At a reading at Windsor Castle years ago, students and their profs nod into craft beer and house wine as the reader perorates with no podium to guard them. In the middle of a passage, their first novel's crux, a drunk pinwheels into the room, blasted and caroming off the tables. Someone stands to calm him. "It's a reading, man. Have a seat." This isn't part of the show. Buddy looks around, walleyed and pre-lingual, muttering in some dreamtongue. It's like he just woke up, or he's still in a nightmare, swaying in this living room retrofitted for a pub, like time's gone wrong and he's stuck in a loop, enacting some drunken performance from a Nowlan New Year's bash forty years before, walking the same drunkard's zigzag path, but there's too many tables here now, and who is that up front with the book? We've entered a Nowlan poem, but this isn't the exalted, exalting drunk of "A Certain Kind of Holy Man," one of "those who've learned / to sit comfortably / for long periods with their hams / pressed against their calves . . . contentedly saying nothing." This man is not comfortable. He doesn't know where he is. He doesn't know whose house he has been visiting all these years.

I pull up to 676 Windsor in Google street view's strange and slanted geometries. It's early fall, a blush of red on the front maple's crown. Thin leaf-cover on the gravel yard. The house is brick and blue-vinyl siding; it looks different from when

Alden and Claudine lived there forty years back. There's a pic of the house from those days in that Nowlan NFB film. You know the film—the opening shot of Nowlan tapping a cigarette from his pack before he reads "The Mysterious Naked Man" in that stuffed-up voice, Nowlan in a dark shirt in a dark room and it's like he's a disembodied head, telling us all he's a congenital liar. Ginsberg reading "Britain Street," really selling it with the neighbourhood voices ("Brian! Marlene! / Damn you! God damn you!"). Each transition accompanied by a clarinet's atonal drone. Back then the house was simpler, all siding, surrounded by foliage like a house in the bush. There's shots of the interior in the film, too—low bookcases surrounding the living room. Is that the main bar area now? Did they take out walls? Still in street view, I swish frames to the back of the house, the lawn manicured, edged with cedar chips and topiary. Boxed ferns on the side path. I want to get closer, to climb the deck, see if it's open, but I'm stuck on Google's delimited and vectored track. Everything is silent and nothing is moving. The house elongates and stretches as I try to gain purchase on it, try to get closer. If only the Google car's panoptic eye had caught someone leaving the house. Maybe they'd have a book. They'd be a blur of movement, two-dimensional and frozen, just starting down the hill. Lumbering.

Bibliography

Alden Nowlan: The Mysterious Naked Man. Directed by Brian Guns, National Film Board of Canada, 2004. *Vimeo*, uploaded by Brian Guns, 14 June 2017, vimeo.com/221605637.

Bartlett, Brian. "Nights in Windsor Castle: Remembering Alden Nowlan." *All Manner of Tackle: Living with Poetry*, Palimpsest Press, 2017, pp. 99-107.

Compton, Anne, Laurence Hutchman, Ross Leckie, and Robin McGrath, editors. *Coastlines*. Goose Lane Editions, 2002.

Dyer, Geoff. "A Note on Photographs." *But Beautiful: A Book About Jazz*. North Point Press, 1996, pp. ix-x.

Easy Reading for Adults. *Alden Nowlan: Writer and Poet*. Literacy Council of Fredericton, 1984.

Houle, Jennifer. *The Back Channels*. Signature Editions, 2016.

Keith, W. J. *Charles G. D. Roberts*. Copp Clark Publishing Co., 1969.

Leroux, John. *Building a University: The Architecture of UNB*. Goose Lane Editions, 2010.

Neilson, Shane. "This Charming Man." *Canadian Notes & Queries*, no. 92, 2015, pp. 52-55.

Nowlan, Alden. "About Memorials." *The Fiddlehead*, no. 137, 1983, pp. 21-29.

____. *Collected Poems*. Edited by Brian Bartlett, Goose Lane Editions, 2017.

____. *Selected Poems*. Edited by Patrick Lane and Lorna Crozier, Anansi, 1996.

Prouty, William. "Atlantic Soundings, New Brunswick." *The Fiddlehead*, no. 137, 1983, pp. 104-106.

Toner, Patrick. *If I Could Turn and Meet Myself: The Life of Alden Nowlan*. Goose Lane Editions, 2000.

THE TRUMP CARD:
WHAT DAVID FRUM IS
MISSING ABOUT AMERICA'S
WORST PRESIDENT

Andy Lamey

David Frum's journey to the White House began in Toronto. In 1975, Frum was a teenage volunteer on a provincial political campaign. The candidate belonged to the New Democratic Party, but Frum, whose political views had yet to solidify, was not supporting him out of solidarity. Frum rather signed on because he wanted to see a political race up close and his family happened to know the nominee. "The campaign's headquarters was a 45-minute bus and subway ride from my parents' house," Frum wrote in the Canadian edition of his book *What's Right* (1996). "I devoted the resulting reading time to a book that my mother had given me: the first volume of Aleksandr Solzhenitsyn's *Gulag Archipelago*. The horror of Soviet communism burst upon me like a bomb. A kind of evangelical fervour gripped me: everybody had to know about this! (Remember, I was fourteen.)"

Frum's encounter with Solzhenitsyn as a precocious Canadian teenager set him on the path that eventually led to writing speeches for George W. Bush. In that capacity Frum is perhaps best known for helping coin the term "axis of evil," a phrase intended to legitimize the invasion of Iraq by depicting it as part of a network of terror-supporting states as dangerous as the Axis nations of the Second World War. Frum's primary career, however, has been as a journalist, and in this role the *Wall Street Journal* has fairly called him "one of the leading political commentators of his generation." Since Donald Trump's rise, Frum has arguably been his most outspoken critic on the right. Less than a week before Americans went to the polls to choose between Trump and Hillary Clinton, Frum published a strongly worded article ridiculing the Republican talking point that Clinton was so vicious that any GOP candidate, even one as offensive as Trump, would be better. "To demonstrate my distaste for people whose bodies contain mean bones, it's proposed that I give my franchise to a man who boasts of his delight in sexual assault?" Frum wrote in the *Atlantic*. "Who mocks the disabled, who denounces immigrant parents whose son laid down his life for this country, who endorses religious bigotry."

Given this background it is no surprise that *Trumpocracy: The Corruption of the American Republic* (Harper) is an indictment of Trump. The book recounts the major moments of Trump's election campaign before cataloguing and criticizing Trump's many scandals. Frum is clear-eyed on the disastrous consequences of Trump's presidency. But one of the questions Trump raises is historical: What is his relationship with organized conservativism? Frum depicts Trump as the corruption of a previously wayward but ultimately respectable political tradition. "He has ripped the conscience out of half of the political spectrum and left a moral void where American conservatism used to be." Such an account requires us to forget the moral void that was already present during the Bush years.

That void is powerfully illustrated by Mohamedou Ould Slahi. Slahi was a prisoner at Guantánamo Bay between 2002 and 2016. In 2005 he managed to complete a 446-page hand-written manuscript in his cell. It was composed in English, a language Slahi achieved fluency in only while incarcerated.

After Slahi tried to have the manuscript released, it was classified secret and deposited in a facility near Washington, D.C., where it languished for years while Slahi's lawyers fought to clear its publication. Eventually a censored version, with 2,500 black-bar redactions, was published in 2015 as *Guantánamo Diary*. Now a second edition has been published without redactions (Back Bay Books, Larry Siems ed.). It documents the Bush administration's embrace of torture and related crimes straight out of Solzhenitsyn. Contrary to Frum's portrait of Trump as a break from a conscientious U.S. conservatism, the real story is one of amoral continuity.

A distinctive feature of Frum's writing, aside from its nimble prose style, is that his brand of conservatism has long been a contrarian one. Well before Trump, Frum regularly criticized American conservatism in the name of making it stronger. He once wrote a magazine article that condemned Pat Buchanan, then on the verge of seeking the Republican presidential nomination, for his "sly Jew-baiting and his not-so-sly queer bashing." Frum's first book, *Dead Right* (1994) was published shortly afterwards. It again took aim at Buchanan-style paleo-conservatism, but also argued that more mainstream conservatives had compromised their commitment to small government in favour of "triviality and faddishness."

After the 2008 financial crisis, Frum's message changed. He argued that conservatives should accept a larger role for government. "There are things only government can do, and if we conservatives wish to be entrusted with the management of the government, we must prove that we care enough about government to manage it well," he wrote in *Comeback: Conservatism That Can Win Again*. Frum's post-2008 writings on issues such as Social Security, health care, and the environment have often staked out positions that a left-wing reader can agree with. The venerable left-wing magazine the *Nation* has gone so far as to call Frum "one of the media's most effective anti-conservative, or at least anti-Republican, commentators."

What makes Frum an anti-Republican rather than an anti-conservative—a critic of a party more than a set of first principles—is his stance on immigration and, especially, foreign affairs and national security. On Iraq for example, Frum has subsequently criticized how the invasion was managed and sold, but not the decision to go to war itself. As Frum told his *Nation* interviewer, "I believe in an American-led world order. I believe in the strength and power of America." If Frum's views on many domestic issues have moderated, he remains recognizably conservative on international issues related to war and terrorism. (Hence the title of his *Atlantic* election article: "The conservative case for voting for Clinton.")

Trumpocracy contains a chapter on Trump's stumbling and farcical efforts at diplomacy, the main outcomes of which have been to alienate the U.S. from its allies and to embolden Russia, whose military intelligence service is widely thought to have hacked the servers of the Democratic National Committee to aid Trump's election. Overall, however, the book focuses on Trump's domestic politics, an area in which Frum, apart from some qualified sympathy for Trump's view on immigration, finds little common ground. The book as a whole offers a sober warning against Trump's ongoing assaults on liberal democratic norms.

Much of Frum's material will be familiar to anyone who follows the news: Trump's pathological narcissism; a White House staffed by fiends and hobgoblins (communications director Anthony "the Mooch" Scaramucci, assistant to the president Omarosa Manigault-Newman); a Twitter account that re-circulates material from Nazis; the constant efforts to delegitimize the press and other organs of accountability; Trump's admiration for the most sadistic and repugnant figures in public life, as evinced by his pardoning of racist ex-sheriff Joe Arpaio, and his dismissal of the sexual harassment accusations against former Fox News CEO Roger Ailes ("It's very sad. Because he's a very good person"). Frum catalogues Trump's depravity in unflinching detail.

Frum aptly identifies Trump's disregard for truth as a defining feature of his presidency. "No American president in history—no national political figure of any kind since at least senator Joe McCarthy—has trafficked more in untruths than Donald Trump," Frum writes. If this aspect of Trump has long been familiar, there is something to be said for Frum bringing many specimens of Trump's dishonesty all together in one place, so as to document the full scope of his mendacity.

Trump's enablers have included Republican media personalities, politicians, donors, and more than a few intellectuals. In some cases Trump's enablers have been corrupted by him. In others their function has been to reinforce Trump's own worst tendencies. Frum notes that Trump has made unprecedented appointments of former or current military commanders to his cabinet and other positions. They include his chief of staff, secretary of defence, homeland security secretary, director of the federal bureau of prisons, and two national security advisors. Given the otherwise incompetent nature of Trump's administration, Frum suggests that this is a dangerous arrangement. "High among those dangers is impatience with law," he writes. A common outcome of military training is a willingness to do whatever it takes to win a battle. "That outlook, good in its place, must always be balanced in a republic of laws by the lawyer's insistence on the supremacy of legality." Trump's contempt for law is likely only to be exacerbated by his decision to surround himself with advisors with military instincts.

Frum argues that Trump ultimately represents an unprecedented assault on the norms that have constrained the American president since Watergate:

Tax disclosure refused for the first time since Gerald Ford. Conflict-of-interest rules ignored for the first time since Richard Nixon. Running a business corporation while in office for the first time since Lyndon Johnson. The first appointment of a relative to a senior government position since John F. Kennedy named his brother Robert attorney general. The first appointment of a presidential son or daughter to a senior White House position since Franklin Roosevelt's son James. The first use of presidential patronage to enrich the president's family since Ulysses S. Grant.

The one positive trait Frum associates with Trump is a lack of hypocrisy. His flaws were plain during his presidential campaign, during which he did not present himself as a traditional politician but as an outsider who would cleanse Washington with fire. In this way he spoke authentically to the concerns of his supporters within the GOP, who felt shut out of the traditional two-party system. "Just 13 percent described themselves as 'very conservative,' " Frum writes. "What set them apart from other Republicans was their economic insecurity and their cultural anxiety." Trump tapped into that insecurity and anxiety in a manner that allowed him to break free of the rules of partisan politics, by establishing a triangular relationship between himself and the two traditional parties. "Donald Trump created in effect a three-party system in the United States, by building a new Trump party in-between the Democratic and Republican parties."

Trumpocracy contains scattered references to the presidency of George W. Bush, not all of which are positive. Their primary function however is to posit Bush and Trump as opposing figures. Trump expects servile deference and hysterical praise from his subordinates. The president whom Frum once served, by contrast, "distrusted flattery and flatterers. His eyes would narrow and a cynical smile would form, as if to say, 'Now I see what you are.'" Trump's rants about the European Union and the North Atlantic Treaty Organization are contrasted with Bush's wise European policy. "During his own tenure in the White House as speechwriter for George W. Bush," the jacket of *Trumpocacy* states, "Frum witnessed the ways the presidency was limited not by law but by tradition, propriety, and public outcry, all now weakened." The Bush years are portrayed as a time when, unlike now, morality and sanity prevailed. But how plausible is Frum's attempt to cabin off Trump from Bush?

"Modern political lies are so big," Hannah Arendt wrote, "that they require a complete rearrangement of the whole factual texture—the making of another reality, as it were, into which they will fit without seam, crack, or fissure, exactly as the facts fitted into their own original context." Arendt, somewhat eccentrically, used "lies" to include false statements a speaker believes but should not. Bush and Trump both created their own alternative realities in this sense.

The basis of Trump's fantasies is mostly egotistical: he has the biggest crowds, he cuts the best deals, he is amply endowed (financially and otherwise). Bush's delusions were geopolitical: Iraq had weapons of mass destruction, mission accomplished. But Trump and Bush both rival Richard Nixon in their propensity to create dream-palaces of the kind Arendt described. Each poisoned the public sphere with enormously destructive falsehoods. If there is a difference so far regarding their alternate realities it is in Trump's favour: his has not yet claimed hundreds of thousands of lives.

American conservatism has long exhibited an antagonistic attitude toward instruments of international justice. Conservative parties in Canada, Australia, and across Europe have reconciled themselves to the fact that their countries are states signatories to the International Criminal Court (ICC), a flawed but necessary institution. The U.S. has never ratified the ICC treaty. To be sure, support for the ICC on the part of the Clinton and Obama administrations was lukewarm at best. But conservative Republicans have long opposed any version of a global court due to their hostility to all attempts to hold the United States accountable for its actions abroad.

During the lead-up to the Iraq war, United Nations weapons inspector Hans Blix warned that Iraq had no weapons of mass destruction. Vice-president Dick Cheney and other Bush administration officials responded by attacking the credibility of Blix, his agency, and the UN as a whole. When Trump, during his campaign, referred to "the utter weakness and incompetence of the United Nations" he was only following the lead of Bush and many other Republicans.

Among the most important issues faced by both Bush and Trump has been human-caused climate change. Rising global temperatures now exacerbate everything from wildfires in California to rising sea levels at Trump's Mar-a-Lago resort in Florida. The Bush administration withdrew the U.S. from the Kyoto Protocol. Rather than replace the problematic treaty with an adequate response to climate change, Bush appointees suppressed the findings of government climate researchers and engaged in repeated "incidents of political interference [as] part of a larger pattern of attacks on scientific integrity by the Bush administration," as a scathing 2007 report by the Union of Concerned Scientists and the Government Accountability Project put it. Trump, who has called global warming a hoax, has announced that the United States will withdraw from the Paris Agreement at the first available opportunity (under the withdrawal rules, the day after the 2020 presidential election). Trump has appointed numerous climate change deniers to high-level positions in his administration, including—tragically, pathetically, inevitably—the head of the Environmental Protection Agency.

Trump may have campaigned as a populist, but he has clearly governed as a conservative. In the Senate, votes by conservative Republican Ted Cruz agree with Trump's views 92 percent of the time, those by left-wing Democrat Elizabeth Warren only 11 percent. In December 2017, after Frum submitted the manuscript of *Trumpocracy*, Trump tweeted on behalf of Alabama senate candidate Roy Moore, who at the time was beset by credible allegations that he had harassed or sexually assaulted teenage girls: "The people of Alabama will do the right thing. [Moore's opponent] Doug Jones is Pro-Abortion, weak on Crime, Military and Illegal Immigration, Bad for Gun Owners and Veterans and against the WALL." One hopes Bush would not have supported an alleged sex offender such as Moore. But the issues cited in Trump's tweet all play to the concerns of conservative Republicans, who largely supported Bush.

Frum, in short, exaggerates the differences between Bush and Trump. This is not to say there are no differences at all. Trump is more hostile to immigration and free trade than the former president, and less enamoured of foreign intervention. But American conservativism has traditionally been a diverse movement made up of proponents who inevitably disagree on some issues.

There is a more significant difference between the two politicians. It can be seen by recalling a description of modern political debate that sees all minimally plausible political theories as occupying an egalitarian plateau.[1] Each theory affirms in its own way that members of the political community are moral equals. This notion of equality is a moral idea, not to be confused with equality of resources or talents. Rather it amounts to the belief that all members of the political community have interests that matter equally. The government therefore must respond to them, not necessarily with equal treatment, but with equal consideration and respect. Where the left and right have historically disagreed, on this account, is on the necessary preconditions for treating people as equals. In the economic sphere for example the left has defended some form of resource equality while the right has emphasized equal rights to one's property and economic opportunity.

It is not hard to name right-wing thinkers whom this model doesn't fit (Ayn Rand, Leo Strauss), but these thinkers are widely considered cranks in part because they do not occupy the egalitarian plateau. The diversity of right-wing thought has long included more respectable voices whose central arguments do endorse moral equality. They range from social conservatives such as Canada's own George Grant to Harvard philosopher Robert Nozick, arguably the 20th century's most rigorous libertarian. This wide acceptance of moral equality is not surprising: in the modern world, it is far more philosophically plausible and politically palatable to argue over what equal respect entails than it is to reject moral equality outright. This is why American presidents have long paid at least lip service to all men, and more recently all women, being created equal.

George W. Bush was no exception. In the same speech in which he referred to an axis of evil, Bush spoke of the "need to prepare our children to read and succeed in school," taking "our children" to include all American children. Today it is normal to extend moral consideration beyond state borders and affirm the moral equality of all human beings, a perspective American presidents have been happy to adopt when convenient. Hence the passages in Bush's speech graphically describing human rights violations the Iraqi regime had committed against its own people.

Critics of American presidents have often charged that their affirmations of equality really are just lip service. Certainly in Bush's case it was a strange response to the Iraqi regime "leaving the bodies of mothers huddled over their dead children," as his speech put it, for him to do the same. Whether it comes to America's school programs or its foreign policy, critics of Bush and other presidents have often called for them to act in a manner that better lives up to their egalitarian rhetoric.

Trump is distinctive for not even paying lip service to equality. His rhetorical attacks on Mexican immigrants, African-American football players, and Muslims; his reluctance to condemn white supremacists; his sympathy for the racist conspiracy theory that denies that the United States' first black president is American—it is impossible to reconcile these nauseating aspects of Trump's record with even a minimal commitment to moral equality. I believe this is what Frum is getting at when he says there is no hypocrisy in Trump. Particularly during the campaign, Trump did not employ noble rhetoric about equality (or anything else). He was instead open about his contempt: for communities of colour; for his female opponent; for everything except himself and his cramped and exclusionary vision of American society.

One of the most extreme things Trump said during the campaign concerned how he would prevent terrorism: "When you get these terrorists, you have to take out their families." Trump was indicating his willingness to disregard human rights in pursuit of national security. For Bush this was not just rhetoric. It was policy.

Aleksandr Solzhenitsyn observed that people who fell into the hands of the secret police usually did not try to escape. "It isn't just that you don't put up any resistance; you even walk down the stairs on tiptoe, as you are ordered to do, so your neighbours won't hear," he wrote in *The Gulag Archipelago*. Because the victims of Stalinism were so often innocent they were unprepared for the knock on the door. This sometimes left them with a nagging sense of complicity after the fact. After his own arrest Solzhenitsyn was haunted by questions he found difficult to answer. "So why did I keep silent? Why, in my last minute out in the open, did I not attempt to enlighten the hoodwinked crowd?"

Mohamedou Ould Slahi had a similar reaction to his own arrest. It occurred in 2001 in his native Mauritania, when members of the West African country's security service showed up at his door. After a week in detention he was informed he was being transferred to Jordan and was taken to the airport by agents who left his legs unshackled, thereby providing an opportunity to break away. Rather than seize it, Slahi co-operated with his escorts. "I could easily have run away and reached the public terminal before anybody could catch me," he writes. "I could at least have forcibly passed the message to the public, and hence to my family, that I was kidnapped. But I didn't do it, and I have no explanation for why not."

Slahi did not know it at the time, but the Jordanian rendition team that brought him to Jordan was following a pattern, one that Human Rights Watch described in a 2008 report. It noted that "from 2001 until at least 2004, Jordan's General Intelligence Department served as a proxy jailer for the U.S. Central Intelligence Agency (CIA), holding prisoners that the CIA apparently wanted kept out of circulation, and later handing some of them back to the CIA." Slahi was originally told that he would be in Jordan only for a few days, but this soon proved false. During his first interrogation his captors asked him what he had done. When he said he had done nothing, they burst out in laughter. "Oh, very convenient! You have done nothing but you are here!" To be a detainee was to be deemed guilty, a rationalization Solzhenitsyn's captors had also employed. As a colonel in the Soviet ministry of state security put it: "We are not going to sweat to prove the prisoner's guilt to him. Let *him* prove to us that he did *not* have hostile intent."

Slahi was incarcerated in Jordan for eight months. Prison rules ostensibly allowed the International Committee of the Red Cross (ICRC) access to all prisoners. Whenever the ICRC visited the prison in which Slahi was housed, however, he was hidden in a cellar, one of several steps taken to deny him contact with the outside world. Throughout his detention Slahi experienced acute stress and depression. His interrogations, which revolved around terror charges he knew nothing about, eventually turned violent. Slahi however suggests that the worst part was the psychological abuse. It involved having to listen to another detainee be beaten with an unidentified hard object outside the interrogation room. This lasted until the detainee was crying for his life and Slahi was shaking with fear.

In July 2002 Slahi was transferred to the Bagram Air Base in Afghanistan, where he was again interrogated about a terror operation he knew nothing about. Two weeks later, Slahi underwent rendition for the third time, to Guantánamo. During his transfer to Afghanistan, Slahi was already so broken that he had to be dragged on board the airplane. During that gruelling flight—prior to which he was made to wear a diaper—he was shackled, blindfolded, and earmuffed. The conditions of his longer flight from Afghanistan to Cuba were even worse. He was again earmuffed, this time with a set that had such an excruciating grip that his ears bled for several days. Equally painful goggles blocked out his sight. Every so often, a guard would remove his earmuffs and speak into his ear, "You know, you didn't make any mistake: your mom and dad made the mistake when they produced you." After being strapped into the plane, Slahi had a mask placed over his face and a bag put on his head. The belt strapping him in was so tight it constricted his breathing. A terrified Slahi did not know how to say "tight" in English: "I kept saying, 'MP, Sir, I cannot breathe! ... MP, SIR, please.' But it seemed like my pleas for help got lost in a vast desert."

At Guantánamo, Slahi was sexually humiliated by female interrogators. He was warned that, if he did not confess, he would spend the rest of his life at Guantánamo; he was told that his family was in danger if he did not co-operate; subjected to extreme noise and light; constantly shackled by his wrists to the floor so that he was unable to stand without stooping, triggering sciatic pain in his lower back; and made to experience extreme cold in a punishment cell known as the cold room. This last technique, Slahi notes, has long-term health consequences that are difficult to trace back to a torturer. "The torture squad was so well trained that they were performing almost perfect crimes, avoiding leaving any obvious evidence."

Slahi's renditions to Jordan and Afghanistan were at the hands of the CIA. After he arrived at Guantánamo, responsibility for his interrogation was divided between different agencies. The redacted edition of *Guantánamo Diary* left open the possibility that the CIA was among them. The restored edition makes clear that it was the work of the Federal Bureau of Investigation and various branches of military intelligence. Military interrogators had a much higher cruelty threshold than their FBI counterparts, to the point that a schism developed between the FBI and military intelligence, due to the latter's adoption of the extreme interrogation methods that the CIA had been employing at its rendition sites. The FBI viewed such tactics as so inhumane and counter-productive that it eventually withdrew from joint interrogations.

Military interrogators subjected Slahi to extreme sleeplessness. It occurred when he was placed in an isolation cell that admitted no light:

> The cell—better, the box—was cooled down to the point that I was shaking most of the time. I was forbidden from seeing the light of the day; every once in a while they gave me a rec-time at night to keep me from seeing or interacting with any detainees. I was living literally in terror. For the next seventy days I wouldn't know the sweetness of sleeping; interrogation 24 hours a day, three and sometimes four shifts a day. I rarely got a day off. I don't remember sleeping one night quietly.

The methods used on Slahi recall those used on Solzhenitsyn. The Russian writer's interrogation had lasted for 96 hours and was made up, Solzhenitsyn wrote, of sleeplessness, lies, and threats. The sleeplessness in particular was "a great form of torture: it left no visible marks and could not provide grounds for complaint even [in] an inspection—something unheard of anyway." Forcing prisoners to go without sleep for days did more than make them experience extreme tiredness. Withholding the biological imperative of sleep "befogs the reason, undermines the will, and the human being ceases to be himself, to be his own 'I.'"

The CIA has long been aware of the lineage of the methods it employs. *Guantánamo Diary* cites a 1956 CIA report titled "Communist Control Techniques: An Analysis of the Methods Used by Communist State Police in the Arrest, Interrogation, and Indoctrination of Persons Regarded as 'Enemies of the State.'" Whereas in recent years apologists for torture have preferred to speak of "enhanced interrogation techniques," and "special interrogation plans," the CIA report is refreshing in its avoidance of euphemism. "These methods do, of course, constitute torture and physical coercion. All of them lead to serious disturbances of many bodily processes."

If Slahi was unable to provide information about terror operations he had no knowledge of, this was not an aspect of reality Guantánamo could easily accommodate. Slahi had to be withholding what he knew. For this reason, a year after Slahi arrived at Guantánamo, he became subject to a "special interrogation plan," approved by then-secretary of defense Donald Rumsfeld. After it went into effect Slahi's captors became less concerned not to leave traces of their work.

The plan saw Slahi removed from his cell by soldiers in riot gear who blindfolded him and placed a bag over his head before placing him on a boat that drove around for several hours. The purpose was to deceive Slahi into believing he was undergoing rendition for a fourth time, to Egypt, where he would experience torture beyond human limit. During the boat ride Slahi nearly suffocated and was beaten so badly he could not stand or speak. When he passed out he was woken with ammonia and beaten again.

Solzhenitsyn observed that greed played a central role in keeping the gulag running. Transportation to the gulag was a long, brutal process. It involved being packed into crowded train cars and unloaded at intermediate transit prisons where non-political prisoners served the role of trustees. Such an arrangement allowed officials to keep a portion of the money budgeted for salaries. Rather than having to pay the trustees, the gulag's managers gave them a free hand in their dealings with newly arrived political prisoners, whom they often robbed. And, as Solzhenitsyn put it, "they also take things from us *honestly*." Political prisoners could pay trustees for various favours, such as changing their departure time or not putting them in a cell with thieves, non-political criminals who were even more vicious than the jailers.

Guantánamo operationalized greed in a different way. This is documented by Murat Kurnaz, whose detention coincided with Slahi's. Kurnaz, a resident of Germany, was on a religious pilgrimage in Pakistan when police at a checkpoint ordered him off a bus and took him into custody before turning him over to the United States. Once at Guantánamo, Kurnaz was told that his arrest had been facilitated by a financial incentive directed at local agencies in Pakistan. "When I was apprehended, everyone knew that there was money to be made by turning in foreigners. Lots of Pakistanis were sold as well. Doctors, taxi drivers, fruit and vegetable sellers, many of whom I later met in Guantánamo." Kurnaz's discussion of his bounty, which he was told was US$3,000, appears in his own 2006 memoir, *Five Years of My Life: An Innocent Man in Guantanamo*. Although Slahi was not brought in this way, Guantánamo as a whole was the product of large numbers of bounties paid in Pakistan and elsewhere.

A major difference between Guantánamo and the gulag is that Guantánamo has been within the reach of law. Human rights groups working on behalf of prisoners launched law-suits that challenged their lack of basic procedural safeguards. One such challenge resulted in the 2008 U.S. Supreme Court decision *Boumediene v. Bush*, which allowed Slahi to challenge his detention in 2009. Thus his case, unlike Solzhenit-syn's, did include a trial to determine whether his detention was justified, albeit one held eight years after his arrest.

Slahi was arrested because he was believed to be an active member of al-Qaeda. Multiple pieces of Slahi's background appeared to suggest as much. He received weapons training in Afghanistan at an al-Qaeda camp; he was in contact with Ramzi bin al-Shibh, who was accused of helping organize the 9/11 attacks, and his cousin was on al-Qaeda's shura council, the body just below Osama bin Laden in the terror organi-zation's hierarchy. Finally, Slahi was thought to be part of the so-called millennium bomb plot. It involved Ahmed Ressam, who was arrested in 1999 after getting on a ferry in Victo-ria, B.C., and trying to disembark in Port Angeles, Washing-ton state. U.S. Customs agents found the makings of a bomb in the trunk of Ressam's rental car, with which he had been planning to destroy the Los Angeles airport. Ressam lived in Montreal, where Slahi also briefly resided. Canadian and U.S. intelligence agencies suspected Slahi, who attended the same mosque as Ressam, of having provided assistance to him.

These allegations were enough for Slahi to be presumed guilty by his torturers. When the case against him was finally subjected to courtroom scrutiny, however, it fell apart. The judge noted that the training Slahi received in Afghanistan had taken place in 1990, before al-Qaeda had taken up ter-rorism against the United States. Slahi's training had been for the purpose of fighting the Soviet-sponsored commu-nist government, a cause the U.S. supported. As for Ahmed Ressam, his time in Montreal did not overlap with Slahi's. The two never met. Slahi did have contact with his cousin who was in al-Qaeda, but this relative had been opposed to the 9/11 attacks and had tried to persuade Osama bin Laden not to carry them out, an effort documented in *The 9/11 Commission Report*. Slahi occasionally performed favours for his relative, but they involved activities unrelated to violence, such as helping to electronically transfer money to a family member. As for al-Qaeda member bin al-Shibh, Slahi barely knew him. Both men were living in Germany in 1999 when bin al-Shibh and two friends met a stranger on a train with whom they discussed jihad and their hope to go to Chechnya to fight the Russians. The stranger suggested they contact Slahi. When the three did so, Slahi put them up for the night and suggested that they could train for fighting Russians as he had, in Afghanistan. But there was no discussion of violence beyond the Chechen-Russian conflict, and no discussion of Slahi harming anyone.

"The evidence does show that [Slahi] provided some support to al-Qaeda, or to people he knew to be al-Qaeda," Judge James Robertson concluded. "Such support was sporadic, however, and, at the time of his capture, non-existent." Slahi's interactions with al-Qaeda members, importantly, did not show he was a member himself, the ostensible grounds for his imprisonment. "Rather, they tend to support Salahi's submission that he was attempting to find the appropriate balance—avoiding close relationships with al-Qaeda members, but also trying to avoid making himself an enemy." Judge Robertson ordered Slahi freed in 2010, but an appeal by the Obama administration meant he was not let go until 2016, 14 years after his initial arrest.

In addition to his civilian trial, Slahi was also subject to military commission hearings at Guantánamo. A primary purpose of his interrogations was to gather evidence that could be used against him in such hearings. A central lesson of his case concerns the profound procedural inadequacy of military terror courts relative to civilian ones. By favouring military tribunals over civilian trials, the Bush administration exhibited a cynical contempt for truth, both factual and moral.

This became clear to the prosecutor assigned to assemble the case against Slahi at his military tribunal, a Marine named Stuart Couch. Couch had joined the prosecution in the hope that, in his words, he would "get a crack at the guys who attacked the United States." In 2003 however, after reviewing Slahi's file, Couch saw that Slahi had falsely confessed to being a terrorist as a result of his torture. Couch was moved in particular by a fake letter that stated Slahi's mother had been detained and threatened to bring her to Guantánamo, as well as a sudden admission of guilt that Slahi offered after being subject to the U.S.-approved torture plan. *Guantánamo Diary* quotes an interview in which Couch describes the effect these discoveries had on him:

> It was at the end of this, [after] hearing all of this information, reading all this information, months and months and months of wrangling with the issue, that I was in church this Sunday, and we had a baptism. We got to the part of the liturgy where the congregation repeats—and I'm paraphrasing here, but the essence is that we respect the dignity of every human being and seek peace and justice on earth. And when we spoke those words that morning, there were a lot of people in that church, but I could have been the only one there. I just felt this incredible, all right, there it is. You can't come in here on a Sunday, and as a Christian, subscribe to this belief of dignity of every human being and say I will seek justice and peace on the earth, and continue to go with the prosecution using that kind of evidence. And at that point I knew what I had to do.

Couch's epiphany amounted to the realization that he had fallen off the egalitarian plateau. Like the FBI, he deemed the methods used against Slahi so objectionable that he removed himself from Slahi's case and refused to be part of his prosecution.

At its height under Stalin, the gulag is estimated to have incarcerated at least two million people. Guantánamo, at its peak, housed 779 prisoners. Even factoring in Guantánamo's network of feeder sites in the Middle East and Afghanistan, there is no comparison in scale. The Center for Constitutional Rights and other non-governmental organizations (NGOs) have also done important work exposing injustices at Guantánamo. The legal universe that generated the gulag permitted no equivalent NGO ferment.

But if Guantánamo does not match the gulag either in size or pure lawlessness, it is recognizably an island in the archipelago that Solzhenitsyn described. According to a Seton Hall University analysis of U.S. government data, less than 10 percent of detainees were classified as al-Qaeda fighters. The same 2006 study, which examined 517 detainees, found that 86 percent were arrested after the payment of a bounty. In addition to Couch, six other military prosecutors requested reassignment or resigned due to concerns that hearings conducted at Guantánamo have failed to meet minimal standards of justice. Opposition to the twilight world described in Solzhenitsyn's prison saga should entail opposition to Guantánamo. Not because the two are identical, but because the affinities between them, which include the imprisonment and torture of innocent people, are terrible enough.

Frum has often retold his origin story tracing his politics back to his reading of Solzhenitsyn. Yet as the axis-of-evil speechwriter, he served the administration that created the Guantánamo Bay detention camp. That administration responded to terrorism in a manner not subject to strong legal oversight. It was, to borrow a phrase, impatient with law. Ironically, the case Slahi was accused of being mixed up with—Ahmed Ressam's bomb plot—ended in what has long been an example of a well-handled terror trial. It demonstrated that suspected terrorists are best tried by open civilian courts, because their respect for the rights of the accused allows them to more accurately address questions of guilt and innocence. Insofar as the Bush administration's response to terrorism was analogous to a war, this entailed that it was conducted with fewer rights safeguards. By coming up with a pithy way of expressing the thought that opposing terrorism, and the regimes that allegedly sponsor it, is akin to waging war, Frum contributed to the climate of unreason in which the methods inflicted on Slahi became possible.

Of course as a mere speechwriter, Frum did not write policy or weigh in on decisions regarding Guantánamo. Accountability, however, is something we face not only for our individual actions, and the differences they make. We can also be judged for our actions as part of a group. Imagine a group of people who decide to hide a body. One of them is physically weak, so that when they all push the corpse into a river one night, her effort contributes nothing.[2] On an individual level she plays no causal role in making the body disappear. She is still complicit in the group's wrong. Frum is complicit in the moral disaster of Guantánamo in a similar way. Not because he caused it, but because he participated in the administration that made it possible. In particular, he participated actively in the project of justifying and selling a war on terror.

Frum has also been complicit as a journalist. Not long after Guantánamo began receiving prisoners, it attracted criticism in the international press. "As American forces advanced [in Afghanistan], Europe's left-wing press invented atrocity stories to keep them company," Frum wrote in *The Right Man*, his 2003 White House memoir. "The left-wing British tabloid the *Mirror* accused the United States of torture for the offence of handcuffing al-Qaeda terrorists in transit to Guantánamo Bay and issuing them plugs to protect their ears from engine noise en route." Accusations of human rights violations were the invention of unreliable critics; all Guantánamo detainees are terrorists; Slahi's bloody ears were for his own protection. The falsehood quotient in Frum's account was high.

Frum's writings have sought to delegitimize not only external critics of Guantánamo, such as the European press, but also internal ones, such as the FBI. The federal agency was deeply implicated in Slahi's ordeal, having twice questioned him in Africa before he was arrested and shipped to Jordan. Nevertheless, the FBI's institutional ethos did not tolerate torture, which made it unwilling to participate in the methods used on Slahi and other prisoners. Frum had this ethos in mind when he called for a transformation of American security institutions in his 2004 book *An End to Evil: How to Win the War on Terror*, co-authored with Richard Perle.

"The transformation must begin with the single worst performer among those institutions: the FBI," Frum and Perle wrote. "The FBI is essentially a police force, and like all good police forces, it goes to great lengths to respect the constitutional rights of the suspects it investigates." This concern with respecting rights renders the FBI "inherently disabled" in dealing with accused terrorists who are not citizens. "Noncitizen terrorist suspects are not members of the American national community, and they have no proper claim on the rights Americans accord one another."

The reference to "suspects" is chilling. This is not because the rejection of torture presupposes that every victim is innocent. Reasons not to torture even convicted terrorists include the fact that people will say anything to make torture stop, resulting in worthless intelligence (such as Slahi's confession). But Frum's reference to suspects takes in a wider class of individuals than those convicted at trial. This is consistent with the view of national security as a theatre of war. According to that view, being unwilling to deprive someone of basic liberties until they have been found guilty is a pathetic feature of procedural liberalism. Slahi was not

American and was a terror suspect. It follows that the methods employed on him were appropriate. Conservatism and Stalinism kiss.

In 2006 Frum took a tour of Guantánamo. One reason the U.S. military may offer such tours is to generate favourable press coverage. If so, Frum's visit paid off. In a *National Post* article about his trip he cited transcripts of detainee testimony given at review tribunal hearings. The detainees' words suggested that they were, in Frum's sarcastic summary, "innocent goatherds and blameless wedding guests swept up by blind American injustice." According to Frum however the testimony was remarkable in each case only for its implausibility. There was no excuse for "those in the west who succumb so easily to the deceptions of terrorists who cannot invent even half-way plausible lies." Frum's account of his visit uncritically recycled the official administration view. Tours of the kind he went on do not permit visitors to speak with detainees such as Slahi, or to concerned military staff such as Couch. This renders them worthless as fact-finding exercises.

Finally, as recently as 2009, Frum defended the Bush administration from criticism of its interrogation practices. Frum was prompted to do so by Barack Obama's admission that the U.S. had used torture. Although Obama's admission was limited to the use of waterboarding, Frum argued that it went too far. "Maybe waterboarding was wrong even in 2002-2003. The Bush administration itself has acted on the understanding that it was unnecessary after 2003," he wrote in his *National Post* column. "But make no mistake: What is going on in this so-called 'torture' debate is an attempt to hijack humanitarian feeling to smuggle into international law new claims on behalf of the world's most conscienceless criminals." The use of scare quotes around torture and the robotic insistence that torture's only victims are terrorists are bad enough. But the most pernicious aspect of Frum's statement may be its insinuation that the use of torture at Guantánamo, which at the beginning of 2018 still housed 41 prisoners, is old news no longer worth dwelling on.

A longstanding fantasy has been that torture can be institutionalized in a controlled way. But torture is like a fire that always escapes the fireplace. It is inevitably directed at the innocent. And on a national level, it inevitably corrupts the institutions of any country willing to use it. During the Algerian war of independence, the colonial French government employed torture on a widespread scale. The phrase "*la gangrene*" was used to describe how torture, in the words of historian Neil MacMaster, "was seen as a form of cancer that inexorably led to the degeneration of the liberal democratic state, its institutions (particularly the army and the judiciary), its core values and fundamental respect for human rights and dignity."

The United States under Bush was infected by the gangrene seen in Algeria and other torture regimes. One of the institutions most affected was the Republican Party. When Trump during his campaign called for "a total and complete shutdown of Muslims entering the United States," he was singling out for abuse a group that had long been mistreated under Bush, the former president's rhetoric about recognizing Islam as a religion of peace notwithstanding. For years, Frum has participated in the gangrene's advance as a Bush speechwriter and a Guantánamo apologist. This prevents him from seeing how the annihilationist conservatism of the Bush years foreshadowed Donald Trump.

In addition to creating Guantánamo Bay's detention camp and invading Iraq, Bush signed the *Patriot Act*, which legalized warrantless wiretapping and indefinite detention. Although his administration took steps to eliminate racial profiling in federal law enforcement, it also instituted regulations that facilitated profiling on religious or national-origin grounds, with the result that "immigrants and visitors from Arab and Middle Eastern countries were subjected to increased scrutiny, including interviews, registration, and in some cases removal," as a 2004 U.S. Commission on Civil Rights report put it. Bush opposed the *Employment Non-Discrimination Act*, which would have prevented discrimination based on sexual orientation, and announced his support for a constitutional amendment to deny legal recognition to same-sex unions. The common theme running through these and other initiatives of Bush's administration is a glaring disrespect for rights. A similar disrespect now emanates from Trump in his utterances on Muslims, Mexican immigrants, transgender people, and countless other groups.

Unlike Bush, Trump has sometimes been too floundering and incompetent to turn his utterances into law. His contributions to public discourse however are bad enough in themselves. The president is a loud voice in the public sphere, and what he says has a huge influence on what counts as acceptable. Hence the renewed prominence of far-right groups since Trump's election. More importantly, equality is the philosophy of democracy. It is naive to think that a president who is openly contemptuous of equality can be a reliable manager of democratic institutions. For these reasons Trump's rhetoric has indeed been a step down from Bush's, which is no small loss. But of course it is not just a president's words that matter. So do their policies. And Bush, unlike Trump, was not so prone to disorganization and chaos that he struggled to implement his deadliest ideas.

The United States may someday have a president who respects moral equality in both words and action. To date, however, few presidents have fallen farther from the egalitarian plateau than Trump and Bush. Frum's view of Trump as a break from his predecessor relies upon a self-serving amnesia we have long been warned against. In Milan Kundera's words, the struggle of man against power is the struggle of memory against forgetting.

Notes

1 Ronald Dworkin, "Comment on Narveson: In Defense of Equality," *Social Philosophy and Policy* 1/1 (1983).
2 This example comes from Julia Driver, "Individual Consumption and Moral Complicity." In *The Moral Complexities of Eating Meat*. Ben Bramble and Bob Fischer, eds. (Oxford, Oxford University Press, 2016), 71.

FIERCE INVENTORY

Ali Blythe

Children's Prison Shower

Don't tell me how it ends. The one about the boy who says everything twice and is therefore sent to children's prison.

Especially don't tell me he eventually stops saying everything twice because of good adult intervention.

Jacob Two-Two Meets the Hooded Fang by Mordecai Richler is a book that has haunted me for more than thirty years. I read it as a kid, and never since. In the original 1975 book, I recall there being a line drawing by Fritz Wegner of six-year-old Jacob completely naked in the prison shower. I found it frightening and attractive. What was happening to him? (I don't even know for certain he was in a shower. I am forever placing people in showers.)

At 10, I find myself in a children's prison called Grade 5, where I'm called *Half & Half*—I still pause, every time I put it in my coffee—and the kids sing a ditty about me being half-man, half-woman, to the tune of the 1985 Halsa Hair commercial. I can only dream of having an alarmingly sized, professional ex-wrestler in a silk robe called The Hooded

Fang to guard me. After that, I spend decades putting myself in a different kind of prison.

We all have prisons. They can be places where we still work and drink nice coffees with people we love.

I have resisted the urge to track down the Mordecai Richler book again, as a small but reverent nod to disappearance. I write a lot about the kinds of creatures who tend to disappear. Mostly two-in-one creatures. To be truthful, I'm also nervous that my sketchy, dreamy resemblance to Jacob will disappear.

Fifth Boot

Though it's decades between encounters, Richard Siken would be the next writer after Mordecai Richler to make me feel the shuddering whump of knowing something is happening, likely irrevocable, but not being able to quite make out what.

It happens seven poems into his first book, *Crush*:

> You're on your back in your undershirt, a broken man
>   on an ugly bedspread, staring at the water stains
>   on the ceiling.
> And you can hear the man in the apartment above you
>   taking off his shoes.
> You hear the first boot hit the floor and you're looking up,
>   you're waiting
> because you thought it would follow, you thought there
>   would be
>   some logic, perhaps, something to pull it all together
> but here we are in the weeds again,
>   here we are
> in the bowels of the thing: your world doesn't make sense.
>   And then the second boot falls.
>   And then a third, a fourth, a fifth.

Every time I get to the part where the fifth boot falls I'm absolutely terrified for the guy in the poem, for Siken, and for myself, too.

Two makes sense. Even four. But five? Where the hell did that fifth boot come from?

The Method

When I read Leslie Fienberg's *Stone Butch Blues* as a teenager, I knew something was coming for me one day. It had to do with precariousness in the body. The chance you might be caught out. The brutish reality of changing form. Ultimately, death. But shit it looked good, too. That said, I never wanted to *be* Feinberg's protagonist, Jess. Though at the time, I couldn't have told you who I *did* want to be.

Harry Dodge is the first person I look at and say, *Oh yes. There. Okay.* I want to be like *that*. I come to know him because he is in Maggie Nelson's memoir, *The Argonauts*. Then I come to know him in his own right. So Maggie Nelson's Harry Dodge then Harry Dodge's Harry Dodge.

They are lovers, he is taking testosterone and undergoing chest surgery while she is pregnant with their son, his art has a "special focus on ecstatic contamination," his hair is growing wilder in each successive selfie. And the lines around his eyes, his eyes, they are deepening. I see a trans male artist growing older. This is something I haven't seen much before.

I have permanently altered a page of *The Argonauts* by pushing a bobby pin under one line. It's about *compatible perversities*. I've done so because it immediately, and out-of-context, made sense as a go or no-go method.

Go or no-go method for what? When I make a decision about what form my body is to take. For instance. Who I want to let take it. I charged the line with this questioning: Are my perversities (both in its definition, "a quality of being contrary to accepted standards" and the more colloquial understanding) compatible with this choice, this moment, this movement, this other?

I pull it out and can still feel its creases, see its shadows.

Am I trusting my desires? Even if there is risk involved. In being seen for what I am.

Vessel of Bottom Smashed Off

If a woman who thinks they are a man
is mad, a man who thinks they are a man

is no less so—via Nelson, via Lacan.
The man slams the door in the wind,

a reverberation of unmet need.
The man is preceded by his substances

of use, the who-said-what to who.
The man's hands are shaking

out masculinity, femininity in the air
—a woman fell from the man's body

when he stood to leave.
She roams the place in a towel

wet, and unresponsive.
The man goes to the toilet.

Empties himself. Comes back.
The man should be working.

He's working. Blinking out and waking up
on a silver and green recovery chair.

He took my glass to the fountain,
tried to fill it to drink. Tried to fill it

and drink. Wet footsteps
lead back to the chair.

The man's chest is numb. Something
must've fallen asleep on it.

The man's mouth paces, unacquiescent,
going through doors just to slam them.

I jump and the man's
skin comes with me.

Bottom

"How has the no drinking plan gone?" my editor Phil
Hall writes to me in larger-than-normal font, "It does change
everything, in some very subtle ways, eh?"

I remember tilting the first vial in the sun. Two years after
starting testosterone, I'd be sober. The statistic for trans men
getting sober is high. High enough someone joked, *you aren't
going to stop drinking are you?* when I told them I was transitioning.

I do wonder about an experiment. 'Men' take a six-month
course of estrogen and 'women' of testosterone. To feel the
changes in how people react to you. In how you react to others. To learn the codes and to forget them. To experience the
subtle shifts. "Subtle" being Phil's subtle code for the also not-
so-subtle.

E.g., I used to feel anger and fear in my chest and stomach.
After transition, I thought these feelings had largely disappeared. But no, I now realize what the new jolting flashes in
my hands and arms are. The feelings snaking outward. And

what to do with the eyes is completely opposite now. I relearn when to look. When not to. At who. For how long. But mostly, I'm let alone now, to do and say as I please. Or not to do or say anything. *Let him be*, everyone seems to say to me with their words and bodies.

In "Bottom," a long poem and essay on drinking and recovery I carry with me every- where, Phil writes about why, to him, "sobriety is a matriarchy."

"I was a drinking 'woman' and now a sober 'man,'" I reply to him, in a more affordable font size. "So sober feels very attached to my masculine being. Testosterone/masculinity drew a line down the centre of me to the earth, which allowed my sobriety, which allowed openness, honesty, the feminine. Anyway, I take a step and it's in my feet."

The right hand of his margin in "Bottom" replies:

Slobber

Sobber

Sober

Masculinity Bookshelf

I wish to write here about masculinity. It doesn't exist. And yet. I take up its space and it takes up mine.

What does it mean that people read me as masculine because of all the gestures that are both completely mine and completely learned? (*This is your life, to do as you please*, I sometimes tell my dog, though he lives within the strange set of rules I create for him.) When I balance this teacup on my thigh it is a masculine gesture because I perform it. I perform the gesture because many years ago at a lecture in Abkhazi Gardens I saw a man who widely and serenely balanced a teacup on his thigh and in that moment I flashed forward to my own possible manhood. It is masculine because my thigh is a location of possible manhood, having hovered over it then jabbed upward of 200 times. This is just one gesture.

And what does masculinity mean in relation to my life-long attraction to femininity? And what is that? Because certainly it is the charge of the connection between the masculine and feminine to which I also say, *Oh yes, there, okay*.

With transition, too, all the private rivers of my own femininity that I had largely abjured (*quit dancing around in your little long johns, Blythe*) are given new freedom to flow in the channel of masculinity. If I were the evangelistic type, I would quote Chapter 28 of the Tao, before wishing to lightly flick the vice versa switch and see what happens.

How do I make masculinity three-dimensional so I can peer at it? I clear a shelf in my bookcase, already seeing the myriad ways this will go wrong, and start moving books over to it. The condition for being moved to the shelf is the book must enact a kind of feeling in me that is *here*. That *here* is masculinity. Gregory Scofield's prayer for the peace of stars. John Ashbery's thing that is prepared to happen. Raymond Carver's boat tugging against its rope. Dean Young's one last wild enjambment.

Sentence

"You need an edge," Michael Cullen tells me, after reading my earliest poems. An edge. I feel in that moment the convergence of the poemself and bodyself. He tells me a Johnny Cash story. The sun is setting and Cash is at the microphone introducing his last song: "If you just keep walking into the sunset, it'll never go down," he says, then starts to sing.

Michael once declared the perfect sentence to be this one, from the insanely attractive messenger of popular music: "You can stand under my umbrella, ella, ella, eh, eh, eh." The commas sound more like periods when he says it. He is big on sentences. Sentences with silences at the beginning and end.

White space. Michael would be dead of a brain aneurysm a couple years later.

In transition, I enter my body. With sobriety, I start to feel my edges. And with those, a fear of death. You can't leave the party until you've arrived.

One moment ago, the exact moment my mind and body put together the words *mortality* and *masculinity,* a bird flies in through the window, bangs into the mirror, and flies out.

Fourm

I am walking in the mountain woods with Tim Lilburn. Not a dream, remarkably. He is talking about a small change he is making in his poetic form, how it will change everything.

I go back to the hotel. I give myself exactly four poetic feet and then I have to return to the left-hand margin. I give myself four lines and then I have to take a stanza break. I'm in a small, beautiful box. Maybe the kind in which a body gets sawn in half and brought back together.

I'm so busy with the sawing I don't see what's going on with the other hand. These are the first poems I will read aloud to people with my new voice. One I have been writing toward. It is felled. It also mispronounces "Ovid."

At the same reading, I meet Betsy/Oscar Warland for the first time. (I keep accidentally retyping a ? instead of a / within their name. I think they'd like that.) They are a reinvention of form, having lived up against constraint in gender and genre. Their kind of masculinity and age is like taking a drink from a fountain you've been walking towards for a very long time.

Silk Chemise

I am surprised to meet a woman with flowing grey hair and a silk chemise. She too, in the process of transition. Autumn Getty admits she thought I'd asked her to do a reading with me because I somehow knew, before she'd let the cat out of the bag. I hadn't.

It's her first reading as herself. She reads some pre-transition poems about living in women's shelters as a kid, poems that conceive the feminine as object of desire, the feminine divine—poems that some folks used to deeply question when they looked at her and saw a man.

It took 40 years for me to take up the word *Him* in public.

With sobriety, with being trans, my edges sharpen as the world's do. Inhabiting the body without the gauze. *Take care, take care,* I want to tell everything. *But live at risk. But take care.*

It's 4 a.m. after the reading in my hotel room. "Sometimes you just have to leap," she says to me, right before I do.

Hymnswitch

In the first four months of sobriety, the ones I spend in a circle looking at the same solid boots, I imagine lying in the desert at the foot of the Sangre de Cristo Mountains with my shirt off. I also imagine a man in white pants coming to check on me once a day, bringing his medicines, before leaving me to it. A little *Man Needs a Maid-y*, I know.

When the program is done, I say goodbye-for-now to loved ones, and pack up the pup for the four-day drive. I also pack 30 poems, having written one a day through one of the tougher months. I take up my unmanageability harmonica to begin to try and talk about it all.

Along the way, I'm invited to not return to Oregon for a good while, due to the speed at which I drive through their state. The extortionate ticket says I'm a six-foot-one man who weighs in at one-eighty. I'll take the ticket. Praxis is expensive.

I pull over at the beginning of the Taos Pueblo Land to take in the landscape that is my every imagining, and chew sage, and let my dog pee. In a field of cactus and jackrabbit.

Whoops. He hates the cold water I use to wash the blood away more than the hundreds of quills I have to pull. But he's happy. We're here.

Every sunset the mountain turns gold then rose before the shadow of the earth runs up it. The nights fall well below our zero. It snows and stays. Here is where I spend half a year, letting my body be.

Once a day I walk the loop in the mesa with my new neighbour and our pups. We talk about our daily projects, whether the mice have hantavirus, if I need a toaster, if she heard the coyotes last night, what will happen to us all now. Her wife takes me up Gold Hill—I climb mountains now. On my one-year, they give me *Out of the Wreck I Rise*, a book of quotes from writers about their relationship to alcohol and being.

I read Eileen Myles' *Snowflake / Different Streets*, enacting a kind of two-thing in the form, with one book headed one way and the other flipped over and headed the other. Myles is gorgeously present throughout. They leave breadcrumbs of themselves down the page and I fly down it hungrily.

I read Lisa Robertson's *Three Summers*, in which I am ravished with her thinking about time and form, hormones and pronouns, and the "narrative of femininity" as she explains it to the dog. At some point in the province of opposites I begin to switch the pronouns to *he* and *him* in my head. I start thinking into my lyric of masculinity. The sketch of my beard grows in and I might look a little like Harry. I lie in the foot of the Sangre de Cristo Mountains. I start to dream in my own body.

Invisible Deck of Cards

I dream that I enter Matthew Zapruder's apartment. Though displeased I haven't knocked, he asks me to sit. His hands are folding together an invisible deck of cards to play a game of solitaire. I realize he can not only memorize a deck that doesn't exist, but shuffle and play.

These mornings in Vancouver, I take his gambolling associations to the dog park and watch my tailless dog play. I wish to give a copy of his *Why Poetry* to every kid who bravely sends a poem to the youth literary journal I edit.

Zapruder says what makes a poem an undependable vehicle for advocacy is that it is easily distracted:

> It wanders away from the demonstration, the committee meeting, the courtroom, toward the lake or that intriguing, mysterious light over there. What is that light? It looks like something, I'm not sure what, I'm sorry to leave this very important conversation but I have to know.

Two-thing

The Little Prince in Antoine de Saint-Exupéry's book *The Little Prince* says that if he were given a pill that saved fifty-three minutes a year because he would no longer have to drink water, he would use those fifty-three minutes to walk very slowly toward a water fountain.

Now that I'm thinking, it was the French version, *Le Petit Prince*, I read, probably around the same time as *Jacob Two-Two*, and I only had rudimentary French. Makes for some translation surrealism. But what immediately mesmerized me was Saint Ex's drawing of a boa constrictor digesting an elephant in Chapter 1. The hat-like creature the two make. I can't stop looking. If it were to come to life, how would that two-thing feel about my particular kind of looking? I wonder.

"Hi Lao," I say to my little desk cactus, which I dreamt I pulled from the flesh of my own left hand, its green protuberances. The quills come with it.

Flower Wars

As I've sat here writing this, a book has arrived. Nico Amador's *Flower Wars*. It has a luminous yellow cover—which I've already mistreated—with four types of scissors on it. The ones for cutting hair are larger and inverted.

Inside, someone will transform. He'll tell you what changed, exactly, if you let him. *Ask me about mazes*, says the button pinned to the business suit of a Minotaur in the pages of the *New Yorker*. Transformation is a disappearing act, where sometimes you get to reappear.

At some point, I looked in the heretofore-evaded mirror to see I'd become my childhood taunt of Half & Half. There must be some kind of celebration when you finally become your childhood taunt. And then I slipped past that.

I do hope I'll always be able to write like that drawing. Of the boy who says everything twice. Naked. In the shower. Afraid is implied all over the place.

"There is the dream of exposure and then there is the act of it—" Amador begins. I turn the page and it's blank.

MÂYIPAYIWIN

Jessie Loyer

Did you know that there's a distinct waver in someone's voice as they say, "Oh my God" that immediately, undeniably means that the person on the other end of the phone is telling them that someone has died?

My family is the part of the extended family that shows up at your house when someone you love has died. We are the ones who remind you where that plot was purchased. We will ask you who will do the eulogy. We will ask you questions about that person, and your answers will become the eulogy— shorter than you could have imagined, but hitting those notes of joy and basic facts and tearfulness. Both funny and plain, raucous and painful. We will sing hymns or rounddance songs or county music. We will pray, in English and Cree. We will say the rosary, in English and Cree. We will tell dirty jokes, in English and Cree. When you break down because someone tells an inside joke and your mind is suddenly flooded with the gross realization that they won't laugh at that joke again, we are the ones who just sit next to you and let you lean into us. We are the ones you cling to as you cry, mouth wide, keening. We will ask you who the pall bearers are going to be. We will help you write the obit; each word costs more than you could have imagined. We help you edit out the things you feel until there are only the facts left: dates, their people, funeral details. We will help you cut that line about how everyone loved them. We will pass you the tissue box when you realize that the person you love is reduced to this tiny paragraph; we tell you a story you've never heard about them. Did you know this one time. . . ? We might say. We will drive from Edmonton to St. Paul at 1:00am in the windy snow to tell your other loved one in person, because they are all alone and the news, if delivered over the phone, might kill them too. While we're driving, we will look over at you hunched forward, head resting on the glovebox, and we will ask you a question that has nothing to do with this horrible moment. We will cry too. We will ask you who will do the readings in church. We will get a smudge going. We will bring some vegetables over, because everyone has been bringing fried chicken. We will make you soup for all the people descending upon your house. We will bring over enough bannock that we will carry it over in a Rubbermaid container. We will go with you to pick up your sister from the airport. We will pick up your brother from the bus depot. We will haul out a mattress and three little kids will sleep on it, while their mom sleeps on the couch. We will ask you who will sing at the wake. We will bring guitars, and maybe a fiddle. We will go to bed very late and we will wake up very early, but we will still be getting more sleep than you. We will be exhausted and you will be exhausted and we will tell you that sometimes fatigue is the only way that grief lets us pause. We will laugh at your one story about the one that you loved, that story that makes the rounds every Christmas. It's a good one. We will laugh so hard we will start tearing up and then the tears will make an abrupt switch in emotion and we will be crying in grief, just a little. But we can't break down; that's selfish; it's not like your grief that sits so close to the surface right now. We will bring babies by so you have something adorable that needs you to remind you, not unkindly, that this is a cycle. We will go through the photos in your drawer, pull out one from a few years ago, and ask "what about this one?" We will hold it up and you might say yes or you might say no. It's a good picture though, either way. "They look good here," we will say. We will sit on the bed as you go through their closet, touching shirts and blazers and dress pants. We will remind you of the time the person you loved wore a red ensemble from head to toe and announced that that was the outfit they wanted to be buried in. When you get to that red outfit you will pull it out and we will fall over on the bed, laughing. We will come and stand next to you and give you a little squeeze when the smell of them, so strong on all their clothes, is overwhelming. When the closet starts to feel oppressive, we will say, "Let's go back in the kitchen for a bit." We will make a lot of tea. We will go to the store and pick up the jumbo pack of Red Rose. We will brew coffee again and again and again. We will run to the store for more milk. We will bring over that braid of sweet-grass that's been sitting on the desk for a little while. We will tell that joke about waniska and one inch cocks. We will light some candles that we brought from Lac Ste. Anne Pilgrimage in the summer. We will bring over our kids so your kids have someone to play with while they're not in school and so that they let the adults do the terrible monotonous paperwork that comes with death. We will let you simply be in your grief.

The halls are always smoky, there are always kids running around in the back, there are always clusters of old people telling real good stories, there are always young guys putting out chairs, there are always women in a kitchen, there are always men smoking outside, there is always some really good ear-ring game, there are always some sweatpants as someone's best clothes, there are always babies crying. Even if the singers at the wake sing the exact same songs in the exact same order and the priest says the exact same homily at the funeral and the exact same food is served at the lunch, it doesn't matter. Every death is its own.

THE HIGH AND
LONESOME SOUND

Robbie Jeffrey

*Our rural culture is in trouble. But where is help
going to come from?*

Mike Hennessy was 10 years old when he jogged his first horse, and it tore flat-out across the farm track so fast he thought his father had pranked him. The speed, the smell of the stables, the thunder of hooves on the track and the mountain air whirling across the northern Rocky plains—Hennessy put his heels along the girth line and breathed it all in. In all its dust and glory, the horse-racing life was his, and he was hooked on the thrill of losing control and the chase of getting it back.

Hennessy, who grew up in Calgary and Airdrie, Alta., became a third-generation harness racer. Alberta has raised some of the world's best, including Red Pollard, who rode Seabiscuit, and Hennessy's own legendary father, Rod. Horse racing used to move trains in this province: on race days, the Canadian Pacific Railway ran a locomotive from Calgary to Cochrane, early Alberta's horse-racing mecca. Into this history came Hennessy in his sulky, assuming his role as its next hero. By his early 20s, he was Alberta's most promising horse racer. His father once said that in racing you've either got all the money in the world or you've got nothing. Boom or bust. Hennessy was smashing track records, stacking wins and raking in prize money. It was boom time.

Drugs were always around. "The horse-racing community isn't exactly spiritually fit," he told me. "The saying is, 'Win or lose, you drink the booze.'" After alcohol he moved on to cocaine. Then, in 2004, he broke his heel and the arch in his left foot collapsed, and his doctor wrote him a prescription for OxyContin. He began using small, "manageable" amounts, and it helped him quit drinking. Then his use became more frequent and eventually he was racing high. OxyContin led to heroin. "Maybe people knew," he said. "But if you're doing well on the track, people believe what they want to believe." Until you get caught, that is. One day, the race track drug-tested him, and when they got the results they told him not to come back for a month. Hennessy sold two horses he was raising and took a 45-day vacation full of the drugs that had got him there. He wound up on the West Coast.

In Vancouver, Hennessy found that heroin was cheap on the streets, until he needed so much that it broke him. He detoxed a couple times, but always came back to drugs. The recovery house he was living in eventually caught him using and kicked him out, and he ended up at the city's infamous Whalley Strip, turning to crime to fund his addiction. He had moments of realization that he was choosing drugs over racing. "But when I was at those depths, people weren't talking to me, they were talking to my disease—and it was talking to them."

At the bottom, he went to jail, got out, and then landed back in for breaching bail conditions. He faced the prospect of two to three years in prison. He spent his days enduring the sweats and at night he kicked so much he put holes in his bedsheets. He'd gone cold turkey, which meant at least he was off the heroin. But he phoned his family and told them he'd be staying inside—he didn't want to try for bail. It wasn't the drugs or the crime that overwhelmed him, but the shame. Plus he could stay clean inside. Generations of his family had pinned their hopes for the future on him, believing he could continue the harness-racing way of life. Here's where it all ends, he thought, I am the broken link.

Mike Hennessy's story isn't unique. While most people might view heroin as an urban drug, today's opioid crisis dovetails with a growing rural alienation and with a lifestyle common to young people in rural and agricultural communities, one of physical labour, social isolation, and dwindling job prospects in shrinking, left-behind towns. As farming communities in Alberta see their communally held knowledge, skills and values disappear, and as rural families break apart in search of work, it makes me think of the "high and lonesome sound" banjo great Roscoe Holcomb created to evoke the void of rural abandonment.

I know the kind of place Hennessy comes from. My family were the descendants of immigrant farmers and had a cattle ranch on a half-section near Islay, a hamlet in eastern Alberta, population 195. It was near the farm my great-grandfather had purchased when he arrived in Alberta from Scotland in the early 1900s, the farm where my grandparents raised my mother, where they grew their own food, sewed their own clothes and got by without running water until 1974. My aunt and uncle still live on that land. I grew up in a community with reverence for the land we worked and the lives we led.

Farmers in Alberta are bound to their traditions because without them they suffer the loneliness of rural life. Yet they know their way of life is vanishing, so they want their children to go off to college and find good jobs, aware the odds are slim they'll return. I had always assumed I'd have to leave and after high school I headed for Edmonton, knowing I'd never move back. I was hardly the only one.

Globalization, capitalism and neoliberalism have normalized ideas that are still radical to those in rural places: that freedom of movement is paramount; that tradition is suspect; that land is a resource to be tapped not a home to be cultivated. In the last few decades, rural Alberta has seen its small-town schoolhouses close and its grain elevators topple. Its grocery stores, banks, entertainment and industry have migrated to urban centres. Crime is up, populations are down, and the cost of farmland has doubled in the last five years. The richest 20 per cent of farms produce 80 per cent of the products.

And there are no jobs, especially jobs young people might stick around for. Politicians pledge to make our cities great places to live, not just do business, but few candidates promise to invest enough money and resources in rural communities. People who live in rural places are acutely aware that this way of life is disappearing, and a sensitivity to the bits of our culture that remain manifests in "Cowboy Pride," as Ian Tyson titled his song. Combine these things—the loss of the agrarian lifestyle, the fight against the inevitable, the shame of wanting to leave, the shame of being left behind—and you can see the kind of hole that opens up, a hole that drugs promise to fill.

In *Writing Off the Rural West*, a collection of essays, former pastor Cameron Harder wrote about farmers who were going bankrupt. Although these communities prided themselves on helping each other in times of need, financial hardships generated silence. The community saw the failure as shameful, and viewed shamed people as unworthy of its respect, or even as threats. *Writing Off the Rural West* was published 17 years ago, and a modern version could easily swap the words "financial failure" for "drug addiction." While much of urban Canada has changed its attitudes toward drugs, primarily in treating addiction as a public health issue rather than a criminal issue, this change has been slower to take hold in rural areas, where there are addicts rather than people with addictions, and where addiction brings shame to the addict's family. Shame compounds over time. We return, as I have off and on, and find the same people in the same bars holding the same grudges, and we feel ashamed again for the failures of rural life. Then the shame transfers to the community's shoulders. I can tell you about many of these things because I have felt them in my own life. "Cowboy pride will always get a man through," Tyson's song goes, "but sometimes it makes a fool of you."

The first call was about a stabbing, the result of a botched drug deal. Tammy Young* was the 911 dispatch supervisor that night, and she listened as a man, who had been left for dead, watched his blood spread out across a stranger's floor. He'd been outside and when things had gone south, he stumbled, severely injured, into the first unlocked house he saw and found the phone. Then Young took a call from a mother who'd discovered her son's body after he had died of an overdose. Young heard the horror in that mother's voice and it portended what her own future in Grande Prairie might be. This was in the early 2000s, when the city was one of Alberta's fastest-growing boomtowns, thanks to oil and natural gas. Like other mid-sized cities in Alberta, Grande Prairie was full of young men making good money, and its prosperity was tailed by vice. The city became known for its supply of cocaine and meth, and Young bore witness to the underbelly of her city every day at work.

Young thought that living in a smaller community would be safer and she'd have more control over what her kids were exposed to. "You get them into 4-H, you get them into high-school rodeo, you do things that centre around the family, around doing it together," Young said. "I thought, 'That's what's going to protect my kids from the world.'"

In 2001, she moved her family to a farm 10 minutes from Sexsmith, once known as the grain capital of the British Empire. Over the years, the family collected six horses. Her daughter, Hailey*, raised one from a foal and later had its name tattooed

---

* Some names in this article have been changed for privacy reasons.

on her back. Hailey was a quiet kid, but "could talk your ear off about horses," Young told me.

Hailey, though, was directionless, thrilled by a few things and uninterested in everything else—and immune to tough love. She was Young's fun-loving flower child, a wayward travel-ler. After she graduated high school, she left the farm for Grande Prairie. Through creeping realization, Young eventually under-stood Hailey was using. When Young visited her, Hailey looked gaunt and her behaviour was erratic. Hailey would say she wanted to go to school and Young told her she was happy to pay the tuition. "No, I need the money," Hailey would snap.

There were pills, and eventually cocaine, pot, acid and heroin. Soon, Hailey only came back to the farm to take some of her old belongings to sell. One day, when there was almost nothing of hers left to sell, Hailey drove to the farm while her mother was at work and sold the horse she'd raised.

When we talk about the opioid crisis, we tend to focus on how and why people get addicted, yet that's the easy part to explain; all it takes is a broken bone and a prescription pad, or maybe a pill pressed into your hand at a party. But to compre-hend why the opioid crisis is so intractable in rural areas, we need to think more about why people stay addicted.

Imagine your city, with its public services, its parks, its people. Think of the cutting edge medical facilities, the safe-injection sites, the preponderance of police, ambulances and doctors, and how a hospital is usually a few minutes away. Remind yourself that even in your city, a drug crisis persists. Now, take away the addiction treatment centres. Take away mental health support. Remove the hospitals. Remove the already small number of physicians trained to administer replacement therapy drugs such as methadone. Locate the police station and ambulances far enough away to render them useless in an emergency. Remove the nearby friend you might call to talk you out of putting that needle in your arm. Now into that emptiness, drop the most potent drugs known to man.

This was what Hailey was up against.

When I spoke with Young, she recounted stories of her days as a 911 operator, with Hailey always on her mind. Alberta had 687 deaths from opioid overdoses in 2017, up about 40 per cent from 2016. Overdose deaths from carfentanil—a synthetic opioid claimed to be 10,000 times more potent than morphine—increased from 30 to 159. Alberta's rate of opioid deaths is about 50 per cent higher than the rate in the United States and almost 15 times higher than in the European Union. In the U.S., the overdose death rate for rural areas recently surpassed the rate in urban centres. Young had always thought of the farm as a sanctuary from this, but Hailey might have been at an even higher risk than anyone in Grande Prairie. A study from U.S. agricultural organizations found that while 46 per cent of rural Americans know someone who's addicted to opioids, 75 per cent of people specifically from farming and ranching communities do.

Young tried to get Hailey into treatment for years, but rural Alberta's only treatment centre was in Cardston, almost 1,000 kilometres away (Edmonton has three and Calgary has four). Opioid-replacement therapy via teleconferencing, which now reaches 45 communities across rural Alberta, hadn't arrived yet. Beds were in short supply in every clinic, and they faced months-long wait times. When Hailey did land on a waiting list for treatment, she'd abruptly back out. She would get a job at an equestrian facility, then go on benders and skip work. Before Christmas 2017, Hailey called Young and told her there was an opening at a rehab centre in Calgary, could she send money? But this wasn't Young's first rodeo: she said no. Hailey didn't come for Christmas.

Young tried to speak with people in her community about her daughter's struggle, but gossip spread like dandelion seeds. Instead of offering support, she said they distanced themselves and kept their children away from her. "People talk, not around the water cooler but around the water trough, about so-and-so's family, but nobody came to help out," she said. "Certainly if there was an illness like cancer, people were always helping each other out, but when it came to drug addiction, it was a whole different ball game." This kind of isolation and stigma isn't uncommon in other towns, as families try to cope with addiction alone.

Stettler is a historic railway town about two hours from both Calgary and Edmonton. It's the kind of town where, by midday, elderly men in suspenders and trucker caps, pens sticking out of their shirt pockets, stroll across the wide, quiet streets to the coffee shop. Whitney Hall is a soft-spoken bookkeeper who lives in Stettler, a single mother with four girls who grew up there. Like Grande Prairie, drugs of all kinds flourished in Stettler when the province's economy was booming and even more so when it crashed.

Hall's partner, Richard, ended up in Stettler after living in various places across Alberta. As a youth, he sold pot and, later, harder drugs, but at first he didn't use them. Eventually he took up cocaine, then pills, and then heroin. He underwent treatment multiple times, staying clean for six months, maybe a year, before starting up again. When he moved in with Hall, she knew his history as an addict. She was naive about those kinds of things, she said, meaning the things that happen in cities but surely not in towns like Stettler.

Hall never did discover exactly why Richard became addicted to heroin. She believes it was tied to a childhood trauma he was too ashamed to speak about. He kept to himself and liked to be alone. He'd read downstairs late at night or go to the garage to tidy up. Around 2014, she began following the news about the rising body count from the synthetic opioid fentanyl, and she and Richard had many conversations about the risks involved. "How can you take it and not be afraid to die?" she asked him. Still, the nighttime treks to the garage continued.

"He used alone because he felt ashamed, like he should be better than this," she said.

Richard's fear and shame were no doubt fuelled by stigmatization because, in a town like Stettler, even if you don't technically know everyone, you know their families, or maybe your children go to school together. You don't go to the hospital and ask for help, because the person behind the desk could be your in-law.

Eventually, though, Hall took him to see a doctor in town, who recommended he quit drugs cold turkey. They looked for help in Edmonton and Calgary, but were afraid it'd be too easy to find drugs there, especially when Richard, who didn't have family in either city, would be alone. Not that he could just up and leave his work, anyway. Time and again, they hit roadblocks. Finally, they found him a spot at Grace House, a rehabilitation centre in Drumheller.

As they prepared to go, they talked about the future: building a gazebo in the backyard, vacationing, having grandchildren—all the opportunities that would open up before them. But then Richard had a gallbladder attack and had to reschedule his trip to Grace House. One night shortly thereafter, Hall awoke alone in bed.

It was three a.m. She assumed Richard had fallen asleep downstairs and so she went back to sleep. In the morning, she walked downstairs and found Richard on the floor in his bathrobe, his body purple and cold, with a needle beside him. He was dead.

Richard's heroin had been laced with fentanyl. His was the first fentanyl-related overdose death in Stettler, so Hall expected to see it in the news. Instead, there was only silence, undergirded by the kind of shame that something like this could happen here.

I knew about that kind of silence, the silence that drowns out the stories everyone knows but won't talk about, like the husbands who beat their wives bloody, like the undisguised racism toward the Indigenous people we share land with, like the story of the gay teenager who ran his car engine in his closed garage until he died and the parents who called it an accident. It is the kind of silence that mutes any voice saying we've failed ourselves and our children. During my research, I called my parents, who live in the Whitney Lakes by Elk Point, two and a half hours east of Edmonton, and asked if they knew much about the opioid crisis. My mother mentioned a name and asked if I remembered playing hockey with him. "He died from an overdose a few weeks back," she said. "And your cousin," she continued, "we're pretty sure that's what he's addicted to, but the family won't talk."

Then she mentioned a man with an alcohol addiction from my hometown. In the city, she said, he'd be just another alcoholic you pass on the street. But in our town, where everyone knew him, they found him a cheap place to live and a job he could hold down. Why couldn't we do that for people addicted to opioids? Maybe, she continued, if losing that sense of community is what's made the opioid crisis so bad, could we reclaim those same values to solve it? Or at least start. "If the stigma in our communities is worse," she said, "maybe that means the bonds are stronger, too? I'm asking. I don't know."

Down the hill from the Blood Tribe community clinic in Standoff, Dr. Esther Tailfeathers pointed from the window of her SUV at people outside a hall. "There's a funeral going on over there," she said. "A young person."

Tailfeathers had invited me on a tour of Standoff, a town in the Blood Reserve in southern Alberta. It was April and already sweltering. The reserve is so close to the U.S. border that the sacred Chief Mountain, in Montana, is almost always visible. She looked from behind her sunglasses at mourners by the hall. Her pain seemed to alter the atmosphere inside the vehicle when she spoke. Tailfeathers, who was born and raised on the Blood Reserve, has a barely audible voice but her words can stop you in your tracks. "Opioid overdose."

I asked her if she knew them. She nodded.

We took a two-lane highway leading out of town, past St. Catherine's cemetery, where there was a pile of unearthed soil for a grave waiting to be filled.

Tailfeathers had left the reserve to become a doctor, and used to split her time between Fort Chipewyan and Standoff. Now she works at the clinic in Standoff full time. The opioid crisis, which has devastated the community since 2014, brought her back. Between August that year and March 2015, when the tribe issued its first state of emergency, almost 20 people died from fentanyl overdoses. Things haven't improved since. One weekend last February, when a snowstorm enveloped the reserve, the Blood Tribe reported 14 overdoses related to a bad batch of carfentanil. By the end of that week, the number of overdoses surpassed 50 in Lethbridge.

The Blood Tribe, or Kainai Nation, has always been a farming and ranching community. The Kainai were in large part responsible for southern Alberta's prosperity in the early 20th century. Settlers needed their commodities, such as coal and hay, and relied on their freighting infrastructure and trade connections. Even today, the Blood Reserve owns the country's largest private irrigation network.

In 1918, the federal government imposed a land-use policy on the Bloods, which opened up leasing on tribal lands to settlers. Soon the Bloods' cattle numbers and grain bushels dropped off. They couldn't sell their cattle, wheat or hay without going through Ottawa, and couldn't borrow money for machinery. After a row of drought years, the cattle starved, and soon the tribe couldn't keep pace with ranchers outside the reserve. In the 1921 book *Our Betrayed Wards*, Indian agent R.N. Wilson called it a deliberate effort by his government to sabotage the tribe. Its legacy is still visible. Today, most of the agricultural land is leased to non-Indigenous people. Tail-feathers' grandparents were farmers, and her brother is still a cattle rancher, but agriculture in the community has become increasingly controlled by fewer and wealthier people.

Days before I visited Tailfeathers, I had met a physician named Ginetta Salvalaggio at the University of Alberta. Salvalaggio's work focuses on social determinants and relationship-building, and she is examining how to support people who use drugs alone, something common in the rural Alberta experience. Childhood experiences of trauma, poverty and growing up in residential schools are strong predictors of drug use, she explained, noting that the rural reality of the opioid crisis can't be uncoupled from community breakdown. Salvalaggio had left me with a question that ran through my mind as I drove with Tailfeathers. "Is it really the opioid causing the death?" she asked. "Or, when the social fabric starts to deteriorate in someone's life, is that the death knell?"

Looking out on the Blood Reserve, however, Tailfeathers didn't want to focus on tragedy. There was an abundance of overdoses in February but just one death. A year ago, she said, it could have been 20. People in this part of rural Alberta were changing how they helped people addicted to drugs.

The tribe used to exile drug dealers and send patients to treatment centres in the major cities, but it learned—as the rest of Alberta has subsequently learned—that abstinence alone doesn't work. The community instead shifted its focus to tradition and ceremony, and to social inclusion. Overdoses still happen, but the tribe is saving lives.

The high school has implemented trauma-informed care, which focuses on the connection between adverse childhood experiences and outcomes. Staff at the high school are volunteering more and the rodeo club has expanded. Both the boys' and girls' high-school basketball teams recently made it to provincials, and there's a rumour that one player is being scouted by the NBA. Every night there's something on at the community centre, from cooking classes to beading courses and, at the health centre, children tend the garden beds outside the windows of the elders' long-term care facilities. In early autumn, the kids harvest what they grow and take it home to eat.

The child welfare program has shifted its focus, too, aiming to keep families together. Chief and council now focus on addressing the social factors affecting the opioid crisis, and have invested in affordable and alternative housing. There are more jobs, and the streets are cleaner and quieter.

I had spoken about the Blood Tribe's approach with Salvalaggio, who said the potential for this kind of community development, and for creating doctor-patient relationships that establish a continuity of care, was far greater in rural areas. Strong, supportive relationships reduce blame, shame and stigma, and shift the focus to healing. When you know that the community has your back, she said, self-confidence in your ability to tackle addiction increases.

Tailfeathers put it similarly: Identity is important to health, just as culture is important in healing. As we drove, she gestured to a street nicknamed Oxy Alley. "There used to be 21 people in a three-bedroom home with one bathroom," she said. That day, it looked like most other streets. Kids wheeled tricycles around and bounced on trampolines while laughter cut through the air. A towering white cross was erected in someone's backyard, behind a fence on which a classic Prairie mural was painted: A man wearing a headdress sits atop a horse facing two tipis and, in the distance, Chief Mountain. The man's head is held high, his gaze unflinching. It looks as if he's simultaneously where he needs to be and scouting where he's going next.

After Mike Hennessy had spent more than 70 days in prison, the Crown Prosecutor's office told him to get help, since he had no criminal history. So instead of two or three years in jail, he spent 13 months in treatment in B.C., then returned to Alberta, and by February he was racing again. That summer he represented Alberta at the Western Regional Driving Championship, and by November he had more wins than anyone else in the province—a record he hit again the next year. In March 2017, he reached the coveted 500-win benchmark driving a three-year-old filly. Rod Hennessy, with more than 2,800 wins, joked that it'd come a little late.

But earlier this year, after returning to rural Alberta and racing at the top of his game, Mike Hennessy quit harness racing. For good, he said. The vices, the people, "the bond at the racetrack"—it creates temptation. Meetings, prayer and meditation were his new benchmarks. Hennessy said he was off to the mountains to work as a farrier and trainer, and told me when he left that what he would miss the most was working with the horses. That, and the rush.

Tammy Young also relocated. After 18 years as a first responder, she left Alberta for British Columbia and now works with an equine-therapy non-profit. She has two horses: a little paint horse and an eight-year-old quarter horse with some colour. She lives in Nanaimo, B.C., and she and her husband board the horses in a facility, avoiding the stress of owning a farm. They should have done it years ago, she said, then offered, unsolicited, that she still hadn't heard from Hailey.

These are melancholy stories, much like the story of our land, especially in that the land I grew up on, that our country grew up on, is not merely land. The marks we make on it, Roger Epp described in *Writing Off the Rural West*, even the collapsing and abandoned houses, halls, and churches, are "repositories of intergenerational family identity and community memory." Epp wrote, "Land is where ancestors are buried. Land is the site of good work that feeds people, that engages parents meaningfully with their children. Land in combination with Prairie sky, light and quiet represents an aesthetic sense of space that is not willingly abandoned."

It's not just the space you miss. You never forget the horses you leave behind: how one would flinch when you'd scrape off the bot flies on her tendons, or the way another would writhe his back and kick his heels up as he bucked. My family had two Tennessee Walkers and a miniature horse named Buffy. One day, I found Buffy dead in the field, her limp body in a pile of hay where we'd ride her in circles. We sold both Tennessee Walkers when we left the farm.

My Tennessee Walkers, Buffy, Hailey's foal, the dozens of all-star Standardbreds that Hennessy raced through his career—this litany of horses gone by reminds me of a line by country singer Corb Lund: "Whenever I see horses, it reminds me of what I ain't."

The horse symbolizes the folkloric rural West, a lifestyle in decline, stubbornly refusing to fully disappear. The rural history of Alberta is full of abandoned company towns like Mercoal, coal-mining communities like Bankhead and railway camps like Coalspur. Kitscoty, where I went to school, was named after a tomb. Its population grows but its culture shrinks. It had a grocery store, but it burned down and won't be rebuilt. The old bank, long ago transformed into an antique store, was finally torn down. Most of the businesses on Main Street have shuttered. Even the liquor store couldn't stay open. I look at our local history and have little hope.

But I do have stories. Clichés about winding rivers or long roads sound trite, like when Lund sings, "You ain't a cowboy if you ain't been bucked off." But such metaphors reconstruct the past to show us who we might have been and who we might still be. When we lose these symbols, we lose our sense of identity, the identity so crucial to our health. We need them to move on. Our stories—our identity and culture—come from the land, as we do, and they affirm it's acceptable, noble even, to stay where we came from.

Yet what are you supposed to do when part of you can't leave and part of you can't stay? That inner conflict sows the seeds for the threat, the loss, the anxiety, the mistakes, the shame. The opioids.

Before my grandfather died from lung cancer, he and my grandmother moved into Vermilion from the farm, and in the backyard of their small house he cut down a branch from a tree and found in its rings the image of a man staring back at him. He began having dreams in which he became this man in that piece of wood, and could observe everything that happened around him but could not move or speak. My grandfather was bedridden, oxygen tank at his side, forced off his farm. I suppose transforming himself into this man in the tree was his psyche's way of capturing what he felt as he prepared to die, helpless as the world left him behind.

When my aging aunt and uncle have passed away, no one will be left to work the farm where my mother and her siblings were raised. I imagine it will be sold to big business, maybe owned by a hedge fund and traded by people who never thought for a second about those who wheeled their wagons through the plains, dying of thirst and poverty, to build a new Eldorado. I certainly won't be taking over the farm. I am my family's broken link, and I still hear it all the time: that high and lonesome sound, that twang of despair. Yes, it breaks the silence. But it deepens it, too.

SIX BOXES

River Halen Guri

One day, finally, after several years of numbtime, and a lifetime before that, when the details were not yet known to me, I went to my shelf and made the section. As I singled out each spine and moved it to the space I'd cleared below, I pictured the blurbs and jacket copy replaced by short, true summaries of violence: *This man beat and bruised women writers without consent during sex. This man attempted to kill his collaborator, a woman writer. This man encouraged his women writing students to drink to the point of passing out; some now believe, but cannot be sure, they were assaulted. This man groped women writers at parties. This man sent a death threat to his ex, a woman writer. This man saddled his ex, a woman writer, with an enormous debt. This man, without warning, shoved his tongue sequentially into the mouths of two women writers who happened to be sitting on either side of him. This man tried to coerce a woman writer into sex by withholding a reference letter at the last minute. This man repeatedly dated his women writing students and assaulted some. This man addressed a woman writer on a ferry deck. He told her he would push her off, then lunged at her, turned, and walked away.* In the way that books all together on a shelf are repetitious—colour, format, author names, paper texture, smell, themes, font, images, letters, words—these acts circled back on themselves. As I made the section I began to access a feeling of vertigo, the way I think you are supposed to feel when you read about Borges's infinite library. People, people, words and people, all of nature, sounds, syllables, the alphabet recombining: Many things on the list had been done by more than one man. Some of the men were the same man. These were just the men I knew about, the books I happened to own. I had been social with everyone. There were more acts than I yet knew about, and more men than I could ever be friendly with or successfully ignore, and some acts committed by people who weren't men, and many people who had written books.

Hello, Literature, I said, addressing it directly for the first time. This love I'd had since childhood. Because the occasion of my standing there, in the lamplight with the scuffed white Ikea unit and the growing terrible pile, was love, just as the occasion of my purchases and attention and friendships and conversation and education and paid and unpaid work commitments and relationships and gifts and time alone with words in bed had been love. People are social creatures. The occasion of everything is love. It is important to remember this.

There was the conversation I had with S about the section. S had been feeling what I had been feeling, and had made a section too, and had put the section in boxes, two of them, and was going to have a book burning. I was in awe of this decision.

She had given it a lot of thought and had arrived at a place of clarity: Thrift shops—not an option. Then other people would buy the books, ignorant of the violence they meant. The street—same. You would not leave a loaded gun in a box by the road. Recycling—a possibility. But the glue in the bindings apparently fucks up the municipal process.

At the same time I felt, acutely, that I could not do this with my own section, not yet. I still had questions.

Here were the words of the rapists and manipulators and assailants written down. If I studied very carefully maybe I could identify the warning signs, learn to spot danger in an aesthetic, in a grammar.

I didn't see the violence because (a) I did not read the book, or (b) I did not see the violence in the book, or (c) the violence was invisible in the book, and then later or beforehand or all along it happened.

Or (d) I saw the violence in the book and everywhere in the world and didn't mind.

Seeing is a skill. Code-breaking is a skill. Minding is a skill. Total rage is a skill. I could keep these books in the closet like dumbbells in escalating stacks, for resistance training.

Was there a system by which I could identify the violence in other books, by authors I did not personally know. Was there a system I could master to NEVER ACQUIRE ANOTHER VIOLENT BOOK.

If I read the violent books I had loved backwards, could I journey back inside myself and extract what I had eaten.

Was there a system of reading and writing and shelving that would lead to justice. I wanted to know.

Was I interested in justice or just having trouble letting go.

I knew these books did not ultimately belong on my shelf. Did this mean I should get a chest freezer.

In the end S did not burn her books either. Blue bin, blue bin, blue bin.

*   *   *

Then I entered the part of my life where I was living beside a known monster, that I had chosen, that people judged me for.

My books took up a whole wall. It was unreasonable to try to hide them.

And I had cultivated the kind of life where it was normal for people to come over to drink and eat and smoke pot and develop feelings about my books, and by extension, me.

It was normal for me to talk about my feelings about my books, or even more normal to talk about something else, with my feelings about my books on display in the background.

As a young bisexual semi-femme repressed genderqueer reader whose tastes were regularly questioned by guy friends, straight friends, even lesbian friends, I had developed some defences against shame. I would feel it begin to well up inside me, and then I would do these little internal curl-ups to keep it down. I was strong. I was reasonably, adequately strong to be living in my particular body.

But now I encountered a different situation. The people judging me were not misguided or uninformed. They knew what I knew: my bookshelf was not a sanctuary or a clear idea or the beginning of an evolution in a positive direction. It was not a worthy love. It was a history of things I had let into my life that had not, for whatever reason, disappeared yet. It was what I had eaten to become who I was.

By this definition it was my body.

It couldn't be.

I wanted to tell people that I knew how bad my books were, that I was keeping the works of the rapists, the attempted murderers, especially, to learn from. That there was something about literature and my relationship to it I still had to figure out. This always seemed to come out wrong.

The people I invited over to drink and eat and smoke pot were not strangers, but beloveds. Maybe they did not judge me. It seems likelier they were only worried for my well-being, confused at my decisions. Maybe it was love. Maybe I was so wholly unfamiliar with the sensation of actual love that when it cut me, when I felt the welling, I did little internal curl-ups to keep it down.

Most of the women and genderqueers and trans guys I know have been raped. When it happened to me it wasn't by an author.

It started in a movie theatre, a full one. My friend from work was sitting two rows ahead. My rapist was sitting next to me. During the previews he put his hand up my skirt and started shoving his fingers inside me, all at once, without warning. My efforts to get him to stop did not succeed. People began to stare.

I stood up, keeping a death-grip on his wrist, and this got his hand out of me. He stood up too, and, as we fumbled to the end of the aisle, tried to put his hand back in. I held it away from me with both hands thinking *I can make this look like hand-holding.*

I took him home to my basement apartment. That seemed less humiliating. On the way there, to keep his hand out of me, I ran. He ran too. For a while I was ahead. When he caught me up, I went back to hand-holding, and we jogged alongside each other in a strange sort of arm wrestle. Google Maps now tells me the distance was thirteen blocks. Did he think this was romantic?

When we got inside I said okay fuck me. I felt clear and on fire and insane in a way that was almost like having power. I felt like I had power. He did not fuck me. He took his limp dick out and slapped it across my face awhile. Slapped it against different parts of my body. Observing a little claw mark on my shoulder from when I'd had sex the week before, he called me a slut. Did he really say it so baldly. I remember the feeling. Then he zipped up his pants and I probably offered him tea or a drink and he either accepted or didn't then left. He complimented me on my books. I think he meant what he said.

At that point in my life I really liked my books. I didn't own that many yet. I had five or six Anne Carsons and a little paperback copy of *Every Building on 100 West Hastings* by Stan Douglas, which has a fold-out photograph, taken from an impossible perspective, of every building on 100 West Hastings, just like the title promises. I liked Gerald Stern. I was weirdly into Gerald Stern.

I could not tell whether those people in the theatre were judging me or whether they were concerned for my well-being. If they were concerned for my well-being, it was not a feeling that led them to any particular action.

I know that there are people who would say, *Well what about your actions.* But I knew, even at the time, that I had aced this. *I aced this.*

I aced it so well I never really became a victim until nine years later, when someone asked me directly: Have you ever been raped? and I had to admit it—I had to realize it, then admit it. It was a safe place to do so. I felt dizzy with the scale of my achievement: the bravery of my body, and the care my body had shown me in keeping this information tightly boxed until we arrived in a safe harbour. And now my mind shaking the contents loose and turning them instantly into conversation. I was having such a beautiful conversation. But at the same time I was sad to understand, in a way that would take time to sink in fully, that I had left my body and its political position just sitting there, somewhere outside myself, for nearly a decade of my life.

This was a decade in which I finished school and wrote a manuscript and became a published author. This was a decade in which I read and acquired a lot of books.

A couple of summers ago I visited a friend in another city. His girlfriend was moving in, and they had made a large bookshelf together, with boards from the lumberyard and bricks, which was kind of in fashion—you stack the bricks four or five high against a wall, then lay down a board, then repeat until you get a grand and precarious structure—and they were deciding how to arrange their books on it. She was hesitant about combining their books. He was enthused. Their books got very mixed up. My friend and his girlfriend were tender with each other as this happened. Between the two of them, they owned many things I wanted to read. At one point in the afternoon, my friend picked a large edition of collected poems, hardcover, very recognizable, up off the floor and said, "I should get rid of this."

I knew what he meant because I owned this book too. In the beginning, it gave me pleasure, but for several years it had sat undisturbed on my shelf in its alphabetical position, in a cloud of difficult emotions that manifested as dust along the tops of its pages. Other books I owned were dusty too, but the dust on this book was meaningful.

The author of this book was wealthy, and his poems were violent and badly written. I had always been aware of this. What changed was my attitude about it. I had thought the violence meant the poems were honest. Wealth *is* violent. What's wrong with showing it. That kind of thing.

Later I realized honesty is facts but also an action. A choice to extend the truth in some direction, like a path or a building. I had only just begun the long and ongoing process of considering this.

When I first read the book I felt relief. Here, finally, was the bad guy, the powerful misogynist who had put me in the cage I'd been living in. I hadn't always thought of it as a cage. But here he was, my jailer. His honesty was the same kind children have, thoughts bubbling over spontaneously as they occurred to him. Power, when you have enough of it, dissolves shame totally I guess. Or shame is irrelevant when you know you will be cared for. And he lied in the same way children lie, transparently. My naked emperor. He was ugly-cute. A twisted little fountain.

I'd been hanging out with all these dishevelled princes. Men who were famous, wealthy writers by birthright but had fucked up the money part, or the fame, or both. I liked to ask them questions about their art. They liked simply to sit with a glass of alcohol and their glowing thoughts. I had crushes on them, or they had crushes on me; it was hard to tell the difference, because I was still in my long phase of learning to distinguish between my self and my surroundings, that will end when I die. They were trying to realize their full potential. I was trying to write my first book and become a prince, too. It was impossible. I felt tight in the chest and masturbated six times a day hard against the floor. I thought that's what crush meant. I lived in a bachelor. I had just this tiny patch of floor space to writhe around in. I was unemployed and running out of money. My pants ripped. No wonder. I couldn't afford to replace them. This was my art. To be zipped up tight inside a life that didn't really contain me.

The emperor's poems explained something. Young women had blank brains until men filled them. A full brain was a ruined one. Men were ruined. He believed this, or it was satire, or both. The emperor had money and was fully aware of the history and present of economic imperialism, and did not let this stop him from continuing it over dinner. He liked to eat as well as possible. He had money and an everlasting sex drive that was almost certainly a fiction, but one so transparent you could see straight through, and this was honest also. He had a limited lexicon of unimpressive rhymes and was not afraid to use them until they ran out completely. Then he started again. He was wealthy. He never ran out. He invited women out for drinks and pictured them in the throes of death or orgasm, which were the same. To be opposite his gaze was to live in a cage. I couldn't stop staring. It didn't matter if the poems were satire. They explained my world to me.

The emperor and I had some things in common. One of these was luck. There were differences of degree and in the combinations of factors that made up our respective lucks. But like his life, my life, in a rich country, in a white body, was upheld and made possible by violence.

It was complicated. One minute I was in the cage the poems made. The next, I was looking in from outside, at that small space containing most of the rest of the world. There were these two positions to choose from, or was it a choice. I'd been given what I'd been given. The poems were the honest poems. Was there anything to decide. I spent a lot of time wondering.

About the bad writing. At the time when I liked this book I had read a lot, but not enough. The bad writing excited me in a way I couldn't explain. I got a little glimpse of what Ariana Reines says, that "literature can be more than good." I hadn't heard of Ariana Reines yet, but I was hungry for her, or maybe deficient is the word, like a person can get for a vitamin. In my condition I did something perverse. I went looking for Ariana's idea—an intervention against the notion that women who write honestly about their real lives write badly, and therefore should not be read—in the work of this poet who wrote badly from a position of enormous power.

Anyway, I read the book and got excited. My excitement was intellectual and sexual. Then I put it on my shelf and did not think about it very much for a long time until, one day in the real world, the racist violence that happens every day, most everywhere, in ways both unique and endlessly repetitive, was met by powerful protests in Ferguson. People who did not normally think about this violence were forced to consider it. The writer, who is by now so old it's crazy he still gets verbs after his name, considered it. Then he published another badly written poem.

People sometimes behave as if words and actions occur in separate realms. They don't. One definition of power is words becoming action, the condition of there being no gap between saying something and causing it to happen. To speak out of turn, to describe real events from a place of ignorance, can be violence—the same violence that enabled the ignorance to flourish in the first place. A loop. This is what the poem did.

What I had to decide was not complicated and had never been. It is embarrassing to revisit. It was huge in my private life and tiny in the world, though these are not separate realms either.

The same afternoon: I tell my friend that I think he should keep the book.

I say this with a weird degree of emphasis, because inside me a voice is bubbling up, *oh no you don't keep it keep it keep it cheater keep it*. This is not a word I would normally use about my friend. It is just what has popped into my head.

My friend is taken aback. I begin to explain. The course of action I am defending does not make logical sense, and therefore cannot be supported by a coherent argument, only fragments of ideas that I have heard or read or invented, interspersed with anecdotes and emotions. But he listens—I make him listen—because each one is important.

When you have eaten a drug, if it is an official drug with packaging, you should keep the packaging. If it turns out you are poisoned, people will know what from. If you are eating a plant from the forest, keep one of its leaves.

When you have made a mistake, like confusing violence for honesty, you should not erase the record of that mistake until you have set it right. Setting literature right will take possibly forever.

I remember once when my friend and I were younger, and he spent the night in my bachelor apartment, which I lived in because it was cheap, and he visited for the same reason. We stayed up, listening to music and falling asleep, but not really, him on the tiny floor space and me in the bed, and he looked at my bookshelf, which had fewer things on it then, and was probably not the same shelf, and he teased me for owning a book by a woman poet I was interested in, whose work he said was terrible.

I believed him. He was wrong. I kept the book and my shame about it for years, until my shame dissolved and the book didn't. This was lucky. I ask my friend if he remembers this. He doesn't. He is genuinely sorry and ashamed. It is hard for him to imagine ever not having been interested in this woman poet—famous, canonical, dead, believed by many people to have been abused by her husband, whose poems overflow with a strange, violent energy a lot of men poets I used to know really seemed to love.

I remember a phase in my life after this when I listened attentively to what men thought I should read. The badly written hardcover was one of the books men recommended, and I agreed with them. I bought it with my own money.

I like my friend deeply, and I would like for him to have an experience of keeping a book he is ashamed of.

I remember a time when another friend of mine lived for a year without adding to the landfill. It was difficult. She failed a little, because at one point she broke a plate and decided not to keep the pieces. But otherwise she succeeded.

Not adding to the landfill can mean not creating any garbage, not bringing any home, or not being the one to throw it out. The lines between these accomplishments are not always clear. Some people live their whole lives without adding to the landfill, and we call this hoarding. Some people spend their whole careers in the humble occupation of garbage collector. I want my friend to think about this with me.

Compulsive hoarding can be the result of trauma, says the *Wikipedia* entry on compulsive hoarding. Trauma is very commonly the result of huge structural forces like racism, patriarchy, capitalism, the state. I can't get rid of the book because—I am just now putting this together—it has injured me, and my injury compels me to keep the weapon close at hand.

And for my friend to get rid of the book while I keep it in shame would be backwards.

I do not tell my friend I am angry at him. I am angry because in the past I listened to him too much, and as a result spent years of my life reading the wrong books. Now he likes different books, ones that I would like to read, too. This structural continuity through our changing tastes is difficult for me to accept. I am at a stage in my life when I would like to listen to my friend less and also read what I want, but now it seems I can only do one of the two. If I cannot change the structure of mainly listening to my friend, is there any point in reading different books at all? It is painful to consider the possibility that what I have learned so far in life is mainly this habit of listening to men.

I have to admit that the night my friend teased me about the woman poet, I wanted to fuck him but wasn't brave enough. Years later, just the other night in fact, I was brave enough. Having such a long delay between an idea and the corresponding action was interesting.

I know what you are thinking, but I'm not angry about the fucking. It was friendly and bold, joyful. It was not shameful or cheating. It was an idea I had, and then it happened.

To get rid of a friend who is alive and changing because of a book that is fixed seems simultaneously very tempting and less than reasonable. "Bibliomania is a disorder involving the collecting or hoarding of books to the point where social relations or health are damaged," says the *Wikipedia* entry on compulsive hoarding.

About moving through the world and discarding things, Maya Angelou says, "Do the best you can until you know better. Then, when you know better, do better."

About the uneven distribution of this labour, Ariana Reines adds, "Why do you always think you / have to do something / I don't know ... maybe / it's because I'm a girl."

About the anxiety that seems especially to accompany the exercise of tiny amounts of power, Anne Boyer says, "I think the real enemy of a just arrangement of the world is not the class of people who stay up all night talking about ideas and waving their hands. We sometimes just think it is because we are the sorts of people who stay up all night talking about ideas and waving our hands."

About people with power, Fred Moten says, "I don't need your help. I just need you to recognize that this shit is killing you, too, however much more softly, you stupid motherfucker, you know?"

About help, Joni Mitchell says, "Help me."

I think that Maya would get rid of the book and Ariana would keep it for performance art and Anne and Fred wouldn't give a fuck though in all likelihood none of them except probably Ariana could have been so turned around as to acquire it in the first place. This is speculation. Joni wasn't talking about the book, just the general condition of men and having feelings.

It is possible I need to discard a lot of what I've known and loved.

There was a paralyzing moment after my friend and I slept together when I proposed, or he proposed, I forget exactly who proposed, that we should have a threesome with his girlfriend. If my interest in my friend was by that point mostly historical, my interest in his girlfriend was more current. The real electricity was a crush I had—a big one, just beginning to unfurl like some springtime thing—on a different woman. I felt swept up in its energy. I couldn't face it yet. So instead of finding a different place to stay I kept on being there one more night, and his girlfriend came home from her travels, and I gave them space to talk and tried to be exactly the right amount flirty and open and filthy and rained on and approachable, and she took me grocery shopping and cooked everyone dinner, and I waited, like a scroll in a vault, to be chosen.

The three of us ate on the balcony in leafy air. Our knees touched. It was delicious. The table was so tiny. Some books spilled from the top of a stack to the floor with slapping sounds. I waited to see if I should make a move. Were there actions in this circumstance that were possible. But if so they were invisible to me, and I didn't take any, and in the end I wasn't chosen.

The next day, I went home on the train. Before I went through my bookshelf and gutted it—and to be clear, I *gutted* it: five boxes into the recycling and six to the second-hand store, where I made the most money I had ever made that way, because violent books have a high resale value; I am sorry if I gummed up the system—I spent five or six months waiting. I was interested in the relationship between myself and my surroundings. I was interested in power: what knowledge is. I was interested in who it belongs to when I have it. I was alone with my body and I was contemplating boxes. How the empty ones are more useful if what you want to do is move. The heart is not infinite. Mine was once again becoming blank.

Note:

When I wrote the list of violent acts that appears at the beginning of this piece, I anonymized the stories to prevent victims/survivors from being identified. I recombined, stripped out, or, in some cases, altered details. As I did this, a new difficulty opened up. Abuse is repetitive and unoriginal to begin with. When I stripped a story of its specificity, the number of people it could apply to multiplied, and it began to encompass experiences I hadn't meant to reference, whether for reasons of accuracy (I never owned that book), safety, or ignorance. And when I invented details to distance a story from the situation I had in mind, there was the potential that these would bring it closer to someone else's experience—abuse is repetitive and unoriginal.

Despite my best efforts to keep the focus off individual victims/survivors, two frightening possibilities persist: One, a survivor of abuse whose story I did not mean to reference will see their experience in what I have written and conclude that their confidence has been betrayed, whether directly by me or through the rumour mill. Two, an abuser will leap to assume that theirs was one of the violent books on my shelf and that their particular actions were the ones I had in mind, and conclude that their victim has spoken up.

I want to greet these possibilities with a basic fact that I hope is more powerful. If you are a victim/survivor of this shit, you are very, very far from alone.

SECRETS ARE A CAPTIVE COUNTRY

Larissa Diakiw

Last November, my grandfather told me that he went to the Soviet Union in 1962 as a roadie for the Montreal Symphony Orchestra. We were eating dinner, spaghetti squash with watery Bolognese, wine from the basement. The table was set with marmalade-colored Ikea napkins on forest-green linen. "We had to put the harp between the pilot and the co-pilot," he said, looking at my step-grandmother. "There wasn't room anywhere else." Outside, the snow had hardened into a crust. It was the first time I had heard him mention this trip. I had no idea he had ever been to the Soviet Union.

My grandfather is in his seventies. If you Google image search his last name, which we don't share, you will see obituary photos of old Polish women with perms and carnations pinned to their blouses. He is balding. His blue eyes pop unexpectedly, frog-like, from behind his glasses. He wears pressed caramel pants, never jeans, and as far as I can tell he has little to no interest in Poland or being Polish. The guest bedroom in his Calgary home has mints on the pillows, bars on the windows, and was renovated to look like Don Draper's living room. When I visit, the first thing we do is go through his version of a safety seminar. He explains how to open the bars and climb out the window in case of fire. I never listen. I figure I'll just go out the back door, but the bars annoy me because they are indicators of anxiety rather than danger. No one walks down the streets there. The little fortified bungalow near the airport will never see a pedestrian, let alone a robbery.

He ladled the tomato sauce onto a pile of squash, and it flooded the plate. "You understand the context, right?" he said. "You have to understand the context. Montreal was invited to perform in Moscow only because the Kremlin wanted to have a musical exchange with the Philadelphia Philharmonic, and Soviet planes weren't allowed to land on US soil." He looked over his glasses at me.

I understood some of the context. In 1962, the Cold War was escalating. It was the same year as the Cuban Missile Crisis. I guess Washington didn't want these musicians—probably spies—landing in their territory. Questions of national security and the fear of nuclear fallout were ever present. A war of culture had started to prove ideological superiority, as though a pianist could affirm that collectivization was better than Liberal market capitalism. By inviting Montreal to participate in the exchange, the Soviet musicians could fly on a Canadian plane to the US, and back to Canada, to play at Place des Arts. Then, the MSO would tour the USSR. At least, that is what I understood from his explanation.

"The place was grey," he said, cutting his food with the mannered precision of someone who has learned table etiquette later in life, a class chameleon. "Was it ever grey." When he talks he uses the cadence of a salesman. Each phrase is constructed towards selling the product of implicit agreement. As I grew older, I learned to not believe everything he said. "You have to understand what was going on there at the time. Bread lines went on forever. All they sold was vodka. Everything was grey, the clothes, the buildings, the sky. It was all grey, so when they saw us, well, that was a different story, but they weren't allowed to talk to us, even if they wanted to."

In 1953, Stalin was found on the floor next to his bed, paralyzed, stuttering, pajamas soaked in urine. In their accounts, witnesses always took note of the urine stain, as though the weakness of the man's body was a surprise, a truth that had to be recorded to be reconciled. Or maybe it was just a crucial humiliation. The paranoid arbiter of life and death pissed himself when he was dying, like anyone else would. He likely lay next to his bed for hours after the stroke. No one wanted to disturb him, because they were afraid of retribution. One of many hundred doctors, imprisoned in the previous months during an anti-Semitic purge, had to be consulted in his jail cell. No free doctors knew what to do. And like those who waited hours and hours before opening his bedroom door, those who attended to the Great Leader in the hospital were terrified. The dentist who removed his dentures was trembling so much that he dropped them on the floor. But none of the nurses or doctors or bodyguards were killed, exiled, imprisoned, or demoted, because Stalin died three days later after an unsuccessful treatment of leeches and oxygen.

"It is difficult for most people to imagine how a nation worshipped such a monster," Oleg Kalugin wrote in his memoir, *Spymaster,* which details his life as a KGB operative, "but the truth is that most of us—those who had not felt the lash of his repression—did. His propaganda machine was all powerful, I revered Stalin."

In '62, the MSO would have landed in a world where, only a decade before, musicians were sent to the Gulag for any misstep, any note that displeased the Party. Up until Stalin's death, music was tightly censored. It had to fit into the aesthetic doctrine of Socialist Realism, or be innocuous enough to maintain the Politburo's idea of a status quo.

"Our bloody tyrant was in a bad mood one day," the composer Dmitri Tolstoy said in the documentary *War Symphonies,* describing how Shostakovich's *Lady Macbeth of the Mtsensk District* was banned, "and then he went to the opera." It isn't clear what Stalin objected to, maybe the plot's moral imperative to kill a tyrant or the sex scenes. Either way, an anonymous letter published in the newspaper *Pravda* a few days later said that the opera "titillates the depraved tastes of bourgeois audiences with its witching, clamorous, neurasthenic music," and signed off by warning "it might end very badly." It was no secret that *Pravda* was the mouthpiece of the communist party, and that this letter was probably penned by the man himself. Shostakovich had to be very careful.

Jazz was suppressed. In 1949 all saxophone players in Moscow were ordered to KGB headquarters, where their instruments were confiscated, and their names put on a list. Musicians were put under surveillance. Jazz was considered dangerous. It had bourgeois implications. It glamorized individualism, and experimentation. Songs like "Yablochko," that mixed traditional folk with military marching music, fit in with the official party line, music that could define the new proletariat, without relying on nostalgia for a Tsarist past. Folk was the music of the common people, so it didn't threaten communist culture, and marching bands were the metaphorical sound of the army. If there was any evidence of a trumpet mute, a brazen bass player plucking instead of bowing, or a flatted fifth, the musician would be immediately arrested and sent to the gulag. A popular phrase was "today he dances jazz, tomorrow he will sell his homeland."

My friend Chrystia's family fled Ukraine during World War Two. She told me that the first time she visited, she was walking through the tangerine light of downtown Kiev. A busker played saxophone, and even then, everyone who passed turned their heads away or stared at the sidewalk. The saxophone was still an uncomfortable symbol. People had been so well trained to disassociate from anything suspect that it was Pavlovian, if no longer imperative, to look away from anything that could be dangerous. This legacy of fear runs deep.

My step-grandmother carried an almond cake from the kitchen and placed it between us as we drank the dregs of a bottle of wine. I could feel the sediment in my mouth. She is beautiful in an unremarkable but relentless way, like Debbie Reynolds in *Singing in the Rain*, with delicate, perfectly placed features and endless small-town Francophone charm. In the '60s she worked as a flight attendant in a dusty blue suit with matching pillbox hat, and spent part of the '70s stationed out of Casablanca working chartered flights from Morocco to Mecca. When I was a teenager she would bring out nail polish and a file. "If you tried harder," she said, "you could marry a rich man."

My grandfather cradled his fishbowl wine glass between his fingers. Sunspots freckled his hands. "At the Kremlin, one of the violinists was wearing a nylon shirt," he said to no one. "Imagine, they hadn't seen synthetic fabric. It caused a stir in the audience, and afterwards the guy exchanged it for a suitcase of rubles. Of course, he was arrested on the spot by his translator." Why had I never heard this before? "Those rubles would do nothing in Quebec. It was basically Monopoly money." I know so little about any of his life.

"Wait, what did your mother think of you going there, being Polish?" I asked.

"I hadn't seen her since I was thirteen."

"Really? Why?"

"Each of us had a translator who doubled as a KGB handler. It was how it was done. The poor dupe just didn't know until it was too late."

I have always wondered why my grandfather refuses to speak about certain subjects. One subject he avoids is my biological grandmother. I know nothing about her. She could be dead or alive. She could be my neighbor. I don't even know her name. When I ask about her, he responds with diversions and evasions. This applies to everything, even his account of this trip to the Soviet Union.

The details are difficult to confirm, but the basic facts are easy to research. The tour was three weeks long, with five stops: Moscow, Saint Petersburg, Kiev, Vienna, Paris. Zubin Mehta, the Mumbai-born conductor, organized the trip. After my visit, I emailed my grandfather several times to ask for more information. The first time I left the question open, hoping he would fill in missing details. The second time I listed specific questions: What was it like to be in a communist country in the '60s? What was Zubin Mehta like? How did Soviets interact with you? What were the musicians like? Tell me more about the concert at the Kremlin? He responded with two short sentences: *It's nice that you're interested. You should do more research.*

Psychologist Michael Slepian published a study called "The Experience of Secrecy" in 2017. The average person, he writes, has thirteen secrets, five of which have never been revealed to anyone. He defines a secret as something that you intend to hide, even if you never have to hide it. The secret exists before and after the point it is concealed. "Secrecy" he writes "is something we do alone in a room." Examining the effect secrets have on mental and physical health, the study concludes that the burden (and there does seem to be a physical toll) comes not only from the content, but from how preoccupied we are with it. The more our mind wanders to the subject, the more difficult simple tasks become, hills seem steeper, distances farther, everyday chores exhausting. The metaphorical language of unburdening the weight of a secret is maybe more tangible than we understand.

Grade five was the beginning of my conscious relationship to secrecy. My friend Mai and I sometimes slipped away from the other kids during recess to talk about what no one talked about. At the edge of the fields and fields of playground, only possible in a prairie city like Edmonton, was a swing set. No one could play on it because fights would break out over whose turn it was, but also because Jared Michaels* said that an old man with a white beard, wearing garbage bags for shoes, hung out there, and had given him a baggie of white powder, telling him to light it. He ended up with second degree burns on half of his face. The adults didn't know what to do, so that entire end of the schoolyard was out of bounds, and carefully patrolled by volunteer lunch supervisors in yellow vests.

The kids knew Jared had lied about the old man, that he had stolen a handful of gun powder from his parents and lit it up as a spectacle for his friends. We were all burgeoning pyromaniacs at the time, so it wasn't a surprise, but I remember feeling the first hints of pride at diagnosing his stupidity, planning my safer, more impressive grass fires as a response to his, and then guilt when he came to class with blisters running up his cheek to his eyelid.

Near the swing sets was an old cedar tree that was perfect for climbing. If you swung back and forth while holding onto the lowest branch, you could use your feet to walk up the trunk, and flip yourself onto the branch. From there, each branch was like a rung on a ladder. When you got to the top, you could watch the playground from above, like a guard in a surveillance tower.

I had a dramatic way of telling secrets. I would whisper "I have something to tell you," in Mai's ear while we sat on the bench in gym class waiting to be subbed on for floor hockey, "let's talk about it in the tree." The recess bell would ring. We would run before anyone else could see where we had gone, and climb up.

I realized quickly that my family had more secrets than the families around me, and I needed to make sense of it.

* Not his real name.

Their secrets weren't veiled translations from the adult world that I could decipher as I got older. They were omissions. No one spoke about my grandmother. No one spoke about my father. When I found out that this was because he was schizophrenic, I told Mai. The fact of schizophrenia was as unusual a revelation as the fact that I was supposed to care that some man I never knew, who existed elsewhere, had the problem. I told her in the tree, and the word, which may be outdated now, felt ugly on my tongue. Stigma was latent in the enunciation. It was a word of consonants, medicalized and complicated, with a suffix that could only mean problems, and by the sound of it should only be repeated in private.

But there were other secrets. We talked about our shared crush, who had perfect dark caterpillar eyebrows. We talked about BDSM, because I had come across the phrase in a newspaper article about a court case. We talked about our bodies. We talked about things which aren't mine to share. When we were up in the tree, nothing else mattered. The football fields that ran along 76th Avenue disappeared. Edmonton became a set designed as a backdrop for us. The younger kids playing freeze-tag disappeared. Naomi and Lena, cross-legged behind the skating rink, playing truth or dare in Chicago Bulls caps, disappeared. Who cared that we weren't invited to French kiss. Who cared that Cam White, brushing his blond hair from his eyes like Leo in *Titanic*, wanted to kiss them and not us. It all faded in favor of excavating the new secret, and sharing the discovery that up until then we had been lied to. And aren't we all lied to, constantly?

After Stalin's death, Khrushchev became the new leader of the Communist Party. His tenure is referred to as the Thaw because repression and censorship were relaxed. Millions were released from prisons and labour camps. Those who had died behind their walls were officially exonerated. In 1958, Khrushchev held the inaugural Tchaikovsky competition.

The Iron Curtain had only barely lifted, and foreign musicians were invited to compete.

A twenty-three-year-old Texan Baptist named Van Cliburn won first prize. He played Rachmaninoff. The musical motifs yearned for a metaphysical Russian past. His fingering lingered emotionally on the notes. It was not the safest way to play music at the time. It would have been discouraged in favor of precise, technically adept fingering. Van Cliburn was humble, boyish. He genuinely, unguardedly loved Russia, and for Soviet audiences it was like someone had cracked open a can, the lid peeled off, the seal broke, he had the effect of Elvis. Teenagers swooned. Thousands camped outside of the concert hall in hopes of getting tickets. People risked punishment to send him tokens of their affection. He left Moscow with suitcases full of gifts. Twenty-five-thousand items: samovars, malachite cigarette boxes, silver cutlery, woodcuttings, music scores, jewelry, photographs, violins, perfume, paintings, letters, valuables that had been hidden away during the terror of the previous decades.

Second-place was shared between the nineteen-year-old Chinese pianist Liu Shikun, and the Georgian pianist Lev Vlassenko. After the competition Liu Shikun was sentenced to six years in a Chinese prison for playing Western music. The Cultural Revolution had hit a shrill pitch. Students from the Beijing Conservatory of Music joined the Red Guards in their denunciation of Western, and feudalist, music, beating professors and classmates with boards of nails and belt buckles. The bone in Shikun's forearm was shattered during an interrogation. After years in the labour camp, one day a guard accidentally left a newspaper in his cell, and the pianist managed to compose a note, attaching characters ripped from the article using pieces of sticky bun as glue. He hid the note in his prison cell until the right moment came years later. He was able to sneak it to a visitor, who then delivered it to a Party member who pardoned him.

The third-place winner, Naum Shtarkman, was sent to prison for eight years after the competition, when a witch-hunt broke out against homosexuals at the Moscow Conservatory. He was arrested on his way to a concert for factory workers in the industrial city of Kharkov.

They were both in prison when my grandfather visited Moscow.

The dry, nearly fat-free cake was brown and deflated. I cut it into bite-sized pieces with a butter knife, because I needed something to do with my hands, and the half-eaten lumps looked like balls of clay. Someone had put on a CD, a Quebecoise chanteuse I had never heard. She was singing from the adjoining pink living room, filling the long silences, so they were less obvious. I had the urge to get drunk. Across from me was a landscape painting. Mountains edged by a lake. I took a bite of the cake. It was dry and difficult to swallow. I washed it down with wine.

How do we understand family secrets without considering their relationship to shame? And how do we begin to consider something so murky, so complicated? Shame is a social emotion, administered by the disapproving gaze of another. It filters our perception of ourselves. It is the feeling that who you are is wrong, that who you are must be hidden from the outside world. Etymologists suspect that the root of the word shame is from Proto-Germanic *skamo*, to cover, and the Greek *aiskhyne*, to put someone to disgrace. The word stigma has a revealing history too. In the 1560s, it was a physical mark scratched into skin with a pointed stick until it would leave a permanent scar, or a brand burned into skin with a hot iron. In the 1600s, stigmata were marks appearing on the body that mirrored the wounds of crucifixion. Now stigma is an invisible mark that everyone can see.

When I told Mai my secrets, I remember trying to fight against a world where appearances were more important than isolation, and self-hate. I thought that if I was open about my father being schizophrenic, then kids couldn't hurt me by saying I was destined to be cuckoo for cocoa puffs. I wasn't hiding anything.

Khrushchev delivered the Secret Speech, officially called "On the Cult of Personality and its Consequences," during a meeting of the Communist Party in 1958. He denounced Stalin's network of prisons and labour camps. On its face, his speech was an investigation into the Great Purge, though it was also an analysis of Stalin's methodology, the machine that revered him and rendered him omnipresent. For his own reasons, Khrushchev wanted to show Stalin's reign of terror for what it was. Stalin, he told his comrades, was a man who gave orders to shoot soldiers retreating from the front line. A man who fabricated crimes and put on show trials to educate his people about the new social order. But, the exposure of this propaganda was disturbing. People in the audience fainted, and later some committed suicide.

When someone is forced to repeat an obvious lie, Hannah Arendt observed, even if they don't believe the lie, through repetition of the lie they submit to the liar. They are forced to choose the world contained by the lie. Self-deception can become a matter of survival. If you are constantly affirming the lie, why not believe it? At least believe it sometimes, or with half of your mind, or because you stop being able to comprehend a world outside of the lie. When do you start to believe that jazz is dangerous, and that it's a slippery slope from loving jazz to betraying your family, to betraying your nation, to betraying yourself? Certain lies are exercises in power and social control. What happens when the lie is dismantled? Were the suicides after Khrushchev's secret speech a reaction to the disclosure of these lies? Was it a question of complicity? Was the horror too much?

I am not interested in a simple narrative where Western musicians go to the Soviet Union and liberate minds through art. I don't consider the West to be a place of freedom. Its prisons are full too. Still, as I researched Soviet music to understand what the MSO would be walking into, it became clear that the double lives of these Soviet musicians and audiences offered insight into the loneliness and horror of extreme social censure.

In 1957, Glenn Gould began to play in Moscow to an almost empty hall. At intermission, the entire audience used the telephone in the lobby, and called their friends, urging them to come to the concert as fast as they could. After intermission, the hall was so packed that people stood in the aisles, and out the door onto the streets. Tatiana Zelikma, a pianist at the Moscow Conservatory, described this concert by saying "we started to live by each new recording of Gould's and until his death, his life became part of our life."

One of the first Western musicians behind the Iron Curtain was the soprano Lois Marshall. She toured in a ball gown with lavish layers of crinoline and her limited mobility, the effect of polio, captivated the audience. They were already breathless before she started to sing. "She represented inner freedom," musician Olexander Tumanov wrote, "which was an absolutely overwhelming concept, because we were all captives in our own country."

"You remember that guy, what was his name?" my grandfather said, mostly to himself. "He rented a white baby grand. The ladies loved him, but he never paid his bill. I had to go up to his hotel the night before he left town to get him to pay up. He came to the door in sunglasses and a bathrobe with a bottle of champagne." He pushed back his chair and crossed his legs. "Dino-something-or-other..."

I put my fork down next to my plate. "I was wondering," I paused. "What was your first wife, my grandmother's, name?" He looked at his watch, then turned to the window. The sun had set outside. It was a dark moonless sky, and the

Milky Way was visible above the snow. He looked at his watch again. "Look at the time, it's getting late. The game should be on soon."

I stared at him, his eyes, his nose, and couldn't help thinking, who is this person in front of me? What is he hiding? Why is he hiding it? I finished my glass of wine. My face was burning. Maybe I didn't need to know anything about him to understand myself better. Somehow, I want to mourn these missing people, lost in the preservation of an acceptable family, but I don't know how. And each time I ask a question that he won't answer I feel it again, the hint of shame, the reminder that there is something to keep secret.

"The Oilers are playing the Flames." He pushed back his chair. "We can light a fire in the Chinook room if you want. I know you like a nice fire."

IN TRANSIT

Melanie Mah

On the last day of their 2017 Xmas visit, you meet your parents underground at the subway station near your sister Laurie's house. Laurie's house is where your parents stay when they're in town and it is beautiful, fancy in the everyday way houses in Toronto, a city chock a block of millionaires, can be. Enter a dark spectre, the comparisons you know are being made. You live in an apartment, one so messy you don't allow anyone but your boyfriend Terry to spend time there. Compared to Laurie's house, your place is small, a little dingy, and lacking a TV, microwave, rice cooker, washer/dryer, and other appliances your parents deem basic for survival. The last time they visited somewhere you were living was 2009. At the time, you were paying five hundred dollars a month for a spot in a student rooming house, where going up the stairs to your floor, you could feel a curtain of heat descend upon you in the summer. If memory serves, that was the season your parents arrived to sweat in your shared kitchen, to speak too loud and try to give you money. Some children with OCD tendencies try not to allow different kinds of food on their plates to touch each other. Each year, funded by American taxpayers, the International Boundary Commission sees as its sole purpose the maintenance and deforestation of the twenty-foot wide line comprising the US-Canada border. And similarly, you'd prefer to keep most aspects of your life separate. It was strange seeing your father splayed on a kitchen chair that may have been scavenged from someone else's garbage heap, that had, in the very best case scenario, been bought at a thrift store. You repeatedly worried over what they thought of you and of the place where you chose to live, and you hoped that none of your eight "roommates" was home to hear this, and that, if someone was, they wouldn't make you feel weird about it later. It's sad and interesting, the amount of money you can make from an old Victorian if you convert living rooms to bedrooms, put locks on all the doors, then charge separately for each bedroom. You apprehended your parents' colossal worry, accepted their money, felt sad and like a loser, and saw them out before going back to your bedroom to work on your novel.

Don't be sad, though. Things have changed in eight and a half years. Or at least you think they have. At the age of 77, your mom has recently started saying she's proud of you, and your eighty-seven-year-old dad, after a Chinatown dinner on the penultimate evening of their 2017 holiday visit, asked if you'd be going back to Laurie's house that night to watch TV with them. This is something you did a few times over the holidays; you watched nature shows with them, explained the animals' behaviours, and your parents were rapt—Attenborough talks too complexly and too fast—they stayed up past their bedtime, they stayed up to spend time with you, the family's dark horse, not anybody's favourite, as you've been told both in actions and in words. Still, when your dad asks after dinner on their penultimate night in town if you'll be going back to watch TV again with them, it takes you aback. He poses it as a thing you'd do to hang out with your mom, as if he wouldn't also benefit. You tell him you'd planned to meet Terry instead, to which your dad says, "Doesn't he have his own house to go to?" He sounded jealous. Seemed like a new thing for him. Plus lately, your dad's been saying to your mom that you've improved. You used to fight with him a lot and for years and at high volume and intensity, though you haven't now for quite some time.

You think your parents have improved as well. For the last many years, you've been saying that you love them, and actions follow these words. When they visit, they are your focus, or one of them, along with Terry and your work. Your work affords you flexibility, so when your parents are in town, you do them favours, take time to give them what they need and ask questions about their lives. Everyone who knows you well knows that you're a great big sap, a mama's girl and daddy's girl who thinks often of her parents' advanced ages. Every time announcements circulate on the news about a famous person dying in their eighties, dread buckles within you like a sidewalk pushed up by the root of a tree. Many years of therapy later, you still think the deaths of your parents will be the hardest things you'll ever face, even more than the decades of trauma at their hands, years of being the other woman to a man you loved who was never really yours, lifelong crippling anxiety and rampant self-doubt, years of yearning for love, and health issues that have given you no pain-free days in fourteen years. Of course, the deaths of parents can be hard, but you, born pessimist, suspect they'll be harder for you. The aforementioned tough past, some unresolved feelings, and your great big, too soft heart might be why.

Anyway, on their last day, you meet underground at Chester Station like you might meet on a street corner; it's sweet like that. You get there early, and when you see them walking towards you on the platform your heart is filled with gladness. Do other people see their parents as cute? Is it infantilizing to do so? Many routes lead to Casa Deluz, a Scarborough restaurant they count as one of their favourites, but you pick the way that'll involve the least walking. It requires getting on an eastbound train, then switching to the Scarborough LRT and then a bus. The whole second half of the journey, your mom's looking around, taking in the scene—she likes traveling above ground so that she can see things—and your dad comments on the huge industrial buildings the train passes on the way to Midland Station, the same as he did last time, three months ago, which he probably doesn't remember, though you do. There's beauty in knowing someone, in being able to guess their reactions to various things in the environment—a curiosity, say, about industrial buildings or strip mall vacancy rates, a swiveling head to read the signs both in English and Chinese, that certain love of certain parts of life.

It takes an hour but you arrive without incident. You get off the bus and cross the street and then a parking lot, your mom twenty feet ahead, but that's just how she walks. It's cold outside. The last days of 2017 and the first of 2018 are some of the coldest you've experienced in more than ten years in this city, and it's certainly colder than they expect. Toronto's shoulder season temperatures suit your parents better, but you love spending Xmas with them, and they like spending Xmas with their kids and grandkids. Plus, there's fun in adversity, a kind of we're-all-in-this-together kind of fun you've been experiencing throughout much of their visit. It's one of the things you love best about your family, the bad times, the emergencies, too much snow on the road, a car accident, too many customers in your family's store during a sale, and the sense that being amongst your kin might protect you, or if not protect you, then help you fumble through. You come in from the cold and order your food—char siu, greens, and fish two ways, which is a dish they get here if they're not with a kid they need to please. Fish two ways is most of the meat sliced off in congee, then the rest of it still attached to the bones and steamed with your choice of seasoning. Times you like best with your parents are full of care. They eat a small amount of the fish and congee; you eat the rest, you eat slow, as is your wont, extracting tiny bits of orange peel from the food—that being a flavour you detest—while your mom urges you to be closer to your sisters with whom you'll be in a business partnership after your parents die. You say you want to but don't know how. You wonder aloud if there's too much water under those bridges, or if the gap between land is too big. "Still, you must be close," your mom says, and she is right, though not just for the reasons she states. No one complains about your slow eating, not even your dad who is definitely the most impatient person you know. He's getting a head start reading the newspaper, ignoring the conversation you're having with your mom—the big lug.

After lunch, you walk around the mall that houses Casa Deluz. It's an Asian mall filled with stores peddling Korean housewares, Hello Kitty things, cheap luggage and cheaper women's clothes in the smallest of sizes. The stores are empty, the mall should be dying, but instead there's a buzz about the place. The food court's full, so full that sometimes strangers share a table. (You love how some malls can be de facto community centres.) Hotbeds of safe activity are totally your mom's thing. You find a seat, buy another newspaper and a large black Timmie's for your dad. Double cup to kill the environment, to protect the man's poor hands. Next, you sit with them awhile, look through the cookbook supplement in the paper for things your dad might like to make, then help your mom with a favour online. When you and she leave him to do his thing, he removes his shoes and puts his feet on the chair she was sitting on. It is then that you see how thin his socks have gone on their bottoms, that you see white spots where his feet shine through the black like lights at the ends of tunnels.

A walk through the mall sends you and your mom into stores where you don't buy anything. Makes sense, since frugality, along with hard work and luck, are the reasons you both have any money at all. You're not really one for shopping— you hate trying on clothes, you have too many possessions already—but your parents are shop owners, inveterate capitalists, so shopping ends up being a thing to do while you look for ways to say the things that matter. You've seen how freely one can speak while occupied by a certain task. You and Terry have had some of your frankest talks while making pasta and dumplings and while going on walks. So it's in a housewares store, while inspecting thermoses and rice cookers, where you end up confessing to your mom how often you've been thinking lately of your dad dying. You say it's why you've been spending so much time with them—science fact: humans are one of the only species that can apprehend a future and act in an anticipatory fashion towards it—and to this, your mother says, "Everybody dies," it doesn't help, but then she adds, "Dad said I have to think about what to do after he's gone. It made me sad."

The assumption in your family is that your dad will be the first parent to go. He's a decade older, after all, has more visible health problems, but—

"What do you think you should do?" you say.

"I don't know."

"I thought you might keep working."

"Can't work forever," she says. She's 77 and still works full days.

"So you should probably live with one of your kids."

"Yah," she says.

"Maybe move around from kid to kid." She has three she'd be comfortable living with, including you.

"Yah."

"But it sort of makes sense for you to live in Toronto." The decent transit system, all the Chinese things. "You can live with us for some of the time," you say, meaning you and Terry. You and he plan to move in together sometime in 2018.

Later on, your dad says he's tapped out on Chinese food, so you decide to bring them out for a light meal at a roast beef sandwich place they'll like downtown. In the half-dark of the bus ride there, you sit beside your mom and tell her that if she moves here, she can get a senior's monthly transit pass, and it causes her to think, her eyes at middle distance, a tiny smile playing on her face. Your dad's across the aisle and behind you on a single seat asleep. Your mom is risk averse, doesn't know how to drive, though she's still relatively adventurous. On a semi-regular basis, she zealously regales you with ancient memories of Paris and Rome, requests that you go with her to Europe someday. Plus, she loves riding the subway. You did it together in Guangzhou and Shanghai. Your confidence and familiarity with transit systems elsewhere, her knowledge of Chinese—those cities didn't stand a chance.

Your dad is the main reason your mom's not independent. Not that she'd do a lot of solo international trips if he weren't around, but maybe she'd come on her own to visit you, or go on her own to visit her brother who lives in Hong Kong. Heaven forbid she go with you or one of your sisters on a trip somewhere else without your dad. Ah, but these are impossibilities. For who but her would supply twenty-four assistance to the daily functioning of your dad? Who would remind him to take his injections and pills, who would watch the road while he drives, tell him what certain words in the newspaper mean, talk to him if he wakes in the middle of the night, explain what's happening on TV, if not your mom?

You watch her smiling on the bus about a senior's transit pass. Perhaps she never considered it before. By the way, you're on a brand new route for her, the Finch Express, it's a fast one, she likes that. She'll get her adventures where she can for now.

As the bus approaches Finch Station, you get up and tap your dad on the shoulder. He wakes from the innocence of sleep so pleased to see you. You stand there quietly. There isn't much to say to him, or maybe you don't know where to start, so you check something on your phone. When you put it away, he tells you about someone in your hometown who has lung cancer now, perhaps from habitually placing his phone in his shirt pocket. He tells you to be careful where you put yours, but there are reasons you put it where you do. You want to tell him it feels essential to keep your phone at the ready these days, and you want to say that your death from cancer or anything else, right or wrong, feels very far away, and you both do and don't want to ask him how it feels to be eighty-seven. Inside the station, you tell him there's a bathroom, and without warning, he goes down the wrong hall to find it. Your dad can be adventurous, too. After the bathroom, you all take the subway downtown. On the way, you periodically quiz your dad on which station to get off at—*Did you hear the name I told you? Have you heard it yet?*—because you want to slow the atrophy of his brain, because if he ever gets separated from the group, you want him to have at least a fighting chance to get where he needs to go.

You ride the subway seventeen stops to St. Andrew, your mom loving every moment of this novel journey, the new bus, the new station, taking the Yonge Line all the way down. You make the streetcar to the restaurant by running for it, or lightly jogging. You think it might be wrong to force them to hurry like this, but your dad laughs at his ability to catch it, and this laugh is one of your favourite sounds. He's old and doubts his ability to do most everything. But you're all in this together, and as long as this is true, you'll try your damnedest to help him feel like he can do things.

At the restaurant, you all order your sandwiches, a big one for your dad, and he tacks on fries and a soup—too much food for just him and for a second you resent the guy for ordering with the expectation you and your mom will have some, too. You find it annoying, it's like he can't trust you to order your own meal or he's expecting you to be responsible for a bad decision he's making. You hate waste. When he's in town, he wastes like it's his job, like he needs to try every single thing he wants to try because when will he if not now? You could get mad, but you don't. You of all people understand the psychology involved. Where else does your anxiety come from other than from past fights with your dad and your parents' unreasonable expectations of you when you were young? As for him, peasants acquire all the food they can afford, so even when a peasant strikes it rich, they'll want to gorge. Plus, he's sharing the soup with your mom. Your mom loves soup. You like French fries. So it's no big deal. Or is it?

The food is good. They like it, too. It's gratifying. All three of you end the night with half a sandwich in a box. Theirs they'll eat on their long travel day tomorrow. Yours will languish in your fridge and eventually go to waste—you hypocrite, you. In the restaurant, you each take a turn in the washroom and when your dad goes, you show your mom the pictures on the walls, old stars from the golden age of Hollywood and rock 'n' roll. It's a moment in pop culture history that's near and dear to her heart. You know who everyone in the photos is but you ask her anyway. She gets all shiny and bubbly telling you about them, what movies she's seen them in, which albums of theirs she owned. Then your dad, king of non-sequiturs, comes out, starts telling you about how they used to make French fries in the cafés he used to work at, and this is the kind of story you love to hear, even if it's not actually a story, and this is but one slice of your life together, a life transformed, the grand result of things changing imperceptibly each year for many years. By the end of it all, your mom is laughing at the audacity of small adventure and she's pretty when she laughs, and pretty when she presses the help button instead of the down button outside the elevator back at St. Andrew Station. A disembodied voice asks her what she wants, and all three of you laugh, though you apologize to the voice, while you scurry in. "Gum batyim," you say to your mom. *So naughty*. You can't help but think of how she might have been when she was younger. The next day is one of the first times you ever accompany them to the airport and drop them off at security without crying.

You tell them both that you love them, your dad smacks your ass while you hug like he does, and you smack his, and your acceptance into their fold comes late in life but not too late and on the other side of the nylon tape at security, you wave and wave and wave. Each time one of them turns around, you wave and smile, then they wave and smile, and when you're forty feet from each other, your dad shows in a gesture that he's thinking to throw the rest of his vacation money at you, he loves you that much, or maybe he's just had time to think about it, but it's impossible, these are the rules of airports. Plus, you don't want it anyway, that's not the prize. People who have had difficult pasts with their parents don't always have reasons, don't always have a chance, don't always get the time to forgive them, to love them, to be loved back. But you do. You don't know how long you'll have, but you'll take what you can get. You'll hold it in your hands and you'll write down the truth. Your parents love you the way they can. It's possible they love some of their other kids more, but you have the relationship you have with them and it's a special one, and finally you know they see it, too.

CANLIT'S COMEDY PROBLEM

Pasha Malla

Derek McCormack did not win the 2016 Stephen Leacock Medal for Humour and its accompanying $15,000 cash prize. Susan Juby did, for *Republic of Dirt*, a sequel to *The Woefield Poultry Collective*, which introduced readers to Prudence, a Brooklynite fish-out-of-water who chances into running a derelict farm in interior British Columbia. The novel's cast of characters includes a septuagenarian named Earl who plays the banjo and cracks wise (refusing Prudence's hot sauce: "I just got over my heartburn from our trip to Ron's Pizza Parlor"), and its scenes rollick along with the joke-per-minute efficiency of a network sitcom.

While the comedy in *Republic of Dirt* may be a matter of taste, the Leacock medal, as Canada's only major award for literary humour, canonizes its victors alongside Important Writers such as Mordecai Richler (the 1998 winner), Farley Mowat (1970), and Robertson Davies (1955). But before we accept the Leacock medallists as a comprehensive representation of our comic elite, consider this: Since 1947 the prize that claims to acknowledge "the best in Canadian literary humour" has never been awarded to a person of colour. By contrast, eight writers of Asian and Afro-Caribbean origin have been awarded the Giller Prize since 1994; M.G. Vassanji has taken it twice, and whether Joseph Boyden's 2008 win jukes those stats depends on how generous you feel about his Indigeneity.

This is not an attempt to instigate a hashtag campaign or lambaste the jurors at Stephen Leacock Associates. The National Magazine Awards didn't fare much better in their humour category before it was suspended in 2016: the last decade of finalists included only three non-white writers, Kevin Chong in 2009, Scaachi Koul (honourable mention in 2015), and yours truly (a bunch of times—toot-toot!). The Leacock medal simply provides an entry point for a larger conversation about what constitutes comedic writing in this country, what role it serves and how it's celebrated. And while the apparent racial bias of the award is, let's say, curious, I'm more interested in it as a symptom of exclusivity, insularity, and a poor understanding of how humour operates in certain overlooked corners of our national literature.

Despite its pretence of scope, the Leacock medal has traditionally been awarded for humour written in the mode of Stephen Leacock. Perhaps this is to be expected. After all, the prize's host organization is expressly mandated to "preserve the literary legacy" and "to honour and perpetuate the name and memory of Stephen Leacock" by continuing "to initiate and support activities which widen interest in Leacock and his writings [and] in the Leacock legend." So it seems predictable that, as a corollary to those activities, the medal honours books that emulate the qualities of its namesake—or at least his fiction.

Assuming that Leacock's various chauvinisms—his contempt for women and Indigenous people, in particular, has been well documented—are not the legacy conscientiously perpetuated by Stephen Leacock Associates, one might take his most famous book, *Sunshine Sketches of a Little Town*, as the medal's exemplary title. The tone is breezy, anecdotal, and archly ironic. The struggle between success and failure (financial, political, romantic) is a consistent theme, and its characterizations traffic in idiosyncrasies and quirky irreverence.

If there's satire or parody at work, it's a particularly gentle and forgiving breed; Leacock's characters are parochial, sure, but that's the source of their charm—and their integrity!

This is not to say that *Sketches* isn't enjoyable or elegantly written. While the citizens of Mariposa tend to be caricatures, they're vividly crafted: the inscrutable hotelier Mr. Smith "makes the Mona Lisa seem an open book and the ordinary human countenance as superficial as a puddle in the sunlight;" more generally, the men of the town are judged per their equanimity: "'Level-headed' I think was the term; indeed in the speech of Mariposa, the highest form of endowment was to have the head set on horizontally as with a theodolite." Zena Pepperleigh, the book's token, summarily humanized woman, sits on her porch imagining rescue by knights in shining armour before capitulating to a more humble, local romance in an artful conflation of fantasy and reality: "Already, you see, there was a sort of dim parallel between the passing of [Mr. Pupkin's] bicycle and the last ride of Tancred the Inconsolable along the banks of the Danube."

Tellingly, Leacock addresses a generic second person with a baseline of familiarity that assumes shared references. "I don't know whether you know Mariposa," the book begins. "If not, it is of no consequence, for if you know Canada at all, you are probably well acquainted with a dozen towns just like it." Ingratiating phrases such as "you will easily understand" punctuate the book, implicating the reader as a presumptive ally of similar experience and social station. (Touchstones include the caprices of the Liberal party, the sinking of RMS Lusitania, and the inadequacy of Greek translation.) The first-person narrator also proxies as an observational "I" slightly peripheral to the action on the page, rendering the reader both "you" and "I" simultaneously—unless "we" don't intrinsically identify with either, of course.

To be fair, most authors of Leacock's era and pedigree might well assume a kindred readership; it's not a project of exclusion so much as obliviousness. And while it can be futile to condemn the past with updated morality, it's worth examining how we deal with history that becomes politicized in retrospect. As such, the Leacock medal feels a bit like a Confederate statue that sits, dutifully tended, in the town square of Canadian literature. But rather than tearing it down, we'd do well to heed Guy Vanderhaeghe's advice in the 1986 anthology, *Stephen Leacock: A Reappraisal*: "We might learn something by taking a walk around the monument which Stephen Leacock has become and taking a look at him from a slightly different angle too."

Perhaps the most Leacockian of medalists in the past couple decades is Stuart McLean, a winner for three separate Vinyl Cafe collections (2007, 2001, 1999). As with Leacock's *Sketches*, McLean's stories boast a folksy, family-friendly appeal and feature "ordinary" people engaged in commensurate affairs. This is comedy for audiences who recognize themselves in the members of a middle-class, nuclear family doing their best to get by, with all the hijinks and teachable moments that come with, say, toilet training a cat or celebrating Christmas with Muslims. Fellow standard-bearers for the Leacock legacy include Trevor Cole's *Practical Jean*, which won the prize in 2011 and takes place in the small, fictional town of Kotemee, and Dan Needles, who won in 2003 for *With Axe and Flask: A History of Persephone Township*, which centres around the small, fictional town of Larkspur. Also operating soundly in the Leacock mode is Terry Fallis, who has seen five of his six books shortlisted for the prize; three have won. His first novel, *The Best Laid Plans*, a mild-mannered send-up of federal politics, was declared by the *Winnipeg Free Press* upon its publication in 2008 to be "the most irreverent, sophisticated, and engaging [satire] CanLit has seen since Stephen Leacock," and was also deemed "the essential Canadian novel of the decade" upon winning the CBC's Canada Reads competition in 2011.

The titles of some other winning books include: *Pardon My Parka*, *Mice in the Beer*, *Saturday Night at the Bagel Factory*, *Beauty Tips from Moose Jaw*, *Gophers Don't Pay Taxes*, *Never Shoot a Stampede Queen*, and *The Night We Stole the Mountie's Car*. There are regional books, such as *The Promised Land: A Novel of Cape Breton*, and Ian Ferguson's *Village of the Small Houses* (i.e., Fort Vermilion, Alberta), and a few through the 1970s and 1980s that, alongside legions of wide-lapelled nightclub comics, mined hilarity from the battle of the sexes, e.g. *Take My Family . . . Please!* and *No Sex Please . . . We're Married*, as well as the less imploring, curiously zoological *Wives, Children & Other Wild Life*. There is wordplay, of course (*Fear of Frying and Other Fax of Life*; also *True Confections*), and eponymous memoirs (Richard J. Needham's *Needham's Inferno* and Max Ferguson's *And now . . . Here's Max*); Arthur Black conflates these techniques with his trifecta of winners, *Black Tie and Tales*, *Black in the Saddle Again* and *Pitch Black* (his *Fifty Shades of Black* was a finalist in 2014, but lost to Bill Conall).

There have been a few aesthetic anomalies among Leacock winners, most recently Gary Barwin's *Yiddish for Pirates* (2017), and *The Sisters Brothers* by Patrick deWitt (2012). These two novels stray from the Leacock formula in some respects—Barwin's postmodern adventure story is narrated by a Jewish parrot; deWitt's postmodern Western suggests a Coen brothers/Charles Portis collaboration—but one wonders if the judges were celebrating the books as works of parody or as further celebrations of masculine nostalgia, here for the swashbuckling and gun-slinging of boyhood fantasies. (Of seventy-one Leacock medalists, only seven, including Susan Juby, have been women.)

As Northrop Frye once noted, "[Whenever] some people get to the point of emotional confusion at which the feeling 'things are not as good as they ought to be' turns into 'things are not as good as they used to be,' back comes this fictional image of . . . the real values of democracy that we have lost and must recapture." The Leacock medal participates yearly in this brand of wistful revisionism, resurrecting the mythos of "traditional values" embodied by *Sunshine Sketches* and emulated by subsequent winners. These books are notable, too, for not only their dramatic content but their comedic sensibility—more Horatian than Juvenalian, certainly, and perhaps best described as safe.

This may be one reason for the unanimous whiteness of the medalists. Voices from the margins tend to deploy humour to question, provoke, and disrupt rather than to uphold the status quo. In *Sunshine Sketches* Leacock claims that, when it comes to comedy, "what the public wanted was not anything instructive but something light and amusing," that "people loved to laugh [and] if you get a lot of people all together and get them laughing you can do anything you like with them," and, finally, "Once they start to laugh they are lost." But the intended reader of Stephen Leacock's stories isn't led afield so much as innocuously distracted; that the prize perpetuates this mode of humour blinds it to any comedic work invested in challenging the modes of power that Leacock and his acolytes tend to reify.

As Margaret Atwood pointed out forty-four years ago, Leacock's stories are based in "the laughter of recognition and identity," such that "the reader, being Canadian, is invited to recognize part of himself and his background in the sketches." Forgiving Atwood some assumptions (and realities) that have shifted in the past half-century—what "being Canadian" entails, exactly, as well as how many of us might recognize exactly nothing of ourselves in *Sunshine Sketches*—the diagnosis is still useful: A Leacock-championed book inspires self-recognition in readers whose heritage and experiences qualify as Quintessentially Canadian—should one, that is, consider the quintessence of our nationhood to be most acutely expressed in the eccentricities of small-town mayoral elections and "whirligigs."

The Stephen Leacock medal has succeeded less at celebrating the breadth of our nation's comedic writing than in substantiating a set of culturally exclusive tropes by lionizing books mostly written by a subset of our population to mollify people just like them. That said, rather than calling for Stephen Leacock Associates to apologetically garland some random writer of colour, which would only achieve a condescending, concessional diversity, let's steer away from Mariposa entirely. This country is home to some very funny writers working outside the artistic and ideological scope of what's traditionally celebrated as "Canadian literary humour," writers whose books challenge readers' comfort and resist dominant narratives in both form and content.

In the interest of scholarship I asked a few dozen literary folks for recommendations of funny Indigenous and Canadian writers of colour. The response was effusive. The names that recurred most frequently included André Alexis, Dany Laferrière, Thomas King, Maria Qamar, Eden Robinson, Leanne Betasamosake Simpson, and Drew Hayden Taylor. Suzette Mayr also got a couple of mentions for her terrific novel *Monoceros*, and by far the most common reply to my survey was Scaachi Koul, whose first book was in fact a finalist, perversely enough, for this year's Stephen Leacock medal. However, even if she had claimed the $15,000 jackpot, a single win for a woman of South Asian heritage doesn't solve the larger problem, and risks being just as tokenistic as cataloguing authors' names in a defiant roll call of BIPOC hilarity.

But let's not abandon that list entirely. Of the above-mentioned writers, many have enjoyed mainstream success far beyond a Leacock commendation—Alexis's *Fifteen Dogs* was a multiple-award winner and runaway bestseller; Robinson won the Writers' Trust Engel/Findley Award in 2016 for her body of work—but few, if they're taken seriously as literary authors, are also lauded for their comedic sensibilities. Contrast this with Will Ferguson, for example, who post-*419* is still recognized, and often defined, as a three-time Leacock medal-winning humourist alongside his Giller Prize accreditation. Some people get to be both; others do not.

A final note about my email query: The most instructive response wasn't reading suggestions, but a thoughtful missive from the Tuscarora writer Alicia Elliott: "To be honest, I feel like 'literary humour' and its attendant whiteness have to do with the ways that white people seem to think there needs to be a separation between being serious and being funny. Indigenous people (and I think black people and other people of colour, as well) have to constantly undergo trauma in a way that makes it impossible for them to have that separation. So to get through really serious, awful shit, we rely on humour almost constantly." This resonates with any community that opposes hegemonic power; consider the absurdism and bold satire practiced by the literary avant-garde who challenged Soviet totalitarianism in the 1920s and 1930s—many of whom were jailed for their efforts.

Any false distinction between literary and humour, or that separate, faintly patronizing category of "literary humour," creates a dynamic in which acclaim is only afforded to writers—and here I mostly mean writers of colour—who forgo their propensity for play in order to be taken seriously. This seems especially true when we look at a few Canadian authors who have achieved global recognition. Of our writers with a major foothold on the world stage, perhaps none is more gravely, beardedly serious than Michael Ondaatje. Yet he used to be pretty funny—or at least playful. Ondaatje's "Application for a Driving License," from his 1979 collection *There's a Trick with a Knife I'm Learning to Do*, reads not just like a parody of lyric poetry, but a parody of the self-aggrandizing, egregiously sombre poet as well. It's also structured like a classic joke, culminating with a deadpan punchline:

Two birds loved
in a flurry of red feathers
like a burst cottonball,
continuing while I drove over them.
I am a good driver, nothing shocks me.

Rohinton Mistry is known for his doorstop social realist novels, but his first collection of stories, *Tales From Firozsha Baag*, exhibits a wit and whimsy that the author has abandoned in his more recent work. "Swimming Lessons," the book's final story, is about an Indian immigrant to Toronto who decides to learn to swim at the local Y, where he becomes obsessed with the pubic hair sprouting luxuriantly from a classmate's bathing suit; "Squatter" features a similar character whose assimilation is foiled by an inability to sit on a Western-style toilet. The book offers one of Canadian literature's most hilarious and honest depictions of the so-called "immigrant experience" (always singular; apparently there's only one), yet one finds little humour in Mistry's mega-selling downer, *A Fine Balance*, and certainly Oprah never championed him as a comedian.

What used to be encouraging about Ondaatje and Mistry, too, was that their humour challenged notions of how New Canadians were meant to depict their engagement with the dominant culture. Should the powers-that-be at Stephen Leacock Associates suddenly about-face and start rewarding more culturally or aesthetically diverse work, little will be achieved if the books merely adhere to and replicate certain tropes of acceptability. Television offers a fine illustration of how this sort of inclusion tends to operate: diverse voices are welcome, provided they either speak the same way as everyone else or operate with the ridiculousness of caricature. We may applaud the cosmetic inclusivity of *Kim's Convenience* and *Little Mosque on the Prairie*, but the formula of the typical network sitcom bulldozes any real idiosyncrasy or difference:

the characterizations are simplistic, the storytelling rote, and each episode relies on the same arcs and narrative beats of most mainstream entertainment. *Kim's Convenience*, in particular, operates under the benevolent but ultimately flimsy banner of tolerance, as if merely showcasing the interactions of people of colour, no matter how banal, is somehow innately progressive.

The best counterexample to this brand of well-behaved comedy is *The Kids in the Hall*, which, over its six seasons on CBC, might have failed to include much racial diversity, but certainly broke the mold for what was allowed on TV. From sketches like "Running Faggot" to the creepy surrealism of Bruce McCulloch's short films, *The Kids in the Hall* refused to placate the average CBC viewer with the broad, facile humour of contemporaries like the Royal Canadian Air Farce, Smith and Smith's Comedy Mill and CODCO. Even now, the "Gay Discount" episode that opens the inaugural series of *Kim's Convenience*, a mostly superficial survey of stereotypes and assumptions, pales when compared to the scathing satire of Scott Thompson's monologues as Buddy Cole. As John Semley wrote in *This is a Book about The Kids in the Hall*, Buddy was "a challenge to any narrow-minded viewer who flipped past the CBC to see a glittering gay caricature waving his rubbery wrists around," and the character embodied the show at its best: confrontational, grotesque, discomfiting, weird—and still the funniest thing on Canadian TV by a considerable margin.

Which brings me, somewhat contrivedly, back to Derek McCormack. Despite being one of the most hilarious, original, brilliant writers in this country—as well as a white man!—McCormack has never been nominated for the Stephen Leacock medal. (In fact I'm not sure that any of his seven works of fiction has been listed for a major Canadian book prize.) His most recent novel, *The Well-Dressed Wound*—"weird, inventive [and] wonderful," according to the *Village*

Voice, "fantastically demented" (*Globe and Mail*), and "radically alive" (*Art Forum*)—is part theatrical performance, part fashion show and part séance. The novel's plot, such as it is, details Abraham and Mary Todd Lincoln's attempts to summon the spirit of their dead son. (If that sounds familiar, *The Well-Dressed Wound* came out a year before George Saunders' *Lincoln in the Bardo*.) As with all of McCormack's work, things go spectacularly off the rails in a raucous, raunchy pageantry of Beckettian farce, haute couture, and scatological obscenity—often at the same time.

Writing for *Vice*, Blake Butler described his response to the book: "You're laughing and then the laughing hurts and then you aren't laughing anymore, which as an experience delivered on paper couldn't feel more immediate." Of course any novel that simultaneously evokes and troubles laughter fails, per Margaret Atwood's analysis of Canadian humour, to comfort readers with familiarity. So perhaps it's understandable that Derek McCormack's work hasn't earned mainstream renown—or a Leacock medal. (Well, that and *The Well-Dressed Wound* features, among other things, a cloven-hoofed, horny devil who declares, "Ladies and gentlemen . . . I give you the future of fashion—AIDS!" and the word "faggot" appears more than three hundred times over the novel's seventy-two pages.) But it's a shame that work this smart, this unconventional, this thought-provoking—and, mainly, this funny—isn't widely celebrated. Beyond the cosmetics of racial representation, we need more writers like Derek McCormack, whose bizarre, wild novel achieves the same effect as any good joke: it disrupts and surprises us, and colours our worlds a little differently.

ON MEANING

Souvankham Thammavongsa

We had not lived there long. A few months, maybe.

The one bedroom, in the apartment, was mine. I had a window and outside was a brick wall. I was happy it wasn't in the basement. We had lived in one before. Mould grew on the walls in the summer, black dots that started in different spots, but then would quickly bloom to reach each other. We used bleach and dishwashing detergent and a cloth to wipe it all away. I was happy I didn't have to do that anymore. That I could open a window and there wouldn't be a parked car there with the exhaust pipe aimed into my bedroom or that I wouldn't wake to some bright lights felt like a luxury.

The brick wall. The brick there was a yellowish brown.

There was no view of sky and I could not see the sun. But I knew when there was sun because there was light. I watched this brick wall and imagined the sun. Where it was in the sky and when it would set. At night, when there was no sun at all, everything out there was dark. I couldn't see the brick at all.

I loved how organized the structure was. That there was a beginning to it, that its assemblage and arrangement had an order, had a purpose, and a responsibility. I loved that it didn't change. Each brick was sealed there by cement. And it would be there forever probably. Forever was an idea that was important to me. I never had that as a child. Forever was something that happened to other people. What I knew and what was always the case for me was: for now. We would live here, for now. We would do this, for now. For now, I knew all about.

I decided then, that this brick wall and the colour of it could mean something to me, would mean something to me.

Yellowish brown was the colour of gravy in the potatoes we ate. Potatoes were not things we ate regularly. They were reserved for special occasions like Christmas or Thanksgiving. My family and I, we didn't know what these things like Christmas and Thanksgiving were but we were told they were occasions to get together and to be together. We would never host. Our place was always too small, too difficult to get to, and my mother never cooked things like that. The people who made the gravy were good people. The kind of people who come to help at a time when those who are supposed to, abandon you.

The grass in the schoolyard gets to be this colour when the snow disappears. I hadn't even known the green was gone. Once, I made up a game and got everyone to join in. We, each alone, spun ourselves, arms lifted. Tornado, I called it.

The colour of the building where I got my university degree. I did not dress properly for the occasion. I had worn jeans and running shoes. I did not know girls wore black stockings and high heels. When my name was called, three hours later into the ceremony, I went up there but I was not alone. It was two-at-time because there were so many of us. I did not know the other person and can't even remember what they looked like. I wasn't looking. I was thinking of the exit, the photo that would be taken afterward in my cap and gown. My parents were outside holding a bouquet of flowers. They asked me if I wanted to go and eat lobster. My favourite. They apologized it was a meal. They wanted to buy me a car I could not drive or a house I could never own.

The colour of hair. The first person I ever loved had this hair colour. The first time I had got close to the idea of forever. He said he was not forever, but what took place, what happened, I carry that with me like it was.

On the last day of a job I held for fifteen years, this colour was on the ceiling. A leaking pipe no one had bothered to fix. I had a coffee cup that had a drawing of a bee and underneath it, the words "Bee-otch." It was something I kept on my desk and turned the word toward anyone walking by to ask how my weekend was.

It's the colour of a book I printed and made myself. The one that made me see and hear my voice. The one that made me feel like I had something forever all to myself.

The colour of the coat my husband wore when I first met him. I knew he'd be someone to me then. He said something, and I said, "It may be naïve, maybe not, but it's decent." I burned the food black, and he ate it.

The last time I saw this colour was in the Serengeti. The grass there was this colour. There wasn't much green. The lions. They were this colour too. I was in a Jeep and it was driven to a tree, where there was shade, and two lions looked at me and then through me. The windows and roof of the car was open. I was sure the lions could smell me. The driver said the lions do not care about us. We are nothing to them. A few hours later, I saw a warthog in the distance. It was on the ground and some part of it had been opened and when the lions lifted their faces there was red. Blood.

The lions hunted in groups. They organized for their kill. They slept during the day and at night you heard them roar. I was in a tent when I heard a roar. I lied to myself that it was far away so I could sleep. When we packed up on the last night there, someone told me baboons know how to open a tent, and they come in there to get chocolate. I'd had chocolate.

Gazelles were everywhere and zebras. I saw a small group of elephants. They were all female, except one. He was obvious. He rolled what he had, out. It was pink and long. We did not laugh. It was that stage in his life when he had to be separated, be on his own. He did not know why he was not wanted. Every time he came near, the biggest female would push him away. His mother, probably.

Nearby, a gazelle was stuck in the mud. Nature, the order of things, don't mess with destiny. Someone could have walked out there and helped it along, given it another chance.

The cheetah I saw had just given birth a month ago. Her cubs were near her. She hid them in a small bush. I counted three cubs. A small number. There is usually at least five, we are told. Two others had died. Eaten perhaps. Or there wasn't enough to eat. The cheetah is female. Males, I am told, can make cubs and don't know. But it is the female who knows and who is responsible for everything after whether she wants it or not. It is not a matter of want, for her. She was trying to hunt now, to get the kill done, for the cubs. Gazelles don't run in straight lines. It takes more energy for the cheetah to pivot, to turn. She chose the smallest gazelle, and it was supposed to be the easiest, but the dirt kicked up was too dusty to see through and the cheetah returned to the cubs without a kill. She too will die if she doesn't make a kill.

Only the Maasai live in the Serengeti. There was a little boy with three goats standing in a field, surrounded by grass the colour of that brick I had always known. It was the sun that made it that way. He wore bright colours, red, purple, green, to let it be known he was coming, that he was there. It was the red that was brightest, that was seen. His back was straight and his chin high. He was alone and brave that day and probably every day. A child, even when you do not have one, can have meaning to you.

I thought of the brick wall I had seen almost twenty-five years ago. How I had always seen that brick wall, that one brick at the centre, and the cement put in around it. The weight of it, though I had never touched it, I could feel it in my chest. A view of the past and a familiar colour in what would be the future.

A poem can be like this with its meaning. Meaning can sometimes blow up, crack something we had not seen, or darken what had been seen so clear to us.

Meaning can happen with so little.

Meaning can sometimes take a long time to arrive, years even, if ever. And it's possible meaning does not mean, and that in itself could be meaningful.

Meaning is not the same thing as clarity. Things can be absolutely clear and mean nothing. Or things can be a mess and still have meaning. Whatever happens to meaning it is always there. It means even when you don't want it.

THE BULL OF CROMDALE

Jessica Johns

My papa used to be called The Bull. Back when he had black hair, styled it like Elvis, and wore cowboy boots with silver heels. He lived with his cousin Dustin in Edmonton's North-side neighbourhood of Cromdale, which was off of 118th Ave, which was also called the Avenue of Champions. If you didn't live in the area, you knew the Avenue of Champions was where johns went to pick up women and where the machete attack happened. If you lived in the area, you knew the things that didn't get reported, but you knew the good things, too. The Cromdale Hotel was a staple of the Avenue of Champions, and that's where The Bull was made. The hotel had forty-four rooms and the attached bar had a pool table with only a couple divots, cheap beer, and country music. Papa and Dustin sharked people every night and could have made a living out of it if they wanted to, but Dustin was a Bellerose, which meant he was small and made trouble. Started fights with moniyaw he knew The Bull would finish. Some people called the Cromdale a hole to house men who didn't know where else to go. My papa called it magic.

I learned about The Bull, this man that my papa used to be, in the same way I learned everything about my family: in

East Prairie, sitting against the backdrop of my papa's farm. Gathering little bits of information and trying to piece them together like shredded paper. I learned that papa and Dustin left East Prairie together when they were fifteen, because even though Edmonton wasn't big then, it was bigger than the Métis settlement where they were born. Big enough for their dreams to fit. Papa and me were playing darts and he skunked me for the millionth time like he could do it in his sleep. I've never seen anyone throw darts like him. Dad just shook his head. He remembered The Bull better than anyone. *The Bull could play poker, darts, and pool at the same time,* dad said. *He could spot a cheater through tobacco smoke and a two-four of whiskey.*

If anyone stepped too close or had eyes too hard, he'd knock them out before they had time to blink.

The Bull, dad said, *never lost.* Then he conjured the man. Dad told stories about how papa used to bring together the whole neighbourhood, how he could strip sound right from the airwaves, how under the wing of The Bull of the Cromdale, you were always safe.

After that, I couldn't stop thinking about him. Even when I slept, The Bull lived in the periphery of my dreams. The dreams started coming in waves in the winters and changed with every new story I heard, but The Bull stayed the same. He was like how I saw him in every old photo stuck to the fridge or creased between book pages: black button-up shirt, arms spread across the shoulders of his cousins, a smile so wide it looked like a wound. He moved like he was floating and I couldn't look at him directly or he disappeared, so I watched him from the corners of my eyes. Tried not to lose him in the rest of the noise or the other people who would come to visit. Most times, he ignored me. Sometimes, he watched me back.

After papa had been living in Edmonton for a while, he started working at McTarin's bookbinding factory where he met my grandma. Papa would sometimes glue pages out of order, and when grandma asked him about it, he said it was because logic was no good for stories or for dreaming. She said that's when she fell in love with him. No one was surprised papa fell for a white woman who already had two kids, my Uncle Will and my dad, but they were surprised about the changes. Papa packed them up and moved to a quiet suburb further south where no one yelled in the streets after dark. Papa started gluing the pages in the right order, and even though he was still The Bull, it was only on weekends. He had people to take care of. And he did.

By the time my dad was twelve and Uncle Will was thirteen, they'd already grown to love the weekends as much as papa. They'd stow away in the backseat of his Ford pickup when he'd head to the Cromdale, hang around papa's old neighbourhood and get into trouble of their own. One night, Uncle Will tried his luck getting into the Cromdale and made it pretty far before getting into a rumble. Nobody believed The Bull at first when he stepped in and said that the white boy getting roughed up was his, but they believed him pretty good after he beat the other guy bloodier than he'd ever beat anybody. When Uncle Will talks about what he saw, he says The Bull grew ten inches taller and five inches wider the minute he stepped into the Cromdale. He says it might have been the smoke or the dark, but he saw the wooden beams of the bar move in waves around papa's body, like it was making room for him. In the Cromdale, uncle swears, The Bull was magic.

It wasn't long after that they left Edmonton behind. They packed up and moved to East Prairie, to build a farm and a life together. But the myth of The Bull still floated through the bar for years to come. Whenever the sound of a pool cue snapping over another man's back rang through the bar, they'd reminisce about The Bull of The Cromdale, blow the memory loose and measure it next to the new ones: *The Bull could crush cue balls with one hand, fight five men at once, drink more than the entire bar combined and then two-step his way home.*

These stories travelled from Edmonton to East Prairie some-how, were repeated like first-hand stories by my other uncles, aunts, and cousins who couldn't have possibly been there. But maybe they saw them in their dreams like I did.

In one dream, the Cromdale was where papa's barn is in waking life, and smelled like hops and sawdust instead of horseshit. The bar stretched back further than I could see and every surface was shiny wet, leaking ocean between cracks and I don't know where else. I put quarters in a jukebox and the lights started to flicker like a rave. Papa moved around the bar in stop-motion, getting closer then further away with every step.

Papa listens to all the stories about The Bull but never confirms or denies anything. He just laughs in his chair, the creases beside his eyes softening the rest of him, his right hand tracing the tattooed B on his left thumb. I try to imagine those hands clenched into fists, meeting another man's face, but I can only see floating and his smile beaming from the juke-box glow. Lit up then dark again. Dad says The Bull's fighting days ended when my grandma had my aunt, her third kid and her first kid by blood with papa. Dad swears he'd never seen someone soften so fast. And then papa grew softer still with the next two of his kids, and then with the grandbabies they made, so by the time it got to me he was malleable, a different mould of a man.

Before I knew about The Bull, I only knew that papa meant summer. Every summer, we'd head out to East Prairie to see my family, because my parents were the only ones who didn't live there anymore. We always knew how far away we were by papa's bridge. We didn't call it that because he helped build it, though he did that too, we called it that because the first right turn after it would lead us to him.

I was one grandchild of ten in the early days. He'd bring anyone who woke up early enough to help him take care of the horses. He taught us how to feed the giants without getting spooked. The magic spot to press on their legs to get them to lift their hooves, check for sticks. How to unhook the burs from their manes without hurting. He let us name the horses and called them ours. They were the first real things we ever owned, though we never really did. Not in the way owning something means caring about it until the very end.

I knew when summer was over when mom and dad would pack up the van and call us. We'd be out somewhere on the farm with papa when we'd hear them. Instead of heading back, he'd take us for a walk along the path behind the barn that led to the river, the path clear from the wear of him walking it every day. Up past the beaver dam, papa would point out the raspberry bushes, and we'd look for walking sticks just like he had. By the time we got home it was too late to leave, and we'd have to unpack, find another place to land for the night. This was how papa gave us one more night of summer. This was how I knew papa was magic everywhere.

With every visit back to papa's farm came some kind of change. It didn't all happen at once because nothing ever happens all at once. Grandma died before anyone. The horses started to go around the same time as his brothers and sisters. His cousins trickled away in between. I dreamt of the Cromdale's death before it happened. A week before it was blown into rubble, it came to me again as papa's barn. It opened like it was a hole in the world, black, sucking in every fleck of light and noise. It started to suck me in too, but I was a mile away, then an inch. I curled up in a ball and counted to ten. Told myself it'd be over as long as I didn't look.

When papa's cousin from the city called and told him the news, he said the city called the demolition an effort for the revitalization of the neighbourhood. That it would be replaced by a Shopper's Drug Mart. I looked to Papa to see if he was sad and he seemed bigger than he had been minutes before. Sturdy in his char, melted to it. We all toasted the Cromdale. Papa said the toast was to honour the old, and the fight the

Cromdale gave. It had been through condemnation, a fire, and court battles. It lived to see Edmonton change. The kids' plastic cups clinked against beer cans and rum glasses and papa grew bigger still, grazed the ceiling with his grey hair.

When I went to sleep that night, I saw the Cromdale again. It sat against quiet, its roof pulled back neatly to let the sky in. The Bull put his head down and queued up a sure shot on the pool table, low-ball corner pocket, when the place groaned like it was watching. Water broke through every crack and seam. The room filled. The horses came in, chests open, organs dripping out of their bodies and moving in the water like jellyfish. Their chests pounded without hearts, nipping at papa's kids, all of them from every generation, sitting around the table. The Bull missed his shot and started swiping at the dead things, but he couldn't hit hard enough or move fast enough. I reached out to help him, but my hands went through his back like butter. I felt nothing but still air and not-body. I blinked and the shadow of him grew, enveloping his family in static. When I tried to yell, my voice caught in my throat, turned around and went back down. Whispered to my gut instead: look at all the new.

OUR COUNTRY — LE CANADA

Jeffery Donaldson

My modest contribution to our sesquicentennial celebrations took the form of a question, one that has been nagging me for a decade or so. I ask you, English Canada, why do we not remind ourselves more often that our country only exists because of Quebec, because Canada was first colonized by the French? Like all questions, this one is built on the rather grand assumption that its premise is true. Follow and judge. It is partly owing to Quebec and the original Quebecois that we are not Americans. That makes us all, if not French-Canadian, then the immediate and fortunate heirs to what the French-Canadian spirit in Canada has fostered.

Something else. I've been trying to work out a puzzle that has to do with poetic thinking and Canadian history and culture. I don't have much expertise in Canadian history, much as I like to read it, and I haven't until now dared to set a toe in the intimidating tides of political commentary. My comfort zone is metaphor and metaphoric thinking, but I have been wondering lately how to apply the caprices of metaphoric relation to my sense of Canadian place and identity.

In metaphor, we say that one thing is another, which is to say that each is both different and the same. Doors open to further thought. There is a tacit futurity in the counter-logic of metaphoric thinking. We reach toward something that vanishes into puzzle and paradox, into a "this is so *unlikely*." Wherever there is tension, a play of differences—in culture, in politics, in religion—there is the puzzle of metaphoric relation. Our challenge is to work out its inferences and *think more*. It is what we find so pre-occupying, but perhaps also promising, in the never resolved, never settled trappings of the Canadian psyche.

My former supervisor Eleanor Cook, Professor Emeritus at the University of Toronto, has written an essay on Canadian literature and identity that reflects on the importance of the hyphen in our mindful constructions.[1] We are French-Canadians, we are Japanese-Canadians, and so on. The expedient dexterity of the Canadian imagination found traction in this shy and diminutive grammatical *trait d'union*. The little hyphen, surely the multicultural *piece de resistance* of grammatical devices, both joins *and* separates. It works like a kind of hinge and recalls the paradoxes of metaphoric relation in a culture such as ours that both is and is not . . . what it is. We have become rather dextrous in our wielding of the hyphen.

Along with the Maritimes, Quebec is *Older Canada*. In my travels to Montreal and Quebec City, I have felt impressed with the sense of reticent maturity, a solemnity that is almost intimidating for a visiting Anglophone bearing his offerings of broken French, a sense that it is about something other than what I know . . . something they know in just being what they are. I wondered whether something of our own origin might be disguised in that reticence.

My French improved enough for me to work through some of the principal histories of New France by the likes of Gustav Lanctot and Marcel Trudel: the Battle of Quebec, the Treaty of Paris, The Quebec Act, Quebec during the American Revolution. I kept thinking, *this is the reason we aren't Ameri-*

cans. I would look up from these revelations of the country's European aspect and how, almost by accident, we still find ourselves here at all. Why, I thought, aren't these books better known? Why aren't their inferences more strongly represented in our Anglophone histories?

I don't mean to ignore the urgent claims of our First Nations. They trump the table. What has puzzled me is, *given* colonization, why Canada did not become part of the United States. We are a child of the French. With English added rather peremptorily to the mix in the middle of the 18th century, and with the First Nations unjustly absorbed into the whole, the country has gone on to parent a great many distinctive cultures among a myriad regions and geographies, applying its hyphen-hinge like a multi-purpose tool. Canada is one of the more improbable political contraptions on the globe. Such is its hybrid history that our many communities have no single common ancestor. But the fact of its existence, that there is a Canada at all today, is an historical curiosity of French providence still under-acknowledged in English Canada. That this should be so is a curiosity in itself. Do we not want to believe it? Do we share a collective guilt that we are indebted to a part of ourselves that we originally, if this is even the right word, defeated? Would we just be making trouble to wander through Ontario or Alberta noising it about that a small population of original *Canadiens* saved our Canadian bacon? The time has come for the rest of the country to lay itself down on the Franco-Freudian couch, confess its suppressed memories, and come clean.

During the last Quebec referendum on separation in 1995, Anglophone Canada tried to assuage the Quebecois by saying "My Canada includes Quebec." How reassuring was this, really? "Hey you, my lawn includes your lawn." "Thanks, but that's actually part of what bothers us." Besides, the adage gets it backwards and inside out. Canada exists even now inside its cultural and political roots in New France—not just historically but in ways that we continue to reveal in our behaviour. Northrop

Frye once had to clarify what he meant by the paradox of radical metaphoric identification. He said, "I am a part of something that is a part of me." It is quite actually meant to be a paradox. It forces you to think more. Let us try it on then: "We are a part of a Quebec that is a part of us."

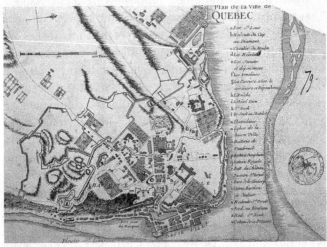

Map of Quebec City, 18th century. Public Domain.

Not as well known as the War of 1812, the original American invasion of Canada happened during the Seven Years' War between the English and the French (1756-1763) and during the American revolutionary war that was fought on many of the same grounds ten years later. The Seven Years' War culminated in the Battle of the Plains of Abraham–a phrase that Quebeckers know very well but other Canadians less reliably–a battle that saw France barely defeated in Quebec City and later removed from North America. The land fell under British rule. This is why English is spoken in Sydney Nova Scotia, Paris Ontario, and Victoria British Columbia. Anglophone Canada likes to believe that its own ancestors won fair and square, flexed a superior brawn, and built a majority demographic that it preserves today. Francophone

Quebeckers were left to come to terms with a truncated heritage and an original dispossession, a sour taste that wears at the heart of our shared identity. How difficult it is to celebrate those years when we end up reminding a large part of our population that its ancestors were conquered! This inconvenience—our version of a civil war before there was a nation to be civil—is a formative part of the Canadian puzzle. Metaphor itself is very comfortable with puzzles of this sort: to identify with limits within itself, to be encircled by an expanding reach. But what especially puzzles me is how even less often we speak of the events that transpired sixteen years after the Battle of the Plains of Abraham, albeit under remarkably different circumstances. For Canada, they were more decisive still.

On New Year's Eve day, December 31, 1775, Richard Montgomery, General of the American revolutionary forces, held a siege around the embattled ramparts of Quebec City. His orders from General Washington were to take the citadel, oust the British from their stronghold, and lay claim to the northern territories on behalf of the continental army of Congress. Montreal was already in American hands; Washington himself had visited the city to bolster support there for his forces. He held the northern military campaign as of the highest importance for the ultimate success of the revolution. The American frontier must be secured against British land invasions from the north.

Montgomery had a difficult decision to make. Many of his troops and militiamen (some 1300 strong) were under contract with terms of service set to expire at the start of the year. If he was going to attack, he would have to move that morning, under the hopeful cover of advancing blizzard conditions, or send his troops home and write to Congress of his delay. Governor Carleton had already retreated behind the walls of Quebec City and ensconced himself there with a mustered militia of some two thousand British and French Canadian soldiers and volunteers. The Governor looked out over the icy St. Lawrence from the citadel and feared for the future. It would be a long winter and no help would arrive from overseas until after the spring thaw.

American Revolutionaries held a bayonet to our nation's neck. One single wintry afternoon in Quebec, Montgomery (along with a now infamous Benedict Arnold) used feint attacks along both flanks of the upper city and led an assault against the walls of the lower town at the foot of Cap Diamant. Had Montgomery's forces made it up the hill, I might well be writing now from some such State of Ontario, no doubt fussing over how to pay my health-care bills.

The Americans stormed the lower walls. Several of the temporary defensive barriers that Carleton had erected were heavily breached. The Americans poured in and advanced, but the rain of gunshot and cannon fire from the upper walls of the city prevailed (Ah, Champlain, you chose well your city on a hill!). Montgomery was killed in action. Arnold was wounded. The Americans were pushed back. The congressional army held its siege until the spring of that year, but the appearance at last of British warships from overseas necessitated its final withdrawal from the northern frontier. Quebec remained in British hands and was formally ceded to the British Empire in the subsequent peace negotiations at Paris in 1783.

That's part of our story—but what does this have to do with the Quebecois? Sure, it was in Quebec that the British fought this important battle, but the French had already "lost" there. Moreover, it was a British army that fought the Americans using British weaponry and British know-how. French Canadians numbered among the volunteers who fought at Carleton's side that winter (some quarter of the total number of men bearing arms), but was their presence decisive? Is it not possible that the British might have held the fort without them? Why should the *Canadiens* be counted as the guardian angels of our commonwealth?

Metaphoric thinking often gets up and running with the sense of something that doesn't fit. Why is this thing here? How do I make room for it? You have to scramble and adjust your sense of *what things are like* in order to make room for the new element. I remember when I was first struck by a curious incongruity regarding the balance of power on the continent at the end of the Seven Years' War. For sixteen years, between 1759 and the beginning of the American Revolution in 1775, *all of North America* (above the Spanish holdings in the far south and west) belonged to the English crown. There were in a very real sense fourteen British colonies: the thirteen New-England states and Quebec, all under rule of the English king George III. The future of North America lay in English hands. Britain was master of its own fate. How did it come about, then, when the Americans went to war in 1775 against their own king (all that business about taxation without representation) and rose finally victorious in 1783, that the entire British continent was not gained in the bargain, including the British province of Quebec?

We might better grasp what was at stake in the question if we pictured a different prequel. Imagine that all of North America had belonged to the English from the beginning. France was never here. Henri IV is never beguiled by Champlain's promise of riches on the other side of the Atlantic. The English settlements spread up the eastern seaboard and its rulers quickly become cognizant of the great resources to be exploited along the St Lawrence. It is all British America. Picture the evolved state of the nation, in turn, when the colonies begin to agitate for their independence, how *all* of the North American territories are equally implicated in the struggle, with equal stakes. Whatever seeds of agitation arise in Boston and New York take root for similar cause in the towns along the St. Lawrence (call them what you will). A General Washington might as easily have been born in what is now Montreal, instead of Virginia. A Paul Revere might have charged on his horse up Yonge Street—"The British are Coming! The British are Coming!"—instead of along the roads to Concord and Lexington.

But that's not how it was. The fourteenth colony of Quebec, as the Americans were inclined to think of it, was unlike any of the other colonies to the south. It was existentially French and had been so for 150 years. It had laboured under English rule for scarcely a decade and a half. Its cultural values, religion, industry, governance, and judiciary held little in common with institutions to the south. Their stakes were different, their priorities and allegiances very much their own. Quebec didn't fit. They hovered between identities, as metaphors often ask us to do. The British said: "You are a part of something else now." The Americans said, "Be like us!"

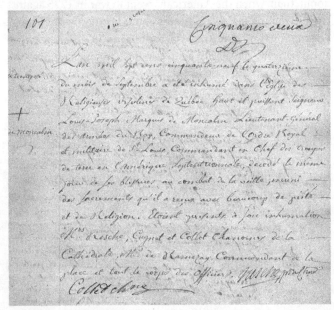

Notice of General Montcalm's internment, September 14, 1759. Public Domain.

Mind you, the *Canadiens* might have had good reason to sympathize with the American cause. The conquering British army in 1759 had not been kind to the rural populations. After the Battle of Quebec, the English moved quickly to subdue any threat of retaliation or resistance in the countryside. There were killings. Houses and granges were burned to the ground. Quebec City fared worse, flattened under a barrage of fire from British cannons during the battle itself. The shelling was merciless. The French had not only been conquered, but actively subdued and brought to heel.

Reconstruction proceeded under the leadership of Governors Murray and then Carleton. Under the Treaty of Paris in 1763, some temporary and practical provisions were made for the French Catholic majority. They were granted the right to own property, practice their religion ("as far as the laws of Great Britain permit"), leave the country, and go fishing. That's it. In the meantime, English colonists were arriving from the south. There was money to be made, and with the territory now in English hands the colonial merchants were moving in. They traded in English currency; they demanded their rights under English law, along with a representative assembly after the model of the established colonies. While permitted to practice their own religion, Catholics were refused political positions and representation on juries. Still worse, the *Canadiens* had been left holding a French currency that was accepted at only a fraction of its original value. It was only a matter of time before the pro-Protestant and Anglican laws of England began to seep into provincial legislation. The English courts with trial by jury were set up to the exclusion of French civil rights. Unrest began to foment among the Francophones, not unlike the unrest that would brew a decade later in the English colonies to the south, and for the similar reason that the local inhabitants were being treated unfairly at the hands of English rulers. What more incentive would the Quebecois need to join the Americans? One thing we know about metaphoric relations, if you leave a thing feeling alienated, *dis-liking* its place in an environment, it will go off and find other likenesses to be itself with.

Governors Murray and Carleton had to walk a fine line. They were cognizant of English rule and the imperatives of the new order, but they were also practical. They governed on the ground. They felt the injustice of disadvantaging a French population of 90,000 in favour of a sometimes-fanatical minority of American and English merchant immigrants. In 1770, Carleton decided to travel to London to press for the adoption of properly Canadian statutes that would observe the rights of a Francophone and Catholic majority. Though they were slow to respond, the British ministers eventually saw the light. They foresaw that the seeds of unrest that had been planted in New England would find a rich soil in Quebec if concessions were not made. On May 2, 1774, British parliament passed into law The Act of Quebec. The law granted that "his majesty's subjects, professing the Religion of the Church of Rome of and in the said Province of Quebec may have, hold, and enjoy, the free Exercise of the Religion of the Church of Rome; and that the Clergy of the said Church may hold, receive, and enjoy, their accustomed Dues and Rights. . . ." An executive council would be appointed with majority representation from the Francophone demographic; the seigneurial system of land rights would prevail.

The *Canadiens* were granted what *they* needed, and *we* all lived happily ever after? By letting the Quebecois join their own cultural dots, did the British convince them, in strong metaphoric fashion, to be *likely* citizens, however *unlike*? Well, it is more complicated than that. Responses were divided. In the cities of Quebec and Montreal there were concentrations of public servants, clergy, elites, merchants, lawyers and judges, all of whom were well-positioned to take advantage of the new allowances. The clergy in particular were quick to recognize the powers that had been restored to them.

They offered a strong endorsement of the king's measures; the trickledown effect of their approbation was intended to spread widely among the urban congregations. The farmers and peasantry outside the city walls however were more detached. Life hadn't actually changed that much for them. They still had the practice of their religion and were free to follow their own customs. They had little interest in the complexities of government and justifiably harboured a general cynicism toward their recent conquerors.

How very close—within the hair's breadth of a year—the British had come to leaving unanswered the *Canadiens'* demands for justice, before the Americans themselves began to woo them to the opposite camp. Even as it was, the new edicts had scarcely enough time to effect broad cultural and political changes in the province. For most of the population, word of new laws from London would have been greeted with a shrug. They would be vulnerable to the propaganda that the American congress was preparing for them. That propaganda was substantial.

The Americans, again, were not happy. Heavy taxes and limited rights of self-determination seemed only to be exacerbated by the encroachment of newly drawn boundaries in the north and west. Now with independence declared, the increasing menace of British power in the form of naval blockades were bearing down on them. Britain ruled the waves off the Atlantic, but their only actual foothold by land was through Quebec. American occupation of Quebec City was, therefore, of the first importance. There was great hope in Congress that this unusual British colony would prove sympathetic to their cause, rise up against its recent conqueror and side with the continental army. They had good reason to hope. But they found themselves in a tricky position. The Canadian demographic was becoming complicated; increasing powers were accruing to the recent English immigrants and there was a

Francophone majority to keep quiet. Congress was in the difficult position of having to win over the English merchants in Montreal by dissing the French, and wooing the French by dissing the English. Some dissembling was in order. Different letters would have to be written and circulated to the appropriate groups. The two sides would have to be played off against one another in order to unite them both against the British. The Americans would have to find "wedge issues," as we call them now, in the Quebec Act that could be used to sow discontent on both sides. Exploitable likenesses. Metaphor offers a great way of finessing complicated relations . . . especially when you use more than one.

Letter addressed to the French by the First Continental Congress, 1774. Public Domain.

The letters of course, had first to address the inconvenient fact of the Seven Years' War, in which the Americans themselves had fought on the side of the British to conquer the French and take Quebec. That, to say the least, would need some finessing: "When the fortune of war, after a gallant and glorious resistance, had incorporated you with the body of English subjects, we rejoiced in the truly valuable addition, both on our own and your account; expecting, as courage and generosity are naturally united, our brave enemies would become our hearty friends." Well played, Congress! That is surely a better way of putting "We had to bomb the bejesus out of you, but it worked out in the end, once you fell, because we could then put all that courage you showed to good use on our side." The writers had next to address the fact that the French had requested and been granted their land rights according to the seigneurial system long-established in New France; an oligarchic system of government had been preserved that was channelled, for their own protection, up through an appointed assembly, the governor, and then the English King. A democratic congress could scarcely approve. A trojan horse was required. A letter would have to camouflage democratic imperatives under the signs of "education" and "equality" and sneak them past what the Americans viewed as a primitive political system: "But since . . . you, educated under another form of government, have artfully been kept from discovering the unspeakable worth of that form you are now undoubtedly entitled to, we esteem it our duty, for the weighty reasons herein after mentioned, to explain to you some of its most important branches." It is on the grounds of democratic and religious freedom that the composers pull out all the stops and employ a dexterity of reasoning that is genuinely admirable:

> These are the rights you are entitled to and ought at this moment in perfection, to exercise. And what is offered to you by the late Act of Parliament in their place? Liberty of conscience in your religion? No. God gave it to you; and the temporal powers with which you have been and are connected, firmly stipulated for your enjoyment of it. Are the French laws in civil cases restored? It seems so. But observe the cautious kindness of the Ministers, who pretend to be your benefactors. The words of the statute are—that those "laws shall be the rule, until they shall be varied or altered by any ordinances of the Governor and Council." Is the "certainty and lenity of the criminal law of England . . ." secured to you and your descendants? No. They too are subjected to arbitrary "alterations" by the Governor and Council.

Translation: *the English cannot be trusted. They may appear to be looking after your interests at the moment, but for how long?* These were genuine concerns. The letter then changes tone. You don't want to listen to reason? Time for some old-fashioned shaming:

> It cannot be presumed that these considerations will have no weight with you, or that you are so lost to all sense of honor. We can never believe that the present race of Canadians are so degenerated as to possess neither the spirit, the gallantry, nor the courage of their ancestors. You certainly will not permit the infamy and disgrace of such pusillanimity to rest on your own heads, and the consequences of it on your children forever. . . . We, for our parts, are determined to live free, or not at all. . . .

And finally, if all else fails, shaming may advance to an unsubtly veiled threat: "As our concern for your welfare entitles us to your friendship, we presume you will not, by doing us injury, reduce us to the disagreeable necessity of treating you as enemies."

In the meantime, Congress was sending letters to the English émigrés in Montreal and elsewhere bemoaning the egregiously oppressive statutes of the new Act that would unfailingly favour Catholics over Anglophone Protestants. That letter speaks of "a religion, fraught with sanguinary and impious tenets ... that has deluged [Britain] in blood, and dispersed impiety, bigotry, persecution, murder and rebellion through every part of the world." While the central complaint in both letters is essentially the same—that democratic rights are being trampled on—the disdain in this letter for the culture and religion of New France is conspicuous:

> An act was passed to protect, indemnify, and screen from punishment such as might be guilty even of murder, in endeavouring to carry their oppressive edicts into execu-

tion; and by another Act the dominion of Canada is to be so extended, modelled, and governed, as that by being disunited from us, detached from our interests, by civil as well as religious prejudices, that by their numbers daily swelling with Catholic immigrants from Europe, and by their devotion to Administration, so friendly to their religion, they might become formidable to us, and on occasion, be fit instruments in the hands of power, to reduce the ancient free Protestant Colonies to the same state of slavery with themselves.

The Americans proselytized out of both sides of their mouths. They borrowed from Pierre to pay Paul. Metaphor says: two things are one. The Americans tried to say: this one thing is two. It put the *Canadiens* in a tight spot. On the one hand, they had the British Parliament and King, former enemies and erstwhile conquerors who had grudgingly appeased their majority demographic. On the other hand they had the American offer to send delegates to the continental congress in Philadelphia and join a revolutionary movement that would correct at last the injustices they had suffered at the hands of the English.

Picture these letters chugging off the printing presses by the thousands in Philadelphia and Boston and being carried by clandestine messengers into the cities of Quebec and disseminated widely in the countryside. The propaganda machine was attaining as near to the power of Twitter and Facebook as could be managed at the time. One can scarcely underestimate the stakes. The Francophone population was some 90,000 in 1770. If the Americans had convinced only ten percent of the rural population to fight with them, leaving the rest neutral, Carleton and his bedraggled militia behind the Quebec ramparts would have been sitting *canards*.

What did the American military encounter as they advanced on Quebec? In the towns, no significant fifth column agitated from within. There was strong support among the clergy and the elite for the British military and its defenses. A quarter of the volunteers in the British militia were of Franco-phone descent. As for the rural areas, the Americans marched over the farmlands and encountered little resistance, but also little support. From the farmers' perspective, the revolutionaries were potential customers who required lodging and food. But in the main, what the soldiers encountered in the surrounding municipalities was an essential withholding, a quite actual *hanging-fire* among the many thousands of potential conscriptees to the revolutionary cause. They demurred before the American offer of salaries and bonuses to any volunteers they could gather on the way.

The *Canadiens*' neutrality was as dangerous and compromising to the British as it was useless to the Americans. The British had answered some of their demands, but, as for fighting at their side, "À ces hommes," writes Gustav Lanctot, "*qui n'avaient pas oublie l'amertume de la défaite ni les ravages des troupes anglaises, il semblait hors de raison de vouloir faire des vaincus d'hier les défenseurs des maîtres d'aujourd'hui dans une querelle de famille, ou ils n'avaient rien à gagner et tout à perdre*" (*Le Canada et la Révolution Americaine*, Beauchemin, 1965: 89) ["To these people, who had not forgotten the bitterness of defeat they had suffered nor the ravages of the English troops, it appeared unreasonable to want to make of yesterday's victors today's masters in a family quarrel in which they had nothing to gain and everything to lose"]. The *Canadiens* were also wary of allying with unproven rebels. Without greater assurance of American success, many *Canadiens* would have counted it foolish to support revolutionary powers against their own masters. Better the devil you know. Their demurring in the midst of the struggle can only seem now all the wiser for its being unconscious or instinctual.

After Montgomery's failed attempt to take the city on New-Year's-Eve of 1775, the scales tipped almost inevitably

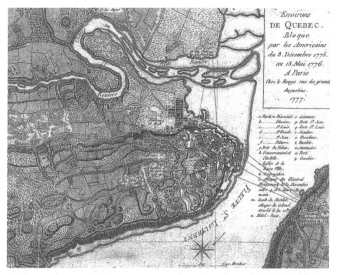

Quebec under siege by the Americans, Dec 8, 1775, to May 13, 1776. 1777. Public Domain.

in Britain's favour. As the siege dragged on and American supplies diminished, the soldiers in the outlying areas became more unruly and demanding, forcing habitants to accept what was highly unreliable credit for food and lodging. The Americans sometimes just took what they needed. Resentment and frustration were building. It is one thing to lay siege to a city when you possess the surrounding countryside or have the free run of it. But to sustain military pressure when you yourself are not especially welcome, *at sea* among a doubtful and increasingly inhospitable populace, is quite another. When the British ships arrived in the spring, the jig was up and the Americans went home. It would be another seven years before Canada was formerly ceded to Britain by Congress in the Paris Treaty of 1783.

Metaphors always make for trouble. That's what they're for! You go along thinking things are *just so*, then in jumps a mess of intervening likenesses and suddenly you don't know where you are. Imagine—to use another metaphor—a chess game involving two parties (American and British) whose allegiances are already complicated and unstable (the younger party born from the elder). They become entangled. Now set among them a third set of pieces—the *Canadiens*—a set that is potentially available to either player and where alliances might easily shift for single moves, and where, further, the pieces speak a different language and have a set of interests entirely their own. Their simply *being there* crowds the spaces on the board. Their very neutrality—coupled with the necessity that they be appeased—infinitely complicates any manoeuvres the attackers might plan. Thus you have the *real* battle for Quebec, a battle for what the *Canadien* metaphor was going to mean.

Our history might have turned out a thousand different ways. Let a butterfly's wing flap at a slightly different tempo in Trois-Rivières in 1702, and we might well be Norwegian. Who knows? Had Montgomery actually taken Cap Diamant and occupied Quebec that winter night, the province might possibly have been given back to the British in later negotiations. It seems unlikely. If the continental army had in fact succeeded in Quebec, the whole war might have turned out differently. With so many military resources drawn off to the northern province to preserve the American foothold there, would Washington's army have been too weakened to fight the British on the eastern seaboard? Might the American revolution have failed? Or consider that the *Canadien* peasantry might have taken up arms and fought with the Americans. They may still, who knows, have been turned back, left to suffer further bitter repercussions at the hands of the British, before whom they would now be traitors, thus souring what were the seeds of a better diplomacy between the British and *Canadiens* in the Quebec Act.

An American Quebec: when one thinks of the anti-French propaganda that the Americans were spreading among the British in Canada, one can't imagine that it would have augured well for a Francophone population subsumed into the American melting pot. Quebec might have become a kind of New Orleans of the North, with a winning carnivalesque character of its own, but almost certainly as watered down as The Big Easy. Though it can be fun to write the histories that never were, we do know this: what governor Carleton and his British militia gave to the Francophone population across Quebec was in every sense a *fighting chance*. What the *Canadiens* gave to the English and their isolated cities surrounded by neutral sceptics was the same thing.

The concern of the Quebecois today over the protection of their heritage, their distinct language, their anxieties in the face of Americanization: we should remember that it was this same reticence in the face of radical change, this tacit withholding from the latest groundswell of political momentum, that opened the road forward for this country in the first place. That spirit left Quebec choosing not to sign the Canadian Charter of Rights and Freedoms in 1982. It spawned the curious and almost inevitable reality of the Bloc Quebecois and PQ. Such socio-cultural puzzles and other anomalies of Canadian regional politics are a naturally evolved expression of something that has been ours from the start. They are the expression in our time of the same spirit, in the same place, that made it possible for Canada to wriggle its way into existence between the last two dominant empires of the west. Quebec left the Canadas free to welcome, as it then did, the United Empire Loyalists, then the immigrants from Europe, from Africa, and still more recently from Asia and the Middle East. The Quebecois became multicultural first by necessity, then by design. They learned how to be, and *not be*, what their government required. Their example has become the pragmatic intuition of an entire country.

The agility of metaphoric thinking has to do with audacious leaps, as in this case, say, between a complex national identity and a series of localized and ill-remembered events 240 years ago. You join a few dots and say ... "Voila! Look who we are!" Metaphors can always be disproven, but the leap must speak for itself. In the end, if I appeal to the relation between a moment in Quebec history and our present character, I do so even more strongly in defense of the Quebecois as historical guardians of a habit of mind that is uniquely metaphoric and uniquely Canadian.

Canadians are by nature agile metaphoric thinkers. Not a global power ourselves, we are the energy of potential relation that moves among powers. For so much of our history we have paddled between the Scylla and Charybdis of British and American influences, past and present. The Quebecois were the hyphen that stood between two insistent nationalities. They represented for the British and Americans an inconvenient but unignorable *between-wheres* that would not be won over by contending forces vying for their allegiance. They had been recently defeated in their own experiment to extend an empire. They were now wary and sceptical. That sense of loss and dispossession that today we shy from naming in provincial relations is actually a defining inheritance. Not yet accepting a name, for a name had been taken away, the *Canadiens* became instead a mark between names, *le petit trait d'union* that slips between cultural signifiers, where two things become, in one thing, both separate and identifiable. I see in the Quebecois a unique and practical reserve, a rejecting of the decade's latest temptations, a holding oneself apart to wait and see. It is the Francophone portion of our Canadian psyche. In every metaphoric sense, it cleared the way for us to become who we are and who we are not.

Notes

1 "A Seeing and Unseeing in the Eye." Canadian Literature and the Sense of Place." *Daedalus*. Vol. 117, No. 4, *In Search of Canada* (Fall, 1988), pp. 215-235.

UVANGA/SELF: PICTURING OUR IDENTITY

Tarralik Duffy

"Lots of times I look in the mirror and I draw myself."
—Jutai Toonoo

The mesmerizing, easy cool of Jutai Toonoo (1959–2015) stares back at you. The edges of his skull fade into a sea of red and spill over a blushing face, the dividing line between internal and external realities has temporarily dissipated. It is equal parts engaging and alarming. His dark, questioning, and perhaps world-weary gaze commands your attention. His thoughts are free from the usual conformity and strict confines of what is expected, an intellect without a linear cage. Toonoo follows no rules. He is his own man, free to express what he wants. His bold, confident presence is palpable even on paper, maybe especially so, and you can't help but feel the pull of his power.

The first time I saw Toonoo's work, I could not look away. It completely obliterated my sense of what I thought I understood about Inuit art. Why had I thought, even as an Inuk woman, that Inuit art had to be a certain thing? Look a certain way? Why had I never before considered the concept of simple freedom of expression? Had I ever seen a self-portrait of an Inuk artist before? I couldn't recall. Definitely not in this way. Not in this form—his black t-shirt casually modern, his slouching posture coolly rebelling against all the stereotypical notions of how an Inuk should look in a gallery space.

"I like faces," the artist recounted in 2011. "Every face is different from the other, like snowflakes. I never run out. I am always inspired by a face. There's so many faces out there, there is no limit to what I can do."[1] He explained that he often draws his own face or the face of his wife, because he felt he was not yet good enough and that he was uncertain that other subjects would like or agree with the outcome. For fear of upsetting the subject, or out of a pure necessity to be completely free to channel his raw emotions onto the page, Toonoo was often compelled to draw his own face—a face that now gazes back at observers in galleries and private collections around the world.

Like many artists, Toonoo spoke about feeling both free and imprisoned by his process and his career as an artist. He described delving deeply into his mind while working, blocking everything else in order to express what he was feeling. "It almost becomes a part of me, what I am putting on paper," he has said. "It comes out of me and it gets transferred onto the paper, and sometimes it drains me and I have no energy left when I am done with a thing." Pieces such as *Self* (2012) and *Seeking Peace* (2015) evidence a process through which Toonoo poured his entire being into the work, leaving all of himself transferred onto the page, so much so that initially he literally hated the finished product, not because he didn't like it, but because it took all his energy to create it.

When asked if he considered himself an Inuit artist or a Canadian artist and how he defines himself, Toonoo answered simply, "I don't."[2] Leaning heavy over his drafting table, filling in the soft blue backdrop of what would later become *Eskimo Tan* (2010), wiping sweat from his brow, he continued, "This is just something I do. I think I am an artist, but then again I am not." Laughter follows in quick bursts, like joyful segues into meditative, humble confessions. "I used to do it for the sake of art, but it became something else. It became something that I have to make a living with—feed my kids and please my wife." Toonoo, a self-aware, sensitive observer of the world around him was not unaware of the weightiness, economic and otherwise, of his work.

The subject of self-portraiture is, potentially, a delicate subject when talking about Inuit art. A field, after all, that has for the past six decades been dominated and shaped by capital. For a very long time, it has been a source of income, an economy, a means to an end for many artists living and working in the Canadian North. This is not to say that Inuit artists, of past and present, don't express themselves in true, autobiographical ways, but it complicates them.

In 1975, three artists from Inukjuak, Nunavik, QC, created, what are likely, the first formal self-portraits of Inuit artists. The bold stonecuts by Thomassie Echaluk (1935–2011), Daniel Inukpuk, and Jobie Ohaituk were released in small print runs in black and white. Though rendered in each artist's own unique style, each work depicts an artist facing forward in a collared shirt with the top button unbuttoned. The catalogue introduction considers that just because an Inuit artist "has never done a self portrait is no reason not to try."[3] The catalogue goes on to indicate that the artists were encouraged by a visiting instructor to make the self-portraits, so the idea to represent themselves was not necessarily their own but perhaps an opportunity to test the market and see if, in the mid-1970s, a southern audience was interested in purchasing unadorned Inuit self-portraits. The records of how well the works sold are unavailable, but the fact that this experiment was never repeated might speak to their performance.

In the decades that followed artists continued to push back on the hungry aesthetic demands of a market fixated on an idealized, romantic notion of the North and its people to increasingly better results. These market desires have had an effect on how even we as Inuit think about Inuit art. I have come to think of the first time I saw Toonoo's work as the moment I vividly let loose my vision of what Inuit art could be. And it can be anything, of course. Toonoo put it simply: "It's not just for the sake of being different . . . I think that's why I don't do the things older artists do, 'cause of our lifestyle today. It's very different from what they went through."[4]

These changes in lifestyle and artistic output are a testament to how quickly our lives have changed in the past 60 years. This dichotomy of worlds, the radical shifts experienced by generations of Inuit, described by Alootook Ipellie (1951–2007) as a "cultural whiteout," is what makes self-portraiture so important, so invaluable. And much like the Arctic storms we endure through the winter, some of these changes have been so powerful that "we are trapped and unable to move forward because we cannot see clearly where we are heading."[5] Our perspective from within the storm is the power we hold. Without Inuit artists expressing themselves and documenting their experiences, we risk looking at ourselves through a tourist's lens or reading our stories from the murky, presumptive ink of a settler's pen, and even the most earnest outsider cannot get it right.

Born in Nuvuqquq, a small hunting camp on Qikiqtaaluk (Baffin Island), Ipellie witnessed first hand "the death of nomadic life."[6] A provocative, political thinker, he was one of the first Inuit artists to begin rapping, both gently and violently, against the glass ceiling of what was both expected and accepted of Inuit artists. Soft-spoken and described by some as one of the most unsung Inuit artists of modern times, Ipellie expresses in stark, graphic, black-and-white imagery the difficult, disturbing, and traumatic transition from a traditional life on the land to life in government-imposed settlements. His book *Arctic Dreams and Nightmares* (1993) is also the first published collection of short stories by an Inuit writer.

A fierce and incisive critic, Ipellie wrote in 2001, "Our society had to rely on another society to be a guide dog to our blind culture."[7] Blinded by the swift commodification and forced conversion to a society so vastly different from our ancient, sacred, self-sufficient ways there was almost no chance of survival. Presented before us was a seemingly fancy, trouble-free, and prosperous life—we were inundated with a new language, a new religion, the introduction of a cash economy, houses, TVs, Hondas, Ski-Doos, and guns. Ipellie's ink drawing *I, Crucified* (c. 1992) confronts this violent, martyrdom of our selves and the crucifixion of our culture and leaves us to question, had we, as Christ, willingly subjugated ourselves? And most pressingly, would there be a resurrection? More than 25 years on, Ipellie's drawing continues to demand sustained, if uncomfortable, reflection on how far we have—or have not—come.

Our warp speed, culture clash progression from a not-so distant, "ancient" nomadic life, illuminated by the warmth of the qulliq (oil lamp), to matchbox houses backlit by the blue-screen glow of Jerry Springer has been most famously documented by the incomparable and prolific work of three Inuit women artists spanning three generations: the great matriarch of Inuit art, Pitseolak Ashoona, CM, RCA (c. 1904–1983); her only daughter, the remarkable Napachie Pootoogook (1938–2002); and of course Pootoogook's own daughter, the enigmatic and dearly beloved Annie Pootoogook (1969–2016), all of whom captured the specific visual language of their lives and generations.

Although few of her works are explicitly labelled as self-portraits, arguably all of Ashoona's work was autobiographical. Like many artists of her generation, Ashoona placed herself, her family, and her community into each piece, from depicting her early years in semi-nomadic hunting camps in the publication *Pitseolak: Pictures Out of My Life* (1971) to her clever commentary on the modern art market with *The Critic*

(c. 1963). This latter vein of self-portraiture in particular, of the artist as artist, made way for both her daughter and grand-daughter to experiment with depicting and ultimately seeing themselves as artists.

As both subject and recorder, self-portraiture gives art-ists complete control over what they want us, as viewers, to see, and this power in the hands of the right artist can reveal volumes of intimate information in a single frame. Author George Orwell wrote, "Autobiography is not to be trusted unless it reveals something disgraceful."[8] Napachie, not one to shy away from difficult subject matter, exposed the darker side of traditional life: spousal abuse, starvation, forced mar-riage, alcoholism and infanticide, ultimately setting the stage for the uncompromising work of her daughter. If Annie broke the ceiling, she was without a doubt standing on Napachie's shoulders as she did it. And the cracks were long present.

In her work Napachie's *Attempted Abduction #1* (1997–98), she records a terrifying moment of having to fight for her dignity and survival while two men with disturbingly serene faces attempt to violently steal her away from her future hus-band. She writes in syllabics that she won the fight because she was terribly frightened, her future husband "just watching." Napachie's image and accompanying narrative reveal the des-perate vulnerability of womanhood within camp life, exposing complex feelings of disappointment, fear, and a near-hopeless dependency on the unpredictable and often abusive men with whom they were immutably connected. A third generation artist, profoundly inspired by her mother and grandmother, Annie Pootoogook skillfully reimagined their artistic legacies while documenting Inuit life as seen through her own eyes. "I only know today," she famously noted. "I must draw what surrounds me."[9] Though the backdrops of Annie's work are contemporary to her generation, her experiences are often strikingly parallel in both tranquility and tragedy to those of her mother and grandmother.

Jamasee Pitseolak is another revolutionary example of someone who, feeling an innate sense of dissatisfaction with his work, moved away from conventional themes to do something different. "As great as traditional Inuit art is, and I am humbled to come from that background, as I grew older," he has explained. "I was getting a sense of emptiness from my work and I wasn't making any connection. There was a sense of dissatisfaction, so I started carving electric guitars. The fulfillment started coming to me and it spoke to me that this is what I want to do."[10] In more recent years, this personal and artistic confidence has led Pitseolak to explore self-representation in his work and, in the process, to bravely reveal something to us that is deeply traumatic. In a work from 2010, *The Student*, we are confronted with a distressing scene.[11] A young child sits in a bathtub, his terror and powerlessness conveyed through harsh, erratic, diagonal lines. A vomitous green is smeared across the abuser's eyes, chest, and genitals as he approaches the young victim. The grotesque slashes of green make their mark across the page and end in succession over the helpless, vulnerable child. It's as though Pitseolak is trying to eradicate this horrific memory, confessing the details swiftly. The pain is still so discernible, the execution so hurried and the trauma still so raw, it's as though it must be drawn as quickly as possible to get it over with.

Pitseolak has said many times that he creates his artworks for himself; he's "not doing it for anyone else."[12] Therein lies the power of self-expression and the power of self-portraiture on a larger scale. When artists are truly free, though it may at times come at a significant cost, the outcome can dramatically shift how we see them, ourselves, and the world around us. When artists exorcise their demons or tell us their most intimate stories, when dissatisfaction leads the way or a relentless thought won't let them rest until it's been transferred onto the page, when they channel their raw emotions to manifest something from their inner world into the tangible, moving it from the unseen to the visible, they are sharing with us a glimpse into their relationship with a shape-shifting muse. When artists do this, not just for themselves but of themselves, without regard for the market or for what an audience might deem too dark or too heavy or too unlike what they've come to know, when an artist is free, you cannot help but feel the pull of their power.

Notes

1 "Jutai Toonoo interview at Marion Scott Gallery, 2011," YouTube video, 6:41, posted by Paul Conroy, July 7 2011, https://www.youtube.com/watch?v=DqpKL38VUFM.

2 CBC, "The Rebel—Jutai Toonoo," YouTube video, 26:04, from Eye on the Arctic interview with Eilís Quinn, posted by Radio Canada International, May 24, 2017, www.youtube.com/watch?v=XlvwvD3BJ00.

3 Marybelle Myers, "Another Reality" in *Arctic Quebec 1975* (Montreal: La Fédération des coopératives du Nouveau-Québec, 1975), unpaginated.

4 "The Rebel—Jutai Toonoo," YouTube video, 26:04, from Eye on the Arctic interview with Eilís Quinn, posted by Radio Canada International, May 24, 2017, www.youtube.com/watch?v=XlvwvD3BJ00.

5 Alootook Ipellie, "People of the Good Land," in *The Voices of the Natives: The Canadian North and Alaska*, ed. Hans Bohm (Newcastle, ON: Penumbra Press, 2001), 26.

6 This is a reference to the title of Alootook Ipellie's work *The Death of Nomadic Life, the Creeping Emergence of Civilization* (2003).

7 Ipellie, "People of the Good Land," 26.

8 George Orwell, "Some Notes on Salvador Dalí," in *George Orwell: As I Please, 1943–1946*, eds. Sonia Orwell and Ian Angus (Boston: D.R. Godine, 2000), 156.

9 *Annie Pootoogook*, directed by Marcia Connolly, (Toronto: Site-Media, 2007), video.

10 "National Gallery of Canada Artist Interview: Jamasee Padluq Pitseolak," YouTube video, 3:40, from interview with National Gallery for Sakàhan: International Indigenous Art, posted by National Gallery of Canada, June 25, 2013, www.youtube.com/watch?v=Jwl4jyzb0Yc.

11 Scott Watson, Keith Wallace and Jana Tyler eds., *Witnesses: Art and*

Canada's Indian Residential Schools (Vancouver: Morris and Helen Belkin Art Gallery, 2013), 48.

12 "National Gallery of Canada Artist Interview: Jamasee Padluq Pitse-olak," YouTube video, 3:40, from interview with National Gallery for Sakàhan: International Indigenous Art, posted by National Gallery of Canada, June 25, 2013, www.youtube.com/watch?v=Jwl4jyzb0Yc.

TERRORIST NARRATIVES

Tanya Bellehumeur-Allatt

April 18, 1983
American Embassy
Beirut, Lebanon
1:05 pm

Each day after lunch, while his ten bodyguards took over the sports field of the American University of Beirut, Robert Sherwood Dillon, the fourteenth American ambassador to Lebanon, jogged three miles around the track.

On April 18, 1983, at one o'clock, when his Lebanese social secretary put her head through the door to tell Dillon that a German banker was on the phone, he pointed at his sneakers and waved her off. It was the last time he would see her alive.

Nine security guards went down to the first floor to wait for him while he changed into his jogging clothes. The tenth guard, hung-over from the celebrations following the Beirut marathon of the day before, waited to escort the ambassador downstairs.

Dillon was standing by the floor-to-ceiling window, wrestling his arms into his Marine t-shirt, when the glass blew in. He shielded his face as the force of the blast threw him across the room, onto his back. Later, he'd listen to other survivors talk about the deafening thunderclap of noise. But the ambassador heard nothing.

The brick wall behind his desk blew out and fell on his body, taking away all sensation in his legs. The office filled with smoke, dust and tear gas.

Secretary Bob Pugh and administrative officer Tom Barron, both white with dust, came running into the ambassador's office. They grabbed the flagstaff and pried up the wall so Dillon could wriggle out. His arms were peppered with bits of glass, his body covered with cuts and bruises.

The three men coughed and retched from the tear gas that had travelled up the air shaft from the first floor, where the blast had set the canisters off. The men got out through a window and stood on a ledge outside, where a salty gust of wind from the nearby Mediterranean brought relief from the sting of the gas.

The central stairway was gone. The men picked their way through the rubble. On the second floor, people staggered around, covered in white dust, or lay motionless on the ground. The top of a man's head had been blown off, his brains spilling out onto the marble floor. The building was crumbling all around them. A woman screamed for help. Her body and face looked like they'd been shredded.

Bill MacIntyre, chief of the Agency for International Development, was dead. His wife, Marylee, couldn't see because her face was cut and her eyes full of blood. The ambassador picked her up, carried her over to the window and helped her down a ladder someone had placed there.

After five days of searching the rubble for the bodies of the dead and wounded, the facts emerged. A few minutes after 1 pm, a man had driven a delivery truck through the embassy gates and crashed through the lobby doors. The driver had two thousand pounds of explosives strapped to his abdomen and tucked around him in the truck.

When he set himself on fire, the explosion was heard throughout West Beirut and broke windows as far as a mile away. The blast collapsed all seven storeys of the central façade of the horseshoe-shaped embassy building. It spewed masonry and glass fragments in a wide swath, and left the wreckage of balconies and offices in heaped tiers of rubble.

Sixty-three people were killed, including seventeen Americans—mostly embassy and CIA staff workers (the entire team, including the agency's top Middle-Eastern expert), several U.S. soldiers and one U.S. Marine Security Guard. Thirty-two Lebanese employees—all clerical workers—were killed, as well as fourteen visitors—visa applicants waiting in line—and nearby motorists and pedestrians. An additional 120 people were wounded.

It was the deadliest attack on an American diplomatic mission since WWII.

2.

April 18, 1983
American Community School
Beirut, Lebanon
Early afternoon

While the suicide bomber was setting himself on fire, fourteen-year-old Etienne Bellehumeur sat at the wooden drafting table in the art room of the American Community School of Beirut, adjacent to the American embassy. The basement classroom was cool and smelled faintly of mildew mixed with bleach and urine from the boys' bathroom.

In preparation for the lesson, their American teacher, Mrs. Gunthrey, had laid pastels and charcoal on the supply desk at the front. It was the first period after lunch, and the handful of students from the grade nine class—all from different countries—were still getting settled. Next door, the grade seven band members were tuning their instruments in a cacophony of squeaks and blurts. Mrs. Gunthrey waited until the instruments were quiet before she addressed the class. "The more pressure you put on the pencil tip, the darker your shading will be. You can also use your eraser nib and finger." She ripped a sheet from her sketchpad and placed it against the blackboard.

Then everything shook, as if in a massive earthquake. There was a huge clap, the loudest sound Etienne had ever heard. It was as if the inside of his ears had been flattened. They throbbed for hours afterwards.

Shards of glass flew everywhere. The lights went out. He put his hands over his head and his face on the desk, then slipped under it the way, a few months before, he'd crumpled behind his mother's seat in the car when they'd missed a PLO checkpoint and had been fired at on the road outside Tripoli.

It was eerily quiet. Afternoon light filtered in from the small casement windows. Etienne righted his chair and brushed the dust and pencil shavings off his jeans. The girl next to him was crying.

The teacher said something about it being too dark to draw. And dangerous with glass everywhere. She announced that she was going outside, to find out what had happened. She said something about her husband. That he worked at the embassy next door, which also housed the CIA. He would know what was going on.

All the students followed her. No one wanted to stay in the dark basement. By that time, sirens were blaring. There was black smoke in the distance. An acrid smell like burning rubber.

Mrs. Gunthrey led the students across the school compound, through the central quad of the American University, in the direction of the embassy. They had to jog to keep up with her—the four boys in a row, the girls in pairs, leaning into each other. Someone had given Milena, the Polish girl, a rag to hold against her arm. It was already soaked through with blood.

Everything said emergency. Strident voices and shouts mixed with sirens and horns. The embassy had been hit. The front façade of the building had sunken in on itself, like an under-cooked cake.

The teacher pressed through the throng of people—soldiers, police, university students, embassy workers, pedestrians—gathering around the embassy.

She stepped over mutilated bodies. Walked by cars wrapped around telephone poles. Hid her face in her sleeve. Behind her, eight students picked their way through the rubble.

Etienne kept his eyes on Mrs. Gunthrey's back. Ash from the smouldering building fell on her head like snow.

3.

April 18, 1983
Sabra and Shatila Palestinian refugee camps
Beirut, Lebanon

Dear God,

I am fourteen years old. I have always been a good girl. Maybe you can give me a sign letting me know what is happening to me.

Thus begins Alice Walker's *The Color Purple*, for which she was awarded the Pulitzer Prize on April 18, 1983. Set in Georgia in the 1900s, the novel tells Celie's story in a series of letters. Beginning when her mother is laid up in childbirth, Celie is repeatedly raped by the man she believes to be her father. When she gives birth, he gives the babies away, then marries her off to Mr. X, a downtrodden farmer who beats her. At night, she parts her legs for him and forces all thought and feeling from her body.

While the literary world was applauding Walker as the first black woman to be awarded this prestigious prize, a teenage girl was giving birth to a baby boy in the Sabra neighbourhood of West Beirut, adjacent to the Shatila refugee camp.

The baby was a secret known only to the mother and the handful of foreign doctors and nurses who volunteered at the Gaza Hospital. Since the Sabra and Shatila massacre, seven months prior, when thirty-five-hundred elderly men, women and children were brutally raped, killed and dismembered by Phalangist terrorists, the hospital had become a refuge, a shelter for the vulnerable, where they received emergency care and food.

"You better not never tell nobody but God. It'd kill your mammy."

When the Lebanese girl realized she was pregnant, Gaza Hospital was the only place she knew to go. If she had told her family about the rape, they would have killed her to save their honour.

"I make myself wood. I say to myself, 'Celie, you a tree.'"

Every month she'd washed and hung her clean menstrual rags, and as her body changed she hid it under layers of clothing. It helped that there was no heating or electricity in her crowded cinderblock home, and the winter had been harsh. The Jewish-American nurse at Gaza Hospital had told her the baby would be born by Caesarian section at seven months. The nuns from the Sisters of Charity would find parents to give it a home.

Her breasts were full and heavy. Some nights, she dreamed of a daughter. Other nights of a son. "Bearing children is a woman's glory," her mother had told her since she was little. "Many sons are Allah's blessing."

This was the day. Would her family believe the story about the emergency appendectomy? Would her future husband be fooled by the scar?

What about her baby? Where would it go?

She pushed images of the rape, seven months before, out of her mind.

"You got to fight. You got to fight.

But I don't know how to fight. All I know how to do is stay alive."

4.

April 18, 1983
Boston, Massachussets
and Beirut, Lebanon

While the suicide bomber in Beirut was getting ready to set himself on fire, the city of Boston was getting ready to run. It was six am. Thirty thousand athletes of all ages were stretching their hamstrings and eating bagels with peanut butter in preparation for the eighty-seventh annual Boston Marathon.

A few minutes before 5 pm Lebanese time, while rescue workers were pulling bodies out of the rubble of the American Embassy in Beirut, five hundred thousand people gathered in the streets of Boston to watch the fittest people on the planet run by.

Greg Meyer knew the course. He'd run it countless times since moving to Boston five years before to train with the city's best. His job as a clerk in a Cleveland Circle store left lots of time for running. But Meyer wanted more. By the end of the afternoon, he wanted to be the fastest man in the city. He wanted to win.

At the start line in the Hopkinton village green, while Meyer was retying his shoelaces, a fine rain fell on his face. The overcast, cool day was perfect for running.

In Beirut, John Reid, the American Embassy spokesman, was buried in bricks, plaster and mortar almost up to his neck. Blood ran from his face and scalp. He could only see out of one eye. He managed to free his arms and throw rubble off his body, grab a pipe behind his head and pull himself free.

In Boston, the starting gun sounded. The lead pack surged forward. Meyer was running with Benji Durden and Paul Cummings. He was getting his splits. He had his sights on the 10 000 metres at the World Championships that summer in Helsinki, and the US Olympic Trials the following May.

An embassy janitor wiped blood from John Reid's face with brown paper towels, then put him in the hands of Red Cross rescue workers, who walked him to an ambulance and sat him inside. Two men came running with a stretcher carrying a dead Lebanese woman, her face black and her swollen tongue hanging out. They shoved the stretcher into the ambulance. But when it lurched forward, the stretcher and the dead woman rolled onto the ground. The rescue workers got the dust-caked body back into the ambulance and started up the hill toward the American University of Beirut hospital. French paratroopers from the multinational force lined the street, sealing off the area.

Greg Meyer was approaching the ten-mile mark, a slight westerly wind at his back. A dense crowd lined both sides of the road. The Boston University track team cheered from the roof of a Brookline T station. At the edge of the crowd, a German shepherd and a Doberman pinscher lunged at each other. The shepherd's owner let go of the leash and the dog ran out into the runners' path. Meyer swerved to the right. Daniel Schlesinger had already been left behind because of a broken shoelace. Meyer didn't want to lose a second. He'd run the first ten miles in 49:11. He had sixteen miles and 385 yards to go.

John Reid's head was bandaged in white gauze. Glass fragments were embedded in his face and neck. One eye was sealed shut. He walked the short distance from the hospital to the embassy, illuminated by an explosion of camera flashes and TV lights from the crowd of journalists.

That night, his bandaged head was seen on TV screens all over America, alongside Greg Meyer, the first man to run towards the television cameras and the state troopers at the Prudential Building finish line. He won the Boston Marathon in 2:09, the third fastest time in the race's history.

5.

April 18, 1983
Corniche, West Beirut

On the other side of Beirut, in the penthouse apartment of a high-rise building overlooking the Mediterranean, Sharon Windsor, a middle-aged Canadian woman, received a phone call from her newlywed husband at the UNTSO headquarters.

An Anglican nun from the Sisters of Charity had a baby for them. Born that day, in the camps. A boy. From a teenage mother.

Outside her living room window, the sun was setting over the five American warships in the bay. Behind the canons, the sky was a cacophony of fuchsia and orange.

At seven months the baby must be tiny—maybe only three to four pounds. Would he survive the night?

Their contact at Doctors Without Borders had never made any guarantees. But Sharon had everything ready—diapers, bottles, powdered milk, godparents, a name.

The TV screen showed Alice Walker winning the Pulitzer Prize, then flicked to scenes from the Boston Marathon and America's fastest man, with his running time of 2:09:00 under his face like a prison mugshot.

New scenes of the carnage in Beirut, followed by lines of Japanese adults and children waiting to ride the roller coaster at the newly opened Tokyo Disneyland.

The nun had said they would receive their baby at 9 am the next day, at the *Couvent Terre Sainte*, the Franciscan Monastery on Gouraud Street. She'd insisted that he be baptized right away.

Sharon decided she would name her son after the Lebanese man, Souhail Abou-Akbah, who worked in the embassy library. She'd seen his startled face on TV all afternoon, squinting at the camera. He'd forgotten his glasses at home that morning, and had decided to go back to get them during his lunch hour. He'd asked his co-worker, the impeccably dressed Riad Abdul-Massih, to drive him, but he'd been too busy. Now rescue teams were looking for Abdul-Massih's body, searching the rubble for shreds of his pearl grey suit and matching silk tie. Abou-Akbah and Elias Kawar, the embassy colleague who'd driven him home, were safe.

Souhail Abou-Akbah blinked at the camera lights while he told his story. When he and Elias Kawar heard the blast, they'd reversed course. He had yet to retrieve his glasses. The myopic, stunned expression in his eyes reminded Sharon of a newborn baby, able to see only as far as the distance from its mother's breast to her face.

POETENT

Sue Goyette

a gopher maybe, a catastrophe, a muskrat, a family, or maybe a river otter

I respond, without thinking, to most situations with fear. This happens when you grow up with trauma. My house was erratic. It could motor along for days in its quiet but off-kilter way and then, out of nowhere, the volume would increase, its intensity and its intolerable, compacted fuck-upedness would hit the fan. In this way, I was wired as a first responder and I often found myself in the trenches. I know how to move fast despite feeling paralyzed. I've known this feeling for decades because it's so deep in my wiring it feels normal. It's a familiar and reliable reaction. Necessary, protective, and, at some point, a fair and worthwhile response to the many situations I experienced. It's got a drone voice and narrates most things with downward dread: *holy shit this is going to be bad, ack.* Don't get me wrong, I have great respect for fear. I appreciate how it shifts my gears to hyper alert, switches my headlights to high beam. But I've been noticing how persistent it's been, how it assumes authority and how much authority I give to it without question.

The Buddhists say we have two dogs in us: love and fear. We're asked by pretty well every situation we find ourselves in: Which dog do you want to feed? The answer is simple enough but carrying out that answer is a little more challenging. Responding to situations and to people with love takes practice. And a generosity I'm working on. Curiosity seems a realistic place to start. It is a reliable negotiator, it can mediate between my racing heart and panic, my dread, and invite me to consider other possibilities, other directions while not quite demanding the outpouring of love which I know to be the golden goal. Curiosity initiates a bonus round or another chance. It's a game changer that widens the horizon line. When I follow its roots, I arrive at awe and the jaw-dropping, unbelievable genius that is our planet's morphology and workings. Awe and then love. The way I see things is refreshed then, invigorated with the resources that bubble up when possibilities are manifesting and anything can happen. And those things may be better than I can imagine. But some days, I can't even imagine that.

If awe is salve for our eyes the way Rumi says it is, then maybe it's balm for our curiosity. There is so much we don't know: how things will turn out, for example. And curiosity, I've been thinking, may be the best greeting for encountering the unknown, the unexpected. Fear has been my reliable first response but curiosity may be a more sustainable fuel. I lean out of myself when I'm curious, I perk up; fear diminishes my primary radiance. It erodes my spirit, it's a pesticide for options and perspective and it robs everyone else of their spirit as well. What first eradicated my fear were encounters with seahorses and a Portuguese man o' war, bats and hummingbirds. A singular pine hit by lightning but surviving with a crooked and vital reach. These encounters claimed me somehow but I'm getting ahead of myself.

A couple of years ago, my friend was camping by a lake. She was sitting by the water in the early evening when she saw something swimming toward her. A gopher, she thought, no, maybe a beaver. Not a beaver, a muskrat? As it swam closer she thought maybe a fisher, a river otter. It gave a shake as it reached the shore then it stood.

I do this all the time. Name things before they're out of the water. I think growing up in the house I did nourished the kind of vigilance that worked hard at making sense of a situation. If I named something then I knew what I was dealing with. It was a way of keeping myself safe. I honed my observation skills, my intuition. *This* usually happens, for example, after *that*. I'd create equations for the unknown, and potentially dangerous, to stay ahead of that danger. And I get why I did it. I still appreciate the skill, the dedication it took. It was spirited. An early form of courage. I bow to that younger version of myself. *Well done,* I say, *and now you can rest.*

Sometimes naming is also a form of control, isn't it? If I name it *this*, it can't be *that*. And the quicker I name it, the faster I know what it is and what I have to do. Another way to stay safe. What would happen if I learned to wait a little longer? What would happen if something was given the space to claim its own name?

The creature shook and then nudged itself forward and up, sort of unfolding itself. A young moose, all legs, dripping the lake back to itself. A moose, my friend said, never would she have guessed a moose.

the moment in which I was lit

I was pedaling a bike with training wheels through two puddles, working on the wet trail of all the tire marks I was leaving. The making of the marks was engrossing, though I was circling something I knew intuitively to avoid. It soon became the hub in my circle, the point from which I navigated. If I had been stopped at this moment and asked what exactly that thing was, I would have maybe said: *wet kleenex.* I would have said: *small clump*. I was four and can still smell the parking lot, see the weeds you can imagine would be growing near an apartment building in the suburbs: long grass, some wild chicory still fisted, new sprouts of goldenrod. The small clump was a bird, fallen from its nest. I remember squatting for a closer look at its workings visible through its translucent skin. Its eyes were planetary, dark and inward. I knew, beneath words, that I was in the company of something important and unexpected. Too important for my parents. I went to the woman who knew birds, the silent old woman on the ground floor who fed them in a way that expanded my idea of family. I don't remember what happened to the bird. What I do remember was the care she showed it, her reverence. It was the nutritional kind of care a child leans into and learns something from. If someone had held a match to her care, it would have lit.

an apparatus, a vortex

I had been conducting the wind to vortex around
our apartment and unearth the root of the basement
from the ground, sending the building swirling to another place
with darker trees and a wider green. The process involved
an open heart otherwise an audience with the wind
wouldn't be given so I put myself in its current
and with wide arms tried to get it to chase me.

This was a couple of years later. I was six or seven running madly around our building convinced I could create an adventure by vortexing our building out of the earth. I had talked a few of friends into joining me but gradually they got bored or distracted so I was running alone.

The apartment building was solid with renters
who didn't have much furniture but had a heaviness

to them that involved shift work and souring.
It was like riding on the back of a mammoth
with nothing to hold on to. It bucked me close
to the bush with thorns but I held on and called it magic.

There wasn't much else in my life at that point. A television. A dark and heavy family. I was convinced I'd been born into the wrong one. Seriously. They just didn't feel right.

My sister yelled stop *every time I blew past her.*
It finally bucked me off and I rolled hard
towards the building, the thorn bush softening
and then stabbing my fall. When I sat up, I was in the same world,
the rocks hadn't grown, the sky still in a hurry. In the bush
above my head was the only clue that something was different.
The unexpected green of it caught my breath, freshened it with
    colour
and then gave it back to me so I could whisper: what are you?

The moment was a chandelier. I was alone in a new and vital silence. The look we exchanged was potent. Or poetent, I just typed by mistake. But that's what it was: the look was *poetent.*

The creature posed all angular and miracle. If it had been
a miniature horse, it would have whinnied and shook its head
at being seen. If it had been a miniature airplane, its propellers
would've started spinning, its engine pulling it down the runway
of the branch and then, unbelievably, airborne
into take-off.

What moments like these share is an expansion and a sense of other, a blueprint for the mysterious and for the totally unexpected manifesting. I was part perk and part bow. Humbled and verging. Fear's blind spot has kept me from knowing that

I'm part of this genius. That I'm unfurling with a delectable spirit honed to that awe, that genius of design all living creatures share. When I forget that, I find myself homesick for the wildness that is inherently part of me.

The creature I found had given me courage,
convincing me that it wasn't an insect but a portal
into the miraculous. If you think I'm special, wait
until you see what else is out here, it telepathed
and I believed it.

I had to. There wasn't much else and my relief was palpable. Ennobling. The luxury of a praying mantis: its colour and unexpected angles, its extensions only hinting at what is possible and how very little I actually knew. I remember the gratitude I felt. My horizon line widened past family. Here was another clue that I belonged to something bigger and my curiosity quickened. Who invented these creatures? And who thought up the apparatus of these perfect and timely encounters? Now I wonder: How do we keep that vitality watered when we find ourselves in a palliative care unit or a mental health ward? How do we keep it fed when all we're given are forms and prescriptions to fill? Or when we feel the heart pain inherent to living on this planet at this time with the deep grief we're experiencing but can't even begin to articulate? What is salve for our care and for our kindness? Our generosity and restoration? I wonder if we're more important to each other than we think.

an attack only better

It was the Summer of Heart Attacks. One after another,
men from Quebec in Speedos, their cigarettes wilting

towards their commendable bellies, this an electromagnetic force

*in the middle of its enduring oui or non argument. The bodies,
   thick*

*logs of sullen nons and the hot tongue of sand licking its yeses.
I counted five attacks before the shark and then stopped counting.*

I was eleven. The first man to have a heart attack on the
beach was an event that afforded me some time to think about
mortality. A voltage into an already present: *Ack, it's going to
happen to all of us??* By the fifth attack, a pattern seemed in place.
I'd have guessed that it would happen again. I would have bet
on it. The next day, however, a shark appeared instead, beached,
and still very much alive. A shark, I remember thinking, who
saw that coming? I'd never encountered anything so stream-
lined and so condensed. It had washed up crammed with ocean
and was the most primordial yet modern thing I'd ever met. It
spiced my summer with something that removed me from the
mundane and wrought company I'd been in. I forged with it,
I melted. There are no reliable patterns, I was learning, and this
was neither good nor bad and sometimes could be spectacular.

*After years of therapy, I unzipped the wetsuit of shark
and found a heart attacking. My mouth to fish, breathing,*

*was replaced with ocean bailed from my eyes and sloshed
on gills. The fish fluttering like a bird, like a new love eager*

for a glimpse of me, another beloved.

synchronizing our watch

I'm still learning to appreciate moments that defy the mundane with their singularity and brilliance. These moments

are like dahlias, each detail a petal contributing to flower. My vocation now is to watch for them, to take notes, to weed around them so they thrive.

An old friend and I were catching up, talking about our lives. Each of us needing answers more than we should have needed anything. Maybe we wanted safety or reassurance. Maybe we wanted affirmation or just company. We both were on our own, facing our singular and private loneliness. The pub we were sitting in was called The Nail and the Kneecap, which is what we were feeling we were up against, emotionally, spiritually even, we had joked. Life, eh? We had so many questions and weren't willing to admit how scared we were, how old we were to be so scared. Here we were, knowing so little. What was it she asked me? If I'd do anything differently? If I had any regrets? The pub's windows were generous: wide and open to the street. Summer was just emerging, the flowerpots vivid and active. My pause after her question was part bafflement, part consideration, and a large part dread. And that's what he drove through on his bicycle. The young person, driving without hands, right in front of us: straight-backed and composed, wearing the biggest, white-feathered wings I'd ever seen: another species of response. His timing, as timing is, was perfect.

CONTRIBUTORS' BIOGRAPHIES

Tanya Bellehumeur-Allatt's stories, poems and essays have been published in *Grain, EVENT, Prairie Fire, Malahat Review, subTerrain, carte blanche, Room, Crux, The Centrifugal Eye, Qarrtsiluni, The Occupy Anthology, Water Lines: New Writing from the Eastern Townships of Quebec* (forthcoming) and reprinted in *Best Canadian Essays of 2015.* Tanya has been nominated for a National Magazine Award as well as a Western Magazine Award and received a Canada Council Grant for her memoir, *Peacekeeper's Daughter.* Tanya holds an MA from McGill and an MFA in Creative Writing from UBC. She has four children.

Ali Blythe is the author of two critically acclaimed books exploring trans-poetics: the debut collection *Twoism*, and the follow-up, *Hymnswitch.* His poems are published in literary journals and anthologies in Canada, England, Germany and Slovenia. "Fierce Inventory" is his first published essay.

Larissa Diakiw is a writer, living and working in Toronto. She has written for *Hazlitt, Brick, The Walrus, Guts, Joyland,* won a silver 2019 National Magazine Award for her essay *Secrets Are* *a Captive Country,* and publishes Comics/Graphic Essays as Frankie No One.

Emily Donaldson is an editor, writer, and book critic whose writing and reviews have appeared in numerous publications including *The Toronto Star, The Globe and Mail, The National Post, The Walrus, Maclean's,* and *Quill & Quire.* Her work has been nominated for National Magazine Awards and for a Governor General's Award. In 2016, she became editor of *Canadian Notes & Queries,* Canada's oldest magazine of literary criticism, for which she is also a long-time contributor. Born and raised in Montreal, she lives in Toronto with her husband and two sons.

Jeffery Donaldson teaches poetry and poetics at McMaster University. He is the author of six collections of poetry, most recently *Fluke Print* (Porcupine's Quill, 2018). His volume *Palilalia* (McGill-Queen's UP) was nominated for the Canadian Author's Association poetry award in 2008. His blog «Jeweller's Eye» offers audio-video reviews of single poems from new volumes of Canadian poetry. He is author of two critical works: *Missing Link: the Evolution of Metaphor and the Metaphor of Evolution* (McGill-Queen's UP) and *Echo Soundings: Essays on Poetry and Poetics* (Palimpsest Press, 2014). A non-fiction work, *Viaticum: From Notebooks,* was published with Porcupine's Quill this past spring.

Tarralik Duffy is a multidisciplinary artist and writer who lives and works between Salliq (Coral Harbour), NU, and Saskatoon, SK. From jewellery and apparel to graphic works, Duffy's creative output shares distinctly Inuit experiences, which are often infused with a dose of humour and pop culture.

Sue Goyette lives in K'jipuktuk (Halifax), the unceded and unsurrendered land of the Mi'kmaq peoples. She has published six books of poems and a novel. Her latest collection is *Penelope* (Gaspereau Press, 2017). She has been nominated for the 2014 Griffin Poetry Prize and the Governor General's Award and has won several awards including the 2015 Lieutenant Governor of Nova Scotia Masterworks Arts Award for her collection, *Ocean*. Sue teaches in the Creative Writing Program at Dalhousie University.

River Halen Guri (previously published as Helen Guri) is a queer non-binary writer of Catalan and Danish descent living on unceded Indigenous land in Tio'tia:ke (Montreal). Their poems and essays dealing with relation, ecology, transformation, and sexuality have been published widely in Canada, as well as in the U.S., Australia, and in translation in Japan. They are the author of *Match* (Coach House, 2011), which was shortlisted for the Trillium Book Award for Poetry, as well as several chapbooks, including *Some Animals and Their Housing Situations* (The Elephants, 2018) and *I looked for the exit, found a sleeve* (Skyebound Press, 2019). Website: helenguri.net

Danny Jacobs' poems, reviews, and essays have been published in a variety of journals across Canada. Danny won *PRISM International*'s 2015 Creative Nonfiction Contest and *The Malahat Review*'s 2016 P. K. Page Founders' Award for poetry. His essay "Rooms" was shortlisted for *The Malahat Review*'s 2018 Constance Rooke Creative Nonfiction Prize. His first book of poetry, *Songs That Remind Us of Factories* (Nightwood, 2013), was shortlisted for the 2014 Acorn-Plantos Award for People's Poetry. His latest book, *Sourcebooks for Our Drawings: Essays and Remnants*, is a collection of lyrical essays and creative nonfiction (Gordon Hill Press, September 2019). Danny lives in Riverview, NB, with his wife and daughter. He works as the librarian in the village of Petitcodiac.

Robbie Jeffrey is a freelance writer in Edmonton. He grew up on a cattle ranch near Vermilion, Alta., and studied at the

University of Alberta. In 2019 he was nominated for three Alberta Magazine Awards.

Jessica Johns is a nehiyaw aunty and member of Sucker Creek First Nation in Treaty 8 territory in Northern Alberta. She is the Managing Editor for *Room Magazine*, and a co-organizer of the Indigenous Brilliance reading series. She has been published in *Cosmonauts Avenue*, *Glass Buffalo*, *CV2*, *SAD Magazine*, *Red Rising Magazine*, *The Rusty Toque*, *Poetry is Dead*, *Grain*, and *Bad Nudes*, among others. "The Bull of Cromdale" was nominated for a 2019 National Magazine Award, and her debut poetry chapbook, *How Not to Spill*, is out with Rahila's Ghost Press.

Andy Lamey teaches philosophy at the University of California, San Diego and is the author of *Duty and The Beast: Should We Eat Meat in the Name of Animal Rights?* (Cambridge University Press).

Jessie Loyer is Cree-Métis and a member of Michel First Nation. She's a librarian, too.

Melanie Mah's debut novel, *The Sweetest One*, won the 2017 Trillium Book Award, and her work's been published in the *Humber Literary Review*, *PRISM International*, *Room*, and *Brick*. She's currently at work on an intergenerational memoir told in essays, and she holds an MFA from the University of Guelph. Born and raised in Alberta, she now lives in Toronto.

Pasha Malla is the author of six books. *Kill the Mall*, a new novel, will be published in spring 2020. He lives in Hamilton, Ontario.

Noor Naga is an Alexandrian writer who was born in Philadelphia, raised in Dubai and studied in Toronto. She is winner of the 2017 Bronwen Wallace Award, the 2019 Disquiet Fiction Prize, and the 2019 RBC/PEN Canada New Voices Award. Her work has been published or is forthcoming in *POETRY*, *Granta*, *The Walrus*, *The Common*, and more. Her verse-novel *Washes Prays* is forthcoming in Spring 2020.

Anthony Oliveira is a writer, film programmer, pop culture critic, and PhD living in Toronto. He is the host of the Revue Cinema's Dumpster Raccoon Film Series and a recurring guest on CBC's *The National Pop Panel*. His pieces have appeared in *The Washington Post*, *Hazlitt*, *Xtra*, *Torontoist*, *Fangoria*, and others. He has been nominated for four National Magazine Awards; "Death in the Village," chronicling the aftermath of the Bruce McArthur murders, won two (Best Essay and Best Long-Form Feature). In addition to several upcoming graphic novel projects, he is at work on his first novel, *Dayspring*.

Meaghan Rondeau is one of Canada's slowest living writers. She grew up in Saskatchewan, spent some years in Alberta, now lives in B.C., and wouldn't mind at all if the final installment of her westerly drifting were a hard shove out into the Pacific in a book- and cat-filled boat. She tries her best to do right by language. She thinks it's obvious that literary rejection is exactly as personal any of the other types. She would give existence a 6/10 overall. You can find her at meaghanrondeau.com, on her couch, or in the ocean, wading, waiting.

Mireille Silcoff is the author of four books of fiction and nonfiction. She won the 2015 Canadian Jewish Literary Award for her short story collection *Chez l'Arabe*, which was also shortlisted for the Danuta Gleed Literary Award, shortlisted for the Vine Award, longlisted for the Frank O'Connor International Short Story Prize, and was voted Canada's favourite work of short fiction on CBC's Canada Writes. She has been a longstanding columnist with the *National Post*, a frequent contributor to the *New York Times Magazine*, and has written extensively for all kinds of publications including *the Guardian* and *Ha'aretz*. Mireille has been a senior editor at numerous Canadian publications, including the *National Post*. She is the founding editor of the literary journal *Guilt & Pleasure Quarterly*, and has organized many events designed to instigate conversations about culture. She lives in Montreal.

Souvankham Thammavongsa is the author of four poetry books, most recently, *Cluster* (M&S, 2019).

Bruce Whiteman was a rare book specialist for over 30 years. He worked at McMaster and McGill Universities in Canada, and at UCLA's William Andrews Clark Memorial Library. He is now a poet, translator, and book reviewer. His most recent books are a collection of prose poems entitled *The Sad Mechanic Exercise* (Gaspereau Press, 2019) and a translation of Fanny Daubigny's study, *Proust in Black* (San Diego State University Press, 2019). He teaches part-time at the University of Toronto and was the poet in residence at Scattergood Friends School in West Branch, Iowa, from 2015-2019. He now lives in Peterborough, Ontario.

ACKNOWLEDGEMENTS

"Terrorist Narratives" by Tanya Bellehumeur-Allatt first appeared in *The Malahat Review*.

"Fierce Inventory" by Ali Blythe first appeared in *Arc Poetry Magazine*.

"Secrets are a Captive Country" by Larissa Diakiw first appeared in *Hazlitt*.

"Our Country—Le Canada" by Jeffery Donaldson first appeared in *Hamilton Arts & Letters*.

"Uvanga/Self: Picturing Our Identity" by Tarralik Duffy first appeared in *Inuit Art Quarterly*, published by the Inuit Art Foundation.

"Poetent" by Sue Goyette first appeared in *The New Quarterly*.

"Six Boxes" by River Halen Guri (previously published as Helen Guri) first appeared in *The Capilano Review*.

"The Weekend God" by Danny Jacobs first appeared in *Hamilton Arts & Letters* .

"The High and Lonesome Sound" by Robbie Jeffrey first appeared in *Eighteen Bridges*.

ACKNOWLEDGEMENTS

"The Bull of Cromdale" by Jessica Johns first appeared in *NDNCountry by Prairie Fire/CV2*.

"The Trump Card: What David Frum is Missing About America's Worst President" by Andy Lamey first appeared in *The Literary Review of Canada*.

"mâyipayiwin" by Jessie Loyer first appeared in *NDNCountry by Prairie Fire/CV2*.

"In Transit" by Melanie Mah first appeared in *The Humber Literary Review*.

"CanLit's Comedy Problem" by Pasha Malla first appeared in *The Literary Review of Canada*.

"Mistresses Should be Muslim Too" by Noor Naga first appeared in *Arc Poetry Magazine*.

"Death in the Village" by Anthony Oliveira first appeared in *Hazlitt*.

"Half-Thing" by Meaghan Rondeau first appeared in *The New Quarterly*.

"Swedish Death Cleaning and the Anorexic Home" by Mireille Silcoff first appeared in *The Literary Review of Canada*.

"On Meaning" by Souvankham Thammavongsa first appeared in *Arc Poetry Magazine*.

"Unc" by Bruce Whiteman first appeared in *Canadian Notes & Queries*.

NOTABLE ESSAYS OF 2018

Allaire, Christian. "The Waiting Room." *Hazlitt*, July 24, 2018.

Al-Solaylee, Kamal. "Unwelcome to Canada." *The Walrus,* April 2018.

Belcourt, Billy-Ray. "Fatal Naming Rituals." *Hazlitt*, July 19, 2018, hazlitt.net/feature/fatal-naming-rituals.

Benaway, Gwen. "A Body Like a Home." *Hazlitt*, May 30, 2018, hazlitt.net/longreads/body-home.

Elliott, Alicia. "Dark Matters." *Hazlitt*, March 27, 2018, hazlitt.net/longreads/dark-matters.

Foster, Karen. "The Right to Be Rural." *Dalhousie Review*, Autumn 2018.

Heighton, Steven. "Everything Turns Away." *Geist*, Fall 2018.

Horne, Lorax B. "O Ye of Little Faith." *Maisonneuve*, Summer 2018.

Leung, Godfre. "Photos Worth a Thousand Houses." *Maisonneuve*, Summer 2018.

McGouran, Anne. "Spinning Thistledown at Midnight." *Queen's Quarterly*, Fall 2018.

Mlotek, Haley. "Searching for the Self-Loathing Woman Writer." *Hazlitt*, January 2, 2018, hazlitt.net/longreads/searching-self-loathing-woman-writer.

Semley, John. "Did Virtue and the Think Piece Ruin Criticism?" *Literary Review of Canada*, April 2018.

Willie, Chris. "My Life and Death on Opioids." *The Walrus*, September 2018.

Magazines Consulted

Arc Poetry Magazine, Border Crossings, Brick: A Literary Journal, The Capilano Review, Canadian Notes & Queries, Chatelaine, The Dalhousie Review, Eighteen Bridges, enRoute, esse, EVENT, The Fiddlehead, filling Station, Geist, Grain, Hamilton Arts & Letters, Hazlitt, Herizons, The Humber Literary Review, Inuit Art, The Literary Review of Canada, Maclean's, Maisonneuve, The Malahat Review, ndncountry: A Joint Issue of Prairie Fire and CV2, The Newfoundland Quarterly, The New Quarterly, ON Nature, Prairie Fire, PRISM, The Puritan, The Queen's Quarterly, Riddle Fence, Room, subTerrain, THIS Magazine, Today's Parent, Toronto Life, The Walrus